50 WALKS IN
Staffordshire

50 Walks in Staffordshire

Published by AA Publishing (a trading name of AA Media Limited, whose registered office is Grove House, Lutyens Close, Lychpit, Basingstoke, Hampshire RG24 8AG; registered number 06112600)

© AA Media Limited 2024
Fourth edition
First published 2003

Mapping in this book is derived from the following products:
OS Landranger 118 (walks 3–7, 10–12, 15, 16, 20, 27, 28)
OS Landranger 119 (walks 1–3, 8, 9, 13, 14, 17–24)
OS Landranger 127 (walks 26–29, 32–35, 38, 39, 41, 49)
OS Landranger 128 (walks 25, 30, 31, 33, 36, 37, 40, 42–45)
OS Landranger 138 (walks 46, 48, 50)
OS Landranger 139 (walks 45–47)
OS Explorer 244 (walks 38–40)

© Crown copyright and database rights 2024 Ordnance Survey. 100021153.

Maps contain data available from openstreetmap.org © under the Open Database License found at opendatacommons.org

ISBN: 978-0-7495-8376-7
ISBN: 978-0-7495-8385-9 (SS)

A CIP catalogue record for this book is available from the British Library.

AA Media would like to thank the following contributors in the preparation of this guide:
Clare Ashton, Tracey Freestone, Lauren Havelock, Nicky Hillenbrand, Lin Hutton, Graham Jones, Ian Little, Richard Marchi, Nigel Phillips, Victoria Samways.

Cover design by
berkshire design company.

Printed and bound in the UK by Oriental Press, Dubai.

A05851

We would like to thank the following photographers, companies and picture libraries for their assistance in the preparation of this book. Abbreviations for the picture credits are as follows:
Alamy = Alamy Stock Photo
Trade Cover, travelib europe/Alamy
Special Cover, Andrew Ray/Alamy
Back Cover Advert, SolStock/istockphoto; 9, Andrew Ray/Alamy; 12/13, shoults/Alamy; 38/39, shoults/Alamy; 55, David Hatfield/Alamy; 62/63, Nick Scott/Alamy; 79, Nick Hatton/Alamy; 89, Robin Weaver/Alamy; 111, Mike Twigg,fotocapricorn/Alamy; 136/137, David Chapman/Alamy; 176, SolStock/istockphoto

The contents of this book are believed correct at the time of printing. Nevertheless, the publishers cannot be held responsible for any errors or omissions or for changes in the details given in this book or for the consequences of any reliance on the information it provides. This does not affect your statutory rights. We have tried to ensure accuracy in this book, but things do change and we would be grateful if readers would advise us of any inaccuracies they may encounter by emailing walks@aamediagroup.co.uk

We have done our best to make sure that these walks are safe and achievable by walkers with a basic level of fitness. However, we can accept no responsibility for any loss or injury incurred while following the walks. Advice on walking safely can be found on pages 10–11.

Some of the walks may appear in other AA books and publications.

Discover and book AA-rated places to stay at www.RatedTrips.com

50 WALKS IN
Staffordshire

CONTENTS

How to use this book	6
Exploring the area	8
Walking in safety	10

The walks

WALK		GRADIENT	DISTANCE	PAGE
1	Flash	▲▲	5.9 miles (9.5km)	14
2	Longnor	▲▲	6 miles (9.7km)	17
3	The Roaches	▲	3.8 miles (6km)	20
4	Greenway Bank	▲	2.75 miles (4.4km)	23
5	Rudyard Reservoir	▲	4.5 miles (7.2km)	26
6	Mow Cop Castle	▲▲▲	6.25 miles (10.1km)	29
7	Tittesworth Water	▲	4.5 miles (7.2km)	32
8	Manifold Valley	▲▲	5.9 miles (9.5km)	35
9	Wetton	▲▲▲	8.5 miles (13.7km)	40
10	Leek	▲▲	4.25 miles (6.8km)	43
11	Endon	▲	3.5 miles (5.7km)	46
12	Cheddleton	▲	3.25 miles (5.3km)	49
13	Grindon	▲▲	4.8 miles (7.7km)	52
14	Beeston Tor	▲▲▲	9 miles (14.5km)	56
15	Stoke-on-Trent	▲	3 miles (4.8km)	59
16	Apedale	▲▲	4.75 miles (7.7km)	64
17	Ilam	▲▲	5.2 miles (8.4km)	67
18	Caldon Low	▲▲	6 miles (9.7km)	70
19	Onecote	▲▲▲	8.25 miles (13.3km)	73
20	Consall	▲▲	3.5 miles (5.7km)	76
21	Froghall Wharf	▲▲	4.5 miles (7.2km)	80
22	Ellastone	▲▲	4 miles (6.4km)	83

WALK		GRADIENT	DISTANCE	PAGE
23	Alton	▲▲	5 miles (8km)	86
24	The Churnet Valley	▲▲	7 miles (11.3km)	90
25	Dunstall Hall	▲	3.5 miles (5.7km)	93
26	Loggerheads	▲	5.5 miles (8.8km)	96
27	Hanchurch Hills	▲▲	7 miles (11.3km)	99
28	Barlaston	▲	3.25 miles (5.3km)	102
29	Downs Banks	▲	2 miles (3.2km)	105
30	Tutbury	▲	2.75 miles (4.4km)	108
31	Hanbury	▲	4.75 miles (7.7km)	112
32	Stafford Castle	▲	4 miles (6.4km)	115
33	Shugborough	▲	5.5 miles (8.8km)	118
34	Great Haywood	▲	4.5 miles (7.2km)	121
35	Union Canal	▲	2.75 miles (4.4km)	124
36	Abbots Bromley	▲▲	5.25 miles (8.4km)	127
37	Rugeley and Colton	▲	3.5 miles (5.7km)	130
38	Cannock Chase	▲▲	4 miles (6.4km)	133
39	Coppice Hill	▲	4.25 miles (6km)	138
40	Cannock Chase	▲	3.5 miles (5.7km)	141
41	Brewood	▲	5.75 miles (9.2km)	144
42	Lichfield	Negligible	2.5 miles (4km)	147
43	Whittington	▲	9.3 miles (15km)	150
44	Alrewas	▲	6 miles (9.7km)	154
45	Chasewater	▲	3 miles (4.8km)	157
46	Trysull	▲▲	6.25 miles (10.1km)	160
47	Wombourne	▲▲	4.25 miles (6.8km)	163
48	Kinver	▲▲	5.4 miles (8.7km)	166
49	Moddershall	▲▲	10 miles (16.1km)	170
50	Kinver to Whittington	▲▲	3.25 miles (5.3km)	173

HOW TO USE THIS BOOK

Each walk starts with an information panel giving all the information you will need about the walk at a glance, including its relative difficulty, distance and total amount of ascent. Difficulty levels and gradients are as follows:

Difficulty of walk
- Easy
- Intermediate
- Hard

Gradient
▲ Some slopes
▲▲ Some steep slopes
▲▲▲ Several very steep slopes

Maps
Every walk has its own route map. We also suggest a relevant Ordnance Survey map to take with you, allowing you to view the area in more detail. The time suggested is the minimum for reasonably fit walkers and doesn't allow for stops.

Route map legend

Symbol	Meaning	Symbol	Meaning
---→---	Walk route	▨	Built-up area
❶	Route waypoint	▨	Woodland area
- - - -	Adjoining path	🚻	Toilet
•	Place of interest	🅿	Car park
⌂	Steep section	▥	Picnic area
☀	Viewpoint	)(	Bridge
ⅢⅢⅢ	Embankment		

Start points
The start of each walk is given as a six-figure grid reference prefixed by two letters referring to a 100km square of the National Grid. More information on grid references can be found on most OS Walker's Maps.

Dogs
We have tried to give dog owners useful advice about how dog friendly each walk is. Please respect other countryside users. Keep your dog under control, especially around livestock, and obey local by-laws and other dog control notices.

Car parking

Many of the car parks suggested are public, but occasionally you may have to park on the roadside or in a lay-by. Please be considerate about where you leave your car, ensuring that you are not on private property or access roads, and that gates are not blocked and other vehicles can pass safely.

Walks locator map

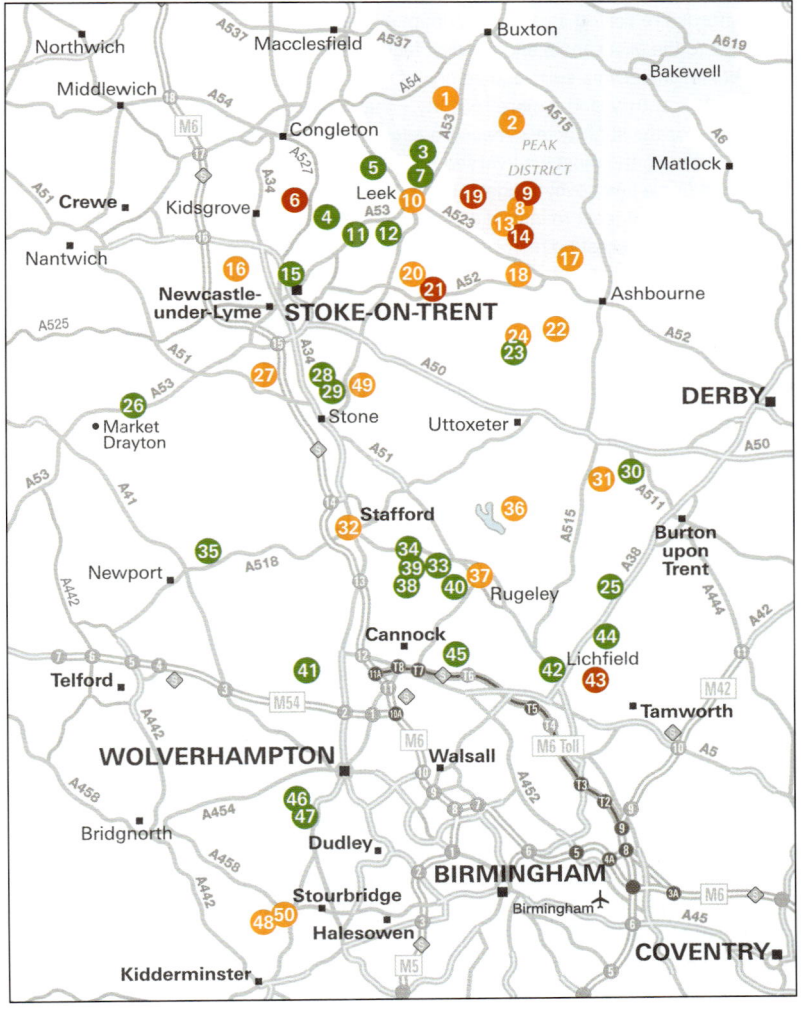

EXPLORING THE AREA

Did you know that Staffordshire bore the brunt of the largest non-nuclear explosion of World War II? Or that the county's regiment once boasted within its ranks the most decorated NCO of World War I? Or going back a little further, that George Handel penned his masterpiece, *The Messiah*, on Staffordshire soil? If so, you'll no doubt also be aware that Staffordshire was home to the first canals and the first factory in Britain, that it had front-row seats for the drama surrounding one of the most notorious murder trials of the 19th century, and – more recently – that it provided the scenery and setting for the slightly less macabre television drama *Peak Practice*.

But even the most well versed of Staffordshire aficionados should still be able to find a few novel nuggets in this little volume, if not to entertain and amuse, then at least to inform and educate. Of course, the county's varied culture and interesting history are all well and good, but what of its potential for walking?

In outline, Staffordshire looks not unlike the profile of a man giving Leicestershire a big kiss (have a look if you don't believe it!). The man's forehead to the northeast of the county is arguably the best region for hillwalking as it comprises a significant chunk of the Peak District. This area is characterised by lofty moors, deep dales and tremendous views of both. In fact seven of the walks can be found in this area, from the great crags of the Roaches to the mysterious Thor's Cave. Further south, at around ear level, are the six sprawling towns that make up Stoke-on-Trent, which historically have had such an impact on Staffordshire's fortunes, not to mention its culture and countryside. This is pottery country, formerly at the forefront of the Industrial Revolution and the driving force behind a network of canals that still criss-crosses the county.

In terms of its scenery, the region around Stoke is surprisingly hilly, thanks largely to vast outcrops of limestone not unlike those found in the Peak District just to the north. In areas where industry once marched rampant o'er hill and down dale, mother nature has recently re-staked her claim on the landscape, which today is typified by peaceful wooded valleys, pond-pearled streams and gently rolling hills.

Next up, hanging like an earring from the lobe of Stoke, is Stafford, home to one of the oldest and most impressive castle earthworks in the country. In fact, glancing at some of the other walks in this area, you'd be forgiven for thinking that it's always been a region of conflict, what with the bloody battlefield of Bloreheath just to the west and the enormous Fauld Crater just to the east.

Just to the south of Stafford is Cannock Chase, arguably the county's best-kept secret. Here, acre after acre of ancient hunting forest has been reclaimed from the devastation wrought by industry to form a huge forested nature park, just a stone's throw from Birmingham. It would take you days, if not weeks, to walk every track in these justifiably popular woods.

And finally, at the southern tip of the county, along the back of our man's neck, are the slopes and ridges that terminate in the impressive vantage point of Kinver Edge, where entire houses are carved into the sandstone cliffs, and where the fine English wine, in a good year, flows freely. Of course, for walking, any year is a good year in Staffordshire.

PUBLIC TRANSPORT
Staffordshire is very well served by public transport:
First Group (www.firstbus.co.uk/potteries) is one of the main operators in the northeast of the county, while Arriva (www.arrivabus.co.uk) services routes throughout the region. Local bus timetables for most major towns and routes can be obtained from Traveline (www.traveline.info).

Walk 3

WALKING IN SAFETY

All these walks are suitable for any reasonably fit person, but less experienced walkers should try the easier walks first. Route-finding is usually straightforward, but you will find that an Ordnance Survey walking map is a useful addition to the route maps and descriptions; recommendations can be found in the information panels.

Risks

Although each walk here has been researched with a view to minimising the risks to the walkers who follow its route, no walk in the countryside can be considered to be completely free from risk. Walking in the outdoors will always require a degree of common sense and judgement to ensure that it is as safe as possible.

- Be particularly careful on cliff paths and in upland terrain, where the consequences of a slip can be very serious.
- Remember to check tidal conditions before walking on the seashore.
- Some sections of route are by, or cross, busy roads. Take care, and remember that traffic is a danger even on minor country lanes.
- Be careful around farmyard machinery and livestock, especially if you have children with you.
- Be aware of the consequences of changes in the weather, and check the forecast before you set out. Carry spare clothing and a torch if you are walking in the winter months. Remember that the weather can change very quickly at any time of the year, and in moorland and heathland areas, mist and fog can make route-finding much harder. Don't set out in these conditions unless you are confident of your navigation skills in poor visibility.
- In summer remember to take account of the heat and sun; wear a hat and carry water.
- On walks away from centres of population you should carry a whistle and survival bag. If you do have an accident that means you require help from the emergency services, make a note of your position as accurately as possible and dial 999.

Countryside Code
Respect other people:

- Consider the local community and other people enjoying the outdoors.
- Co-operate with people at work in the countryside. For example, keep out of the way when farm animals are being gathered or moved, and follow directions from the farmer.

- Don't block gateways, driveways or other paths with your vehicle.
- Leave gates and property as you find them, and follow paths unless wider access is available, such as on open country or registered common land (known as 'open access land').
- Leave machinery and farm animals alone – don't interfere with animals, even if you think they're in distress. Try to alert the farmer instead.
- Use gates, stiles or gaps in field boundaries if you can – climbing over walls, hedges and fences can damage them and increase the risk of farm animals escaping.
- Our heritage matters to all of us – be careful not to disturb ruins and historic sites.

Protect the natural environment:
- Take your litter home. Litter and leftover food don't just spoil the beauty of the countryside; they can be dangerous to wildlife and farm animals. Dropping litter and dumping rubbish are criminal offences.
- Leave no trace of your visit, and take special care not to damage, destroy or remove features such as rocks, plants and trees.
- Keep dogs under effective control, making sure they are not a danger or nuisance to farm animals, horses, wildlife or other people.
- If cattle or horses chase you and your dog, it is safer to let your dog off the lead – don't risk getting hurt by trying to protect it. Your dog will be much safer if you let it run away from a farm animal in these circumstances, and so will you.
- Everyone knows how unpleasant dog mess is and it can cause infections, so always clean up after your dog and get rid of the mess responsibly – bag it and bin it.
- Fires can be as devastating to wildlife and habitats as they are to people and property – so be careful with naked flames and cigarettes at any time of the year.

Enjoy the outdoors:
- Plan ahead and be prepared for natural hazards, changes in weather and other events.
- Wild animals, farm animals and horses can behave unpredictably if you get too close, especially if they're with their young – so give them plenty of space.
- Follow advice and local signs.

For more information visit www.gov.uk/government/publications/the-countryside-code

FLASH – THE HIGHEST VILLAGE

DISTANCE/TIME	5.9 miles (9.5km) / 3hrs 30min
ASCENT/GRADIENT	1,080ft (330m) / ▲▲
PATHS	Field and rugged moorland paths, can be boggy after rain, some roads, many stiles
LANDSCAPE	Hills, moorland and meadows
SUGGESTED MAP	OS Explorer OL24 Peak District – White Peak Area
START/FINISH	Grid reference: SK026672
DOG FRIENDLINESS	Keep on lead near livestock, cattle may be present
PARKING	Small car park on Brown Lane, near church
PUBLIC TOILETS	None on route

At an altitude of 1,519ft (463m), Flash proclaims itself the 'Highest Village in Britain'. At this elevation, winters come early and linger long. They can be cold too. Once, during wartime, it got so cold that the vicar had icicles on his ears when he reached the church.

Despite being a devout community, Flash also has the dubious honour of giving its name to sharp practice. The terms 'flash money' and 'flash company' also entered the English language as a consequence of events in Flash.

A group of peddlers living near the village travelled the country hawking ribbons, buttons and goods. Known as 'Flash men' they initially paid for their goods with hard cash but, after establishing credit, they vanished with the goods and moved on to another supplier. Their name became associated with ne'er-do-wells in taverns, who helped people drink their money and were never seen again, as typified in the 18th-century folk-song, 'Flash Company':

Fiddling and dancing were all my delight
But keeping flash company has ruined me quite

'Flash money', on the other hand, referred to counterfeit bank notes, manufactured in the 18th century by a devious local gang using button presses. They were captured when a servant girl informed on them to the authorities. Some of the gang members were hanged at Chester. Flash was the ideal location for avoiding the law because of its proximity to the borders of three counties; police in one county could not pursue miscreants into another.

A local beauty spot called Three Shires Heads, about a mile (1.6km) northwest of the village, by a packhorse bridge, is the meeting place of Derbyshire, Cheshire and Staffordshire. Illegal bare-knuckle fights were held here and, when the police arrived, the participants simply crossed the bridge and continued their bout on the other side. More peaceable inhabitants formed the Tea Pot Club. This fund, set up in the centuries before the NHS, helped members who were sick or who needed money to pay for a funeral.

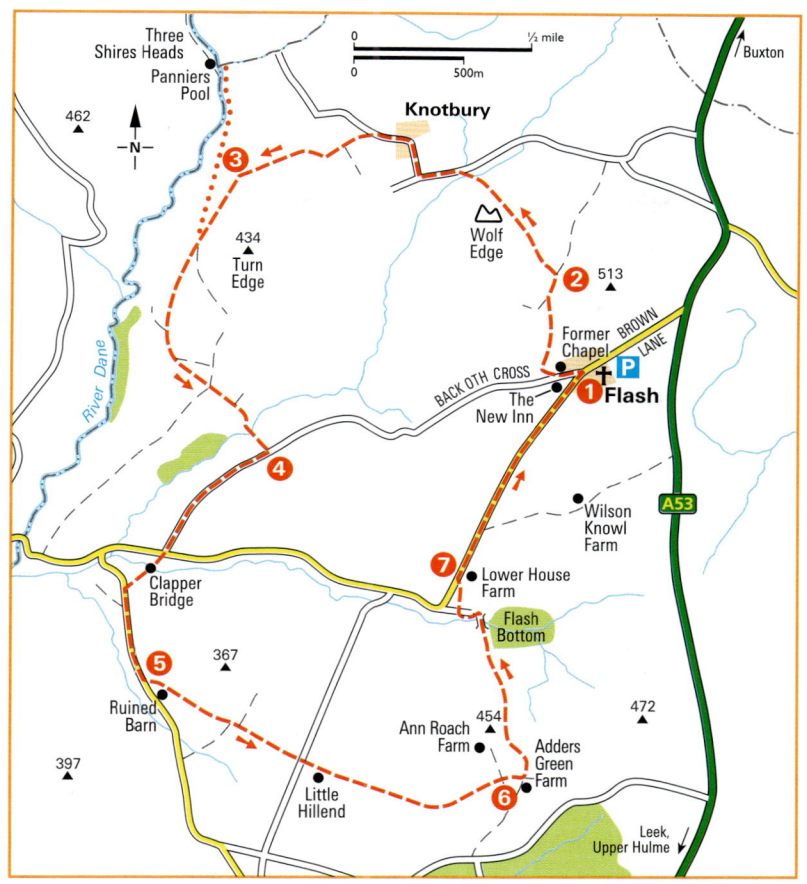

1. From the church gates walk down Back Oth Cross passing The New Inn. At the edge of the village, branch right on a track bending past Bank House and Far View Cottage. Fork right at a bright yellow fingerpost and into fields. Enter a walled track, ending as you cross a stile. Continue at the edge of rough pasture, then turn left through a gate on to a short grassy track.

2. At the track's end, bear right over Wolf Edge. Descend the right boundary past a redundant stile. Cross to the far side, then cross back towards the bottom of the slope, angling down towards a lane. Go left, then right into Knotbury. Pass Knotbury Lea Cottage, then fork left at a fingerpost. Head downhill beside the wall, ignore a track left, and continue with the moorland path, bending right then left at the field end. Rise on to Turn Edge, maintaining your direction at a stile.

3. Over the crest, descend left, passing through trees to a track. Detour right here for the Panniers Pool; otherwise go left. Branch off at a tall waypost, along another falling track. Maintain a slant over rough enclosures to a gravel track. Go left to an easily missed waypost on the outside of a bend left. The grassy track runs almost parallel with, but below, the gravel track. Maintain your direction past a gate, the way eventually steepening into a deep valley. As

the track drops towards the stream, it zigzags to meet a ford. The footbridge lies to the left (not the crash-barrier bridge to the right), and is hidden by gorse; a wooden pole supporting a power cable guides you to it. Climb uphill over rough ground to a lane.

4. Turn right. At the junction, cross slightly to the right and through a squeeze stile. In wet conditions, follow the road right then left instead. Go downhill through scrub to a clapper bridge, then rise, bending gently left, across a field to a lane. Follow this uphill.

5. Near a ruined barn, fork left through a squeeze stile. Cross a pasture diagonally right, then follow a faint path across moorland grazing. Pass a building, then keep ahead on a track. Cross a lane and continue opposite through Little Hillend's driveway. A distinct, rough path leads on to the moor, eventually crossing a track from Ann Roach Farm. Cross a broken stile, through a couple of gates, and turn right to Adders Green Farm.

6. At the entrance, go left through a gate towards Flash Bottom. Follow the left wall at a corner and through a large gate. Continue ahead then bear right below a rise, the path soon descending to a plantation at Flash Bottom. Cross a footbridge then walk left up a rough track. Cross a stony driveway, taking a faint grassy path opposite towards Lower House Farm.

7. Go up steps to the road. Turn right and follow this lane gently uphill back into Flash.

Extending the walk To extend the walk to visit the Panniers Pool, turn right on the track near the start of Point 3. Return the same way, forking left at a track junction halfway.

Where to eat and drink
The Winking Man pub, a few miles down the A53 towards Upper Hulme serves good hearty food and has a range of decent ales. Walkers are welcomed and the pub is open every day of the week except Mondays.

What to see
Look for evidence of the network of packhorse trails on the moors. These routes were used from medieval times to transport goods between communities, and several of these routes converged at the Panniers Pool at Three Shires Heads. Packhorse trains could have up to 50 horses and were led by a man called a 'jagger' (their ponies were Galloway crossbreeds called Jaegers). Today you will find their paved routes descending into the valleys in distinctive 'holloways' or sunken lanes.

While you're there
Visit Buxton, England's highest market town. Founded by the Romans after they discovered a hot spring in AD 79, it became a spa town in the 18th century. Home to Buxton Spa water, there are many fine buildings, and a publicly available street fountain is still fed from St Ann's Well.

AROUND LONGNOR

DISTANCE/TIME	6 miles (9.7km) / 3hrs 30min
ASCENT/GRADIENT	459ft (140m) / ▲▲
PATHS	Some on road, otherwise good footpaths; can be muddy; many stiles
LANDSCAPE	Valleys, hills and meadows
SUGGESTED MAP	OS Explorer OL24 Peak District – White Peak Area
START/FINISH	Grid reference: SK089649
DOG FRIENDLINESS	Suitable for dogs, but keep on lead near livestock
PARKING	Longnor village square
PUBLIC TOILETS	Longnor village square

Longnor, a charming Peak village situated on a high ridge between the Dove and Manifold rivers, developed as a meeting place on the ancient trade routes that once crossed these hills from Sheffield, Chesterfield, Nottingham and the Potteries. More recently it became famous as the location of the television drama *Peak Practice*. First screened in 1993, the series put Peak District scenery on the television map and attracted countless visitors. The earlier episodes took many different parts of the area to establish fictional Cardale – particularly Crich. Real life in Longnor, though, is somewhat quieter than the TV version, which ceased filming in 2002.

There is plenty that will be familiar to viewers of the series. The fine brick frontage of the fictional Cardale Tearoom is actually a Georgian hotel built to serve the needs of the Harpur-Crewe Estate; it was used as a meeting place for the local farmers when they came to pay their annual rents at the end of March. The Horseshoe had the honour of being the TV doctors' local, the Black Swan. Dating back to 1609, it was an important staging point for the packhorse and carriage trade that crossed these hills. Both the Crewe & Harpur Arms and The Horseshoe are now self-catering establishments. The one remaining pub in the village, Ye Olde Cheshire Cheese Inn, in the village, had its origins as a cheese store in 1464 and it still has a reputation for fine food.

The ancient pubs and cobbled market square are a reminder of Longnor's importance in days gone by as a market town. The turnpike roads with their tolls, and the lack of a railway link, prevented Longnor's development as a major trading centre, but the village retains its Victorian market hall. Now a craft centre and coffee shop, it still has the old market toll charge board, with a list of long-forgotten tariffs, above the front door.

One of the highlights of a visit to Longnor is the churchyard of St Bartholomew's. Although the church is 18th-century, the churchyard has some ancient graves, including that of the remarkable William Billings, who lived to the ripe old age of 112. Born in a cornfield, he was at the capture of Gibraltar in 1704, saw action at the Battle of Ramillies in 1706 and fought against the Stuarts in the Jacobite Risings of 1715 and 1745.

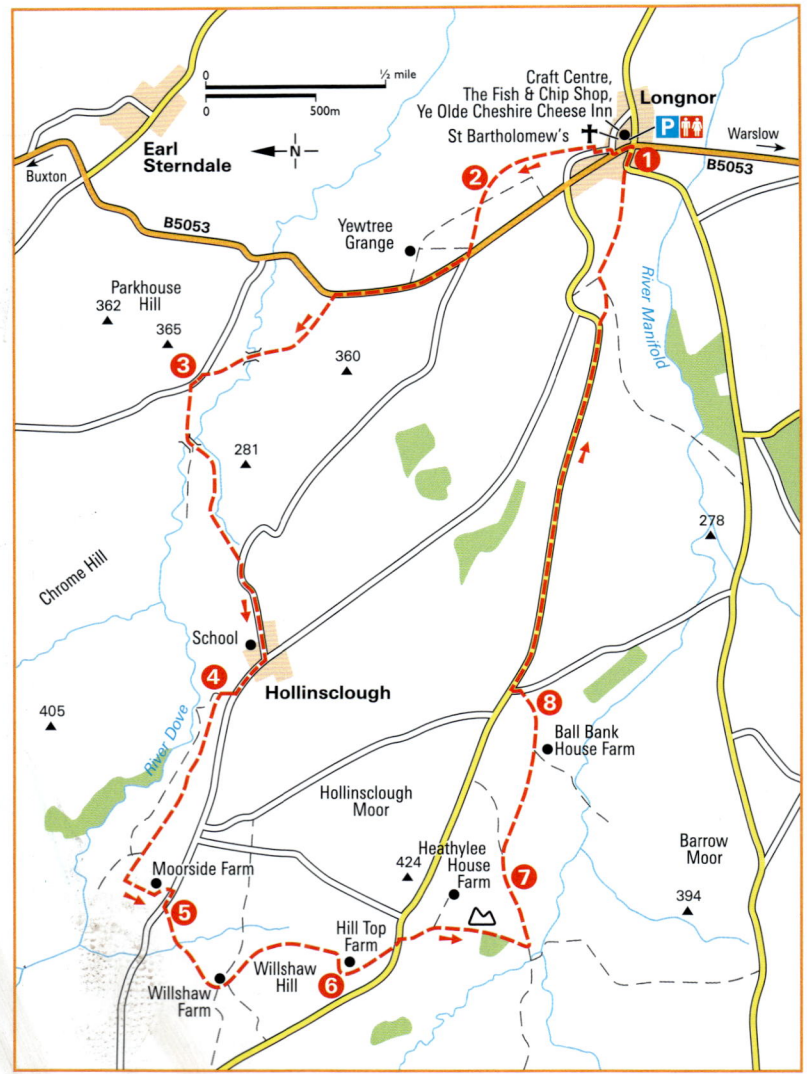

1. From the square take the road towards Buxton. Take the first right to turn into Church Street, and then go immediately left, up Lane Head and right up steps to the footpath. Follow the waymarkers, behind some houses, over a stile and along a wall. Cross another stile, go downhill and turn left onto a farm road.

2. Go straight on and turn right onto the road. Just before the bend towards the bottom of the hill, take the farm road on the left. At the end, continue through a gate onto the footpath, through a gap stile, downhill, across a bridge

and continue straight ahead. Eventually go through a gate and turn left onto the road.

3. Fork left onto a farm road, following the waymarked path. Cross a bridge by a ford and turn left to follow the river bank to the road. Turn right, through Hollinsclough, following the road to the right and uphill. Turn right onto a bridleway, go through a gate and downhill.

4. After 50yds (46m) fork left by two stones and continue along the flank of the hill. Cross a stile and continue until the path meets a stone wall, then veer left and uphill. At the top, turn left at a stone gatepost, and walk through Moorside Farm, through a kissing gate to the road. Turn right then cross a stile to a public footpath on the left.

5. Follow a line downhill from the fingerpost, aiming for the gate in the field beyond the trees and the brook. In very wet weather this is a quagmire. Cross a stile and the brook and head uphill, through a gap in the wall by a gate at the top and turn left through Willshaw Farm. Fork right for the well-signposted path to Hill Top Farm.

6. Follow the path over stiles and past the farm to the road. Go straight over for the track signposted 'Heathylee House Farm'. Approaching the farm go right, steeply downhill, over a stile and follow the path along the wall. Just before the stream, cross a stile on the left and head uphill to the left of some trees.

7. Continue walking uphill, through a gate in a stone wall to a ruined building. Follow the track to the next farm, bear left after the barn, then go left onto a footpath uphill.

8. Go through a stile and follow the wall uphill to the road. Turn left then right towards Longnor. Just as the road bends left, cross a stile on the right, go downhill and over several stiles and gates to a farm road. Turn right and follow this back to the village and your car.

Where to eat and drink
In Longnor, there's the fish-and-chip shop and tea room with indoor seating. The Craft Centre and Coffee Shop at the former market hall, serves home-made cakes and cream teas, and refurbished Ye Olde Cheshire Cheese Inn offers a varied pub menu.

What to see
Some 350 million years ago, Britain lay south of the equator and the Peak District enjoyed a tropical climate. The Peak limestones were built up over millions of years from the remains of shells, corals and tiny aquatic creatures called crinoids. Parkhouse and Chrome hills, two prominent landmarks on this walk, are limestone reefs, that formed, rather like mud or silt piles, during this period.

While you're there
Well dressing is a centuries old tradition in this area. A wooden framework holds a bed of clay, into which flower petals, moss, berries, cones and seeds are pressed in an intricate design. The display is then placed over the well in a special ceremony. Each village has its own design and date. Dressings take place throughout the summer.

THE ROACHES

DISTANCE/TIME	3.8 miles (6km) / 2hrs
ASCENT/GRADIENT	625ft (191m) / ▲
PATHS	Rocky moorland paths, forest tracks and road
LANDSCAPE	Moor and woodland
SUGGESTED MAP	OS Explorer OL24 Peak District – White Peak Area
START/FINISH	Grid reference: SK004621
DOG FRIENDLINESS	Access land, keep on lead
PARKING	In lay-by on lane below The Roaches
PUBLIC TOILETS	None on route
NOTES	This route was ravaged by wildfire in 2018. It is hoped that the outstanding natural beauty of this area will recover to some degree, but it may take a few years to return to its former glory

The jagged ridge of The Roaches is one of the most popular outdoor locations in the Peak District National Park. The name is a corruption of the French for rocks: roches. It was here on the gritstone crags that the 'working-class revolution' in climbing took place in the 1950s. Manchester lads Joe Brown, a builder, and Don Whillans, a plumber, went on to become legends within the climbing fraternity by developing new rock-climbing techniques wearing gym shoes and using Joe's mother's discarded clothes line as a rope.

Look out for Rockhall Cottage, built into the rock and containing at least one room that is a natural cave. The cottage was a former gamekeeper's residence and is currently owned by the Peak District National Park. Restored in 1989, and now known as the Don Whillans Memorial Hut, the bothy can be booked through the British Mountaineering Council by small groups of climbers. Otherwise, you can glimpse the listed building from a distance.

Other less tangible legends surround this long outcrop, several of them attached to Doxey Pool. Locals speak in hushed voices of a young mermaid who lived in the pool but was captured by a group of men. If the stories are to be believed, her ghost can still be heard singing through the mist. Lurking in the darkest depths of the pool is Jenny Greenteeth, a hideous monster with green skin, long hair and sharp teeth, who grabs the ankles of anyone unfortunate enough to get too close, dragging them to a watery grave. Another myth says the pool is bottomless and will never dry out. Sadly this myth was busted in the heatwave of 2018, when it did indeed dry out, leaving little but damp peat on its surface.

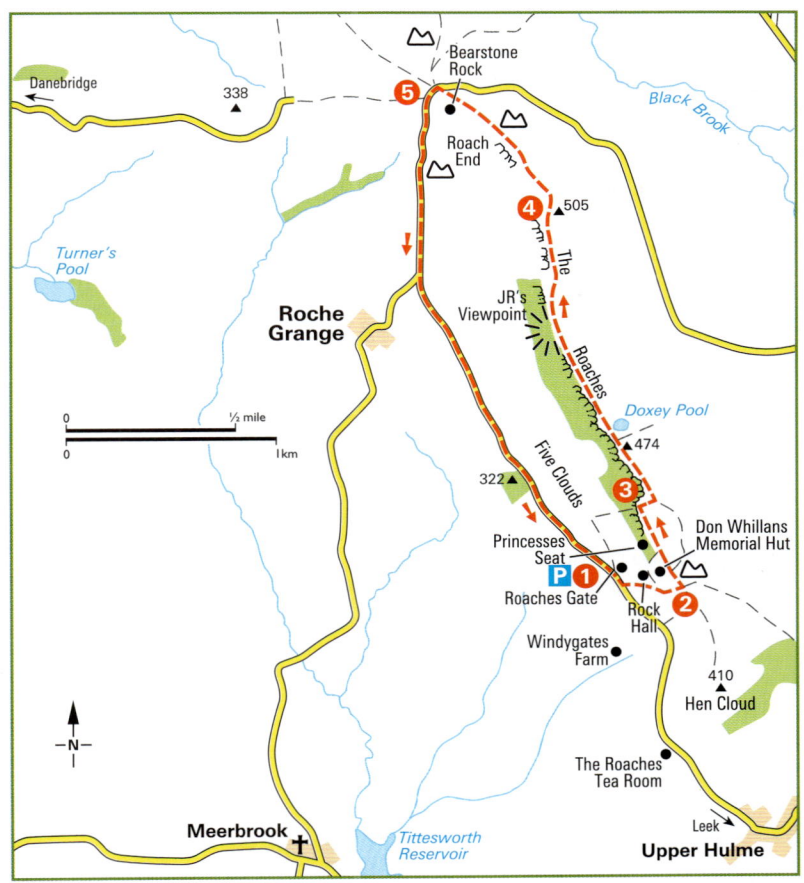

1. Descend the lane from the long parking lay-by below The Roaches. Turn left through the main gate into access land, by the interpretation panel at Roaches Gate. Follow the main path which gently rises to the southern end of the rocks. On the way there are a couple of tracks which lead left to Rock Hall, but ignore all side turns until you reach a crossing track. (This leads to the top of the angular cliff wall of Hen Cloud on your right.)

2. Fork left on to a broad rocky track to begin the ascent to The Roaches ridgeline. Take the next fork left on to a narrower sandy track leading between two distinct levels of rock crags. Go left through a pair of stone gateposts and continue right on a well-defined track. The path is flanked by rocks on the right and woodland to the left and below. Follow it under the rocks to a sandy T-junction.

3. Turn right and rise up a stepped path through a gap in the rocks to the ridgeline. Turn left and follow the ridge path, passing to the left of Doxey Pool. Look out for JR's viewpoint with its fabulous views as far as the North Wales hills on a very clear day. It's roughly halfway between Doxey Pool and the trig point.

4. From the trig point summit, descend on a sandy path through bouldery rocks. As the outcrops fade, this becomes an easy-going paved path. Continue past the Bearstone Rock, to join the road at Roach End.

5. Turn left down the road, pass through a gate, and go back to the start point.

Where to eat and drink
The Roaches Tea Room & Restaurant at Paddock Farm sits beneath the rocky outcrop of Hen Cloud, just down the road towards Leek. There's a conservatory overlooking a herb garden and superb views across Tittesworth Reservoir. It's open daily all year. Ye Olde Rock Inn at Upper Hulme also does great bar meals and real ale.

What to see
Part way along the ridgeline, look out for a small grassy ledge with a fantastic viewpoint. The rock at the back of the ledge is inscribed with the initials JR, carved with a degree of skill into the rock. From here you can see as far as The Wrekin on a clear day, with nearer landmarks such as Croker Hill (with its transmitter), Jodrell Bank and Tittesworth Reservoir.

While you're there
Leek is a magnet for antiques hunters. As well as having a host of antiques dealers, there's an open-air craft and antiques market each Saturday in the historic Market Square. Other markets include the indoor Butter Market, selling mainly fresh traditional produce, on Wednesday, Friday and Saturday.

GREENWAY BANK

DISTANCE/TIME	2.75 miles (4.4km) / 1hr 30min
ASCENT/GRADIENT	295ft (90m) / ▲
PATHS	Field paths and firm woodland tracks, one long flight of steps, 7 stiles
LANDSCAPE	Undulating farmland and woodland
SUGGESTED MAP	OS Explorer 258 Stoke-on-Trent & Newcastle-under-Lyme
START/FINISH	Grid reference: SJ889552
DOG FRIENDLINESS	Signs request on lead in Country Park
PARKING	Greenway Bank Country Park visitor centre, closes at dusk
PUBLIC TOILETS	By visitor centre

Greenway Bank Country Park, a scenic mix of lakes and craggy woodland, is located a mile to the southeast of Biddulph and was formerly part of two large estates. To the north was an enclosed deer park belonging to Knypersley Hall, while the rest belonged to the Greenway Bank estate that was owned by canal-building entrepreneurs.

At the heart of the estate are The Serpentine (or Serpentine Pool) and Knyperseley Pool, strictly speaking two man-made watercourses. The former was constructed in the early 1780s as a feeder reservoir for the newly-built Trent & Mersey Canal, developed by Greenway Bank owner Hugh Henshall who was the successor (and brother-in-law) of the great canal-builder James Brindley. The larger Knyperseley Pool, which is also called Knypersley Reservoir, was built afterwards and still feeds the nearby Caldon Canal. Together with the ponds below the dam, the pool is a popular venue for local anglers and notable for its plentiful perch, bream and roach, as well as carp and pike.

Now demolished, Greenway Bank House once stood near the car park at the start of the walk. You can still make out the landscaped grounds and enjoy surviving details like the miniature grotto, while its former stables and outbuildings now form the visitor centre, with a delightful brick-walled courtyard that is a sun trap in summer. However, spring is perhaps the best season to visit Greenway Bank when the extensive woodland floor is covered with bluebells, ramsons, wood anemone and red campion.

Indeed, the trees themselves are also noteworthy and in particular the Jubilee Arboretum beyond the head of The Serpentine that you visit at the end of this walk. What's claimed to be a complete collection of native and long-established trees and shrubs has been planted, many with name plates to help you identify the different species – from beech and wych elm to dogwood and rowan. At the foot of the wooded slope is a marshy area of reeds, where plants like ragged robin, meadowsweet and marsh marigolds can all be found.

On the eastern side of Knypersley Pool is the Warder's Tower, a Gothic castellated building built in 1828 that stands on a crag among the trees, but it is in a poor state of repair. From here you can follow a there-and-back path beneath the wooded crags to see Gawton's Well and Gawton's Stone. It's named after a man named Gawton who, in the 18th century, lived as a hermit beneath the stone, apparently curing himself of the plague by bathing in a nearby well.

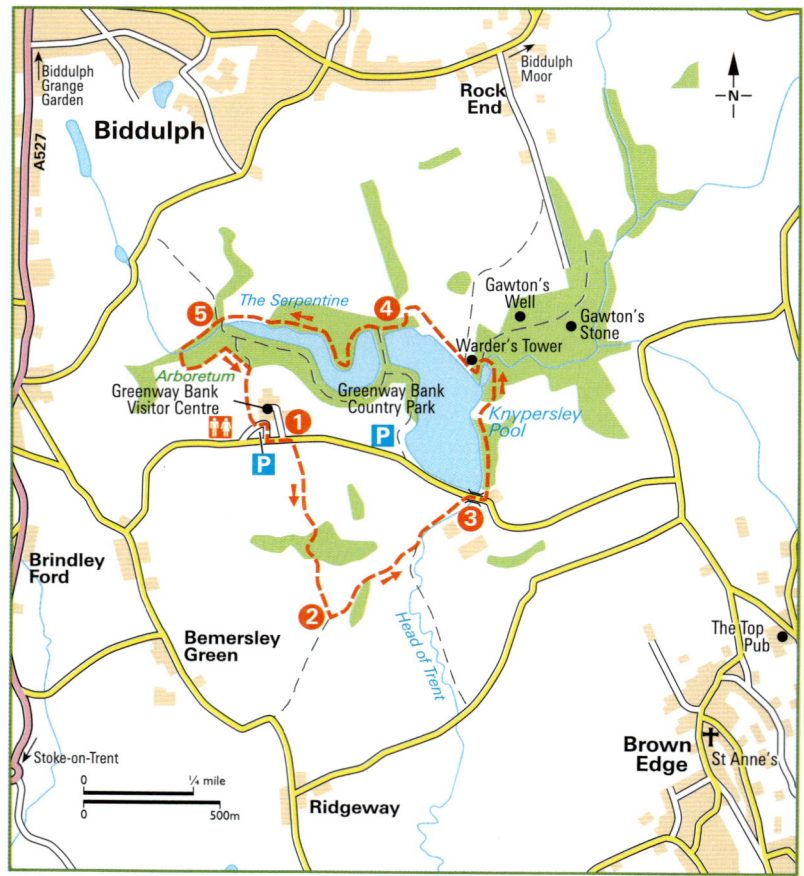

1. Walk out of the car park exit and cross the road. Turn left then almost immediately right for a footpath along the top edge of a field. Continue through a wooded dip and ahead across another field, this time drifting half right uphill to reach a stile in the far corner.

2. Don't cross the stile but turn hard left, almost back on yourself. Walk down the steepening slope above the trees, aiming for the reservoir glimpsed ahead, until you come to a stile. Beyond this continue in the same direction across undulating ground to join a path beside a stream. Go up a long flight of steps to the road.

3. Turn right and once across the black girder bridge turn left for the popular path beside the reservoir. At the path junction by the Warder's Tower you can divert right to visit Gawton's Well and Stone among the wooded crags, otherwise continue ahead with the reservoir on your left.

4. When you come to a path junction just before the dam of The Serpentine go right, across a small bridge, and follow the path to the right of this long, sinewy lake. Ignore all paths off and continue to the far end.

5. Swing sharply left, over a short wooden bridge, then turn immediately right for a narrower path above a marshy area. At the far end follow the path around to the left for a gentle, stepped ascent of the wooded slope. Continue past a path junction to the very top and go across a farm track via two gates. Fork left through the Grotto to return to the visitor centre and the start of the walk.

Where to eat and drink
There is generally a van or kiosk onsite at the Visitor Centre selling snacks and hot drinks. For more substantial fare visit The Top Pub at Hill Top, above Brown Edge, a popular freehouse with a good selection of real ales. It also has a beer garden and serves food every day.

What to see
The stream that issues from the two lakes is marked on Ordnance Survey maps as 'Head of Trent', although the real source of the river appears to be further upstream near Biddulph Moor. Below Greenway Bank it goes on to flow through Stoke and Stone before swinging northwards via Burton and Nottingham to join the Ouse near the Humber Estuary.

While you're there
Biddulph Grange Garden was created by Victorian James Bateman and is an extraordinary collection of plants from around the world, laid out in separate gardens and shrubberies and separated by steps, terraces, hedges and tunnels. From springtime rhododendrons to late summer dahlias, pinetums to Chinese Gardens, it's a mesmerising trip around the continents of the world via their flowers and plants. The garden is now owned and run by the National Trust.

RUDYARD RESERVOIR

DISTANCE/TIME	4.5 miles (7.2km) / 1hr 45min
ASCENT/GRADIENT	180ft (55m) / ▲
PATHS	Gravel bridleways, footpaths and roads, several stiles
LANDSCAPE	Lakeside and woodland
SUGGESTED MAP	OS Explorer 268 Wilmslow, Macclesfield & Congleton
START/FINISH	Grid reference: SJ939611
DOG FRIENDLINESS	Good, but care should be taken near wildfowl
PARKING	Car park at northeast corner of reservoir
PUBLIC TOILETS	Opposite visitor centre at reservoir's southwest corner

Rudyard Reservoir was created in 1800 to provide an adequate water supply to the region's canals. It wasn't until the second half of the century, however, that it was commercially exploited as a major tourist attraction, thanks to the fast-growing popularity of boating and picnicking among the Victorian middle classes.

In its heyday, the waterfront would have been awash with holidaymakers escaping from the smoggy industrial towns at weekends, with a funfair, bandstand and dance floor for the adults, and carousels, slides and swings for the children. Ice skating was very popular in the winter, when fairy lights were hung from trees, and great fires on the shore enabled night skating and dancing. The reservoir was also the scene of some amazing spectacles. In June 1861, the memorably named African Blondin walked over the reservoir on a tightrope. (He was a pupil of the great Charles Blondin, renowned for crossing Niagara Falls on a tightrope.)

However, it was at a Victorian picnic in April 1863 that the reservoir's name was assured its place in literary history, when renowned pottery designer John Lockwood Kipling met his bride-to-be Alice Macdonald. History has it that the courting couple spent much of their time here and were so fond of the memories that they named their first son after the reservoir. Rudyard Kipling was born in Bombay on 30 December 1865 and spent his first five years in India, before being sent to England to stay with a foster family. After finishing his schooling he returned to India to work as a journalist on the Civil and Military Gazette, but during his spare time he wrote the first of the poems and stories that would later make him famous. He went on to write many more, including his most famous poem, *If*. Despite his popular and critical success, Kipling declined many of the honours that were offered to him, including a knighthood, Poet Laureateship and the Order of Merit, but in 1907, aged 42, he accepted the Nobel Prize for Literature.

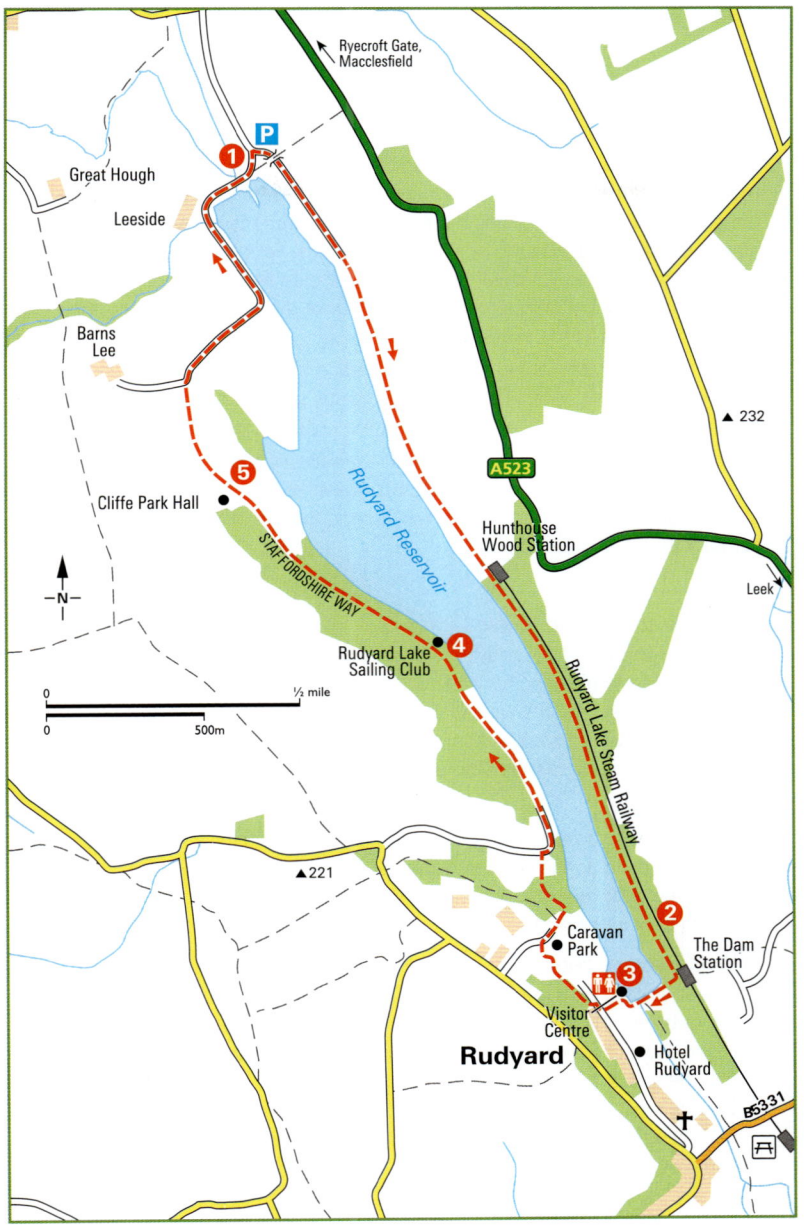

1. From the car park, which is at the far end of a potholed dirt track off Beat Lane, take the left fork underneath the obvious bridge. Follow the wide, gravel bridleway along the shore, with a mini-gauge railway just to the left (see While You're There). Continue towards the end of the reservoir.

2. Nearing the end and just after the Lakeside Loop signal box there's a short track to the right of the main path up to a scenic picnic area. After this cross

the dam at the head of the reservoir (a pay telescope gives wider views). Bear right to the visitor centre and toilets.

3. From the visitor centre and toilet block head away from the reservoir up the footpath beside some prominent black railings (not the vehicle drive through the wide gate). At the top is a metalled road. Turn left to reach the Hotel Rudyard, otherwise turn right and then fork left at The Crescent, after which the road becomes a gravel track. Where the track veers right, take the narrow footpath straight ahead (avoiding the private road into the caravan park). Just after the brow of the rise is a junction of two paths. Fork right, then go straight ahead along the road. Go downhill and left on a path before a private drive. At the far end turn right onto a road. Continue above the shore until it becomes unsurfaced at Rudyard Lake Sailing Club.

4. After 400yds (366m) along the wooded path, cross the stile into a clearing with views over the water. The path eases gently uphill to a gate with a chain, which signals your arrival at the vast Victorian pile of Cliffe Park Hall.

5. Continue past the building and down the gently sloping drive. At the far end turn right onto a small, surfaced road, back towards the reservoir. Go over the stile beside the cattle grid and continue around the end of the reservoir to the car park.

Where to eat and drink

The Rudyard Lake Café near the visitor centre offers snacks and light refreshments, including hot and cold drinks, all year round. For those after something more substantial, the Hotel Rudyard offers a selection of main meals and bar snacks, Tuesday to Sunday evenings, as well as a Sunday lunchtime carvery. There's also a dog-friendly café open daily.

What to see

The various structures along the lakes edge, including the visitor centre are often home to the nests of migrating swallows. You can see the adults flying low over the lake catching small insects for both them and their young back in the nest.

While you're there

At weekends during the summer, you can hire rowing boats. Alternatively, the Rudyard Lake Steam Railway offers a 3-mile (4.8km) round trip along the side of the reservoir on a mini-gauge railway about half the size of a standard narrow-gauge railway. Steam-hauled trains operate most weekends from March to end of October, including bank holiday weekends, and on most weekdays during school holidays. See www.rlsr.org for details.

MOW COP CASTLE

DISTANCE/TIME	6.25 miles (10.1km) / 2hrs 30min
ASCENT/GRADIENT	660ft (201m) / ▲▲▲
PATHS	Gravel bridleways, footpaths and roads, many stiles
LANDSCAPE	Escarpment top, farmland, canal and woodland
SUGGESTED MAP	OS Explorer 268 Wilmslow, Macclesfield & Congleton
START/FINISH	Grid reference: SJ856573
DOG FRIENDLINESS	Should be kept on lead in fields
PARKING	At Mow Cop Castle (closed at dusk)
PUBLIC TOILETS	None on route

The tiny village of Mow Cop and the escarpment on which it is perched has a rich and fascinating history that goes back thousands of years. Its prominent position, visible from five counties, made it the perfect spot for a beacon. It's thought that the Romans may have had a watchtower here; it's known they built a road from nearby Astbury to Biddulph, passing over Nick i' th' Hill, which would have brought them very close to Mow Cop. There's also an abundance of coal, millstone grit and limestone in the region, all of which the Romans would have used.

During the reign of Elizabeth I, beacons were lit throughout the country warning of imminent invasion by the Spanish Armada, and there is little doubt that Mow Cop would have been part of this chain. More recently it has been used as a beacon site for special royal events. As part of the Her Majesty Queen Elizabeth's Diamond (2012) and Platinum (2022) jubilee celebrations, a beacon at Mow Cop was lit. It was just one of the long chain of beacons around the world. The queen was also honoured in this way for her 25 years and 50 years on the throne, and for her 90th birthday in 2016. The UK's tradition of lighting beacons began in 1897 to commemorate Queen Victoria diamond jubilee and has been continued ever since for marking coronations, jubilees and royal weddings, and very special royal birthdays.

Given the village's lofty position, it perhaps comes as no surprise to learn that Mow Cop is famed for its castle which, situated as it is on the massive stone outcrop right at the top of the escarpment, is visible for literally miles around. But this is no ordinary castle and it certainly wasn't built for defensive purposes. In fact it is not a real castle at all, but an elaborate folly made to look like a ruined medieval fortress, as was fashionable at the time. It was built in 1746 by Randle Wilbraham I of Rode Hall as a summer house and as a means of enhancing the view from Rode Hall some 2 miles (3.2km) to the west.

The castle's tower and wall (the latter little more than a façade) still present a striking silhouette to the east as well as the west, and would certainly have impressed, or riled, rival landowners on both sides of the border. A century or so after it was built, the owner of nearby Keele Hall claimed that part of the summer house was on his land and therefore that part ownership should fall to him. It was eventually ruled that both parties should share the building, but that the public should also have free access. The castle and its surrounds were threatened by excessive quarrying in the 1920s and 1930s, but in 1937, after another legal wrangle, the deeds were donated to the National Trust.

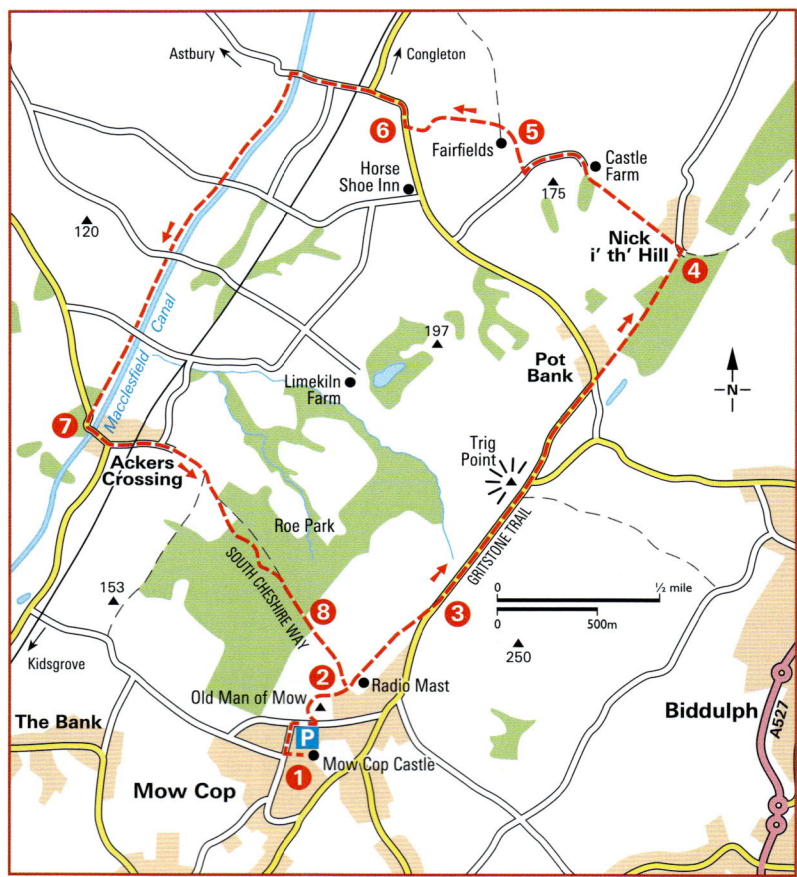

1. From the castle, turn right along the High Street, then right again up Wood Street. Before you reach the brow of the hill, turn left on the Gritstone Trail to the Old Man of Mow, which is situated on the site of a cairn.

2. Continue along the track to a junction of three paths. Keep ahead, signposted the Gritstone Trail, just to the left of the radio mast. Go down steps, and at the end of the narrow field take the upper path (not the more obvious lower track) through woodland.

3. Go left on the metalled road and walk this along the ridge for 0.75 miles (1.2km) until it bends left at Pot Bank Farm. Go straight ahead on the obvious path.

4. Follow this path until it reaches another road. Turn left down the hill and continue straight down another track, to the left of the former Methodist church. Just after a house on the right, the path squeezes through a slot in the wall. Stay straight down through the fields, over the stile. At Castle Farm, go through the gate and follow the road round. After 250yds (229m), after a brick shed on your right, go through a gap in the hedge.

5. Keeping to the right of Fairfields, cross the stile under a tree and head left across the field to cross a farm driveway. Keeping the same direction, cross a succession of fields and stiles, aiming to the left of the white house in the distance ahead. In the last field, follow the hedge around to the left before crossing another stile onto the road.

6. Head right along this road, going left on Dodds Lane to cross the railway and then the canal. Drop down to the tow path on the Macclesfield Canal and turn right along it for 1.25 miles (2km).

7. At Bridge No. 85 cross the canal and, after 200yds (183m), go left up Yew Tree Lane. Go under the railway, keep right at a wide fork, and after 300yds (274m) take a left fork up a steep track and, soon after, the less obvious gated track, right, into a field. Head right of the farm and follow the hedge up. At the top, cross a stile into the wood.

8. At the top of the wood, cross another stile into a field and continue to the top of the ridge. Turn right and make your way back past the Old Man and into Mow Cop.

Where to eat and drink
Half way around the walk, a little off route, is the Horse Shoe Inn, open every day from noon and serving both traditional pub meals and sandwiches. A beer garden is available to eat and drink in when the weather is nice enough or besides an open fire inside when it is not.

What to see
The Old Man of Mow, 65ft (20m) high and 1,100ft (335m) above sea level, is situated on the site of a cairn that is thought to have been an ancient burial mound, although it may also have served as a simple boundary marker separating Cheshire and Staffordshire. The cairn has been reduced to its present slimline status by years of quarrying, although quite why this single column was left is unknown. It may have been used to raise large slabs of gritstone, or as a reminder of the original cairn.

While you're there
Little Moreton Hall is an eye-catching, half-timbered Tudor house surrounded by a moat built in the 1500s for the prosperous Cheshire landowner William Moreton. Its irregular, top-heavy design has seen it likened to a gingerbread house. Now owned by the National Trust, the hall is visible from the walk at the top of the escarpment.

AROUND TITTESWORTH WATER

DISTANCE/TIME	4.5 miles (7.2km) / 2hrs 30min
ASCENT/GRADIENT	345ft (105m) / ▲
PATHS	Good well-made footpaths, forest tracks and roads
LANDSCAPE	Reservoir and woodland
SUGGESTED MAP	OS Explorer OL24 Peak District – White Peak Area
START/FINISH	Grid reference: SJ993601
DOG FRIENDLINESS	On lead at all times and under control
PARKING	Tittesworth Water Visitor Centre
PUBLIC TOILETS	At Tittesworth Water Visitor Centre

Tittesworth Water and dam were built in 1858 to collect water from the River Churnet and provide a reliable water supply to Leek's thriving textile and cloth-dying industry. By 1963 work to increase its size had been completed, and local farmland was flooded to create a reservoir capable of supplying drinking water to Stoke-on-Trent and the surrounding areas. When full it can supply 10 million gallons (45.5 million litres) of water every day.

The land around the reservoir provides a habitat for a wide variety of wildlife, and many creatures can be seen in the course of this walk. Look out for brown hares in the fields near the car park. You can tell them from rabbits by their very long legs, black-tipped ears and a triangular black and light brown tail. Otters were once hunted almost to extinction by dogs, and although the sport is now illegal their numbers remain low, but look out for the tell-tale prints of their webbed feet and wavy line of tail prints in the sand and soft mud. Look also for holes in the banks along the River Churnet, where otters enter the reservoir. Although it's a difficult little creature to spot, a hole may just be the entrance to a vole burrow and home to a water vole.

Europe's smallest bat, the pipistrelle, suffered a severe decline in numbers in the last decades of the 20th century due to loss of hunting habitats like hedges, ponds and grassland. Pond restoration near Churnet Bay is encouraging their return and they can best be seen here near dusk, flying at an incredible speed as they dive to gobble caddisflies, moths and gnats. Bird life around the reservoir is also abundant and there are two bird hides for visitors' use. Look out for skylarks, small birds with a high-pitched continuous warble, that nest in the meadows around Tittesworth. The song thrush, another bird that has been in decline, also finds a home here, as does the linnet. Look for the male of the species in spring and summer when it has a bright blood-red breast and forehead. At various times of the year you might spot barnacle geese, great crested grebes, pied flycatchers, spectacular kingfishers, cormorants and even a rare osprey that has visited here.

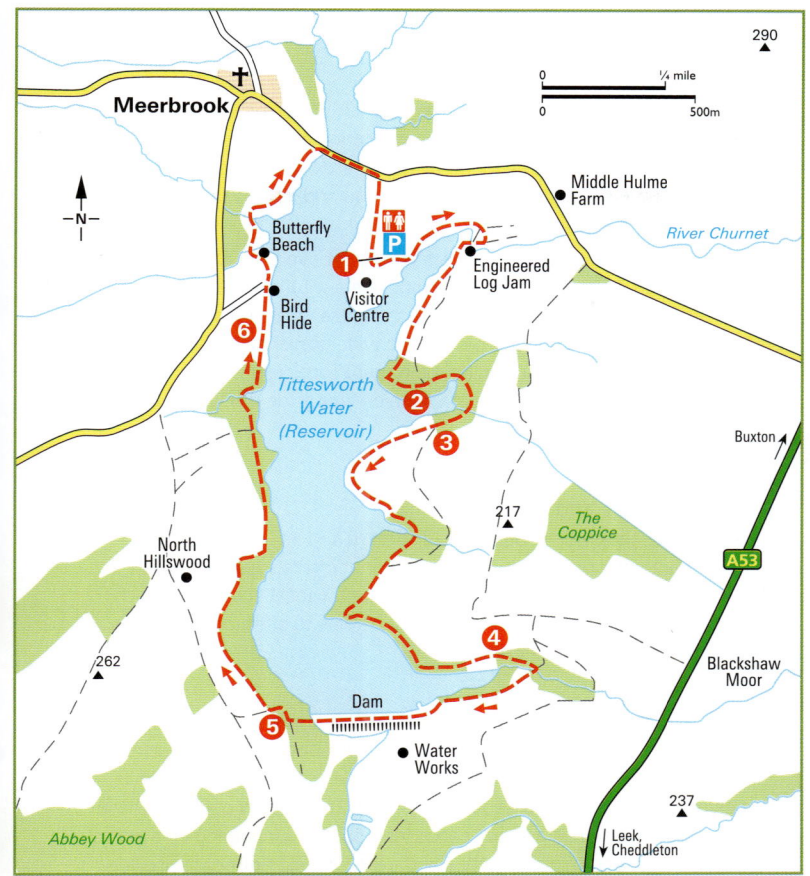

1. Facing the entrance to the Visitor Centre cross the car park to your left and follow a path signed 'Waymarked Walks'. Bend left at an early junction then pass the main car park and a play area. Ignore side paths on a twisty section to pass an engineered 'log jam' then cross two bridges. Fork right from the main trail to take the 'Water's edge path'. Ignore all side turns along this, bending left at a small headland and past some woodland. Now bend left into the woods and fork right at a track junction to rejoin the 'Long Trail' (unsigned).

2. Follow the Long Trail through the wood, crossing two small bridges. As the path leaves the wood fork right on to a grassy track, again signed 'Water's edge path'.

3. Continue along the bank of the reservoir, then re-enter the woodland and cross some duckboards. Cross a bridge by a picnic table, ascend some steps and turn right to rejoin the wide main track once more. Skirt the edge of a wood, keeping a fence on your left, then go downhill through a wood and along the reservoir bank before rising back into thin woodland.

4. Pass a 3km waymarker on a slight rise in the track, then cross a bridge. Rise steeply uphill on a graded track (replacing older steps), staying on the main path as a path joins from a field. Go downhill towards the dam wall on a

33

graded path (again passing older steps) and take the footway across the dam wall. Climb up steps beside a woodland conservation area, then turn right on to a track, which soon bends left to a junction.

5. Bend right here, staying on the 'long trail'. This keeps just right of fields, bending right and briefly downhill into undulating woodland and passing a 5km waymarker. Cross some metal-grilled boardwalks either side of a bridge, then head up over a small knoll of mixed woodland. This is followed by steps either side of a boardwalk bridge.

6. As you exit woodland you gain a pleasant view over Hen Cloud and The Roaches ahead. Stay on the stone path beside a wildflower meadow. Join the end of a tarmac road past the watersports centre, then cross over a junction by a metal barrier and open bird hide. The wide gravel path ahead leads past the Butterfly Beach, then out to the main road. Turn right along the grass verge then right on to a tarmac path running alongside the Visitor Centre driveway to return to the start.

Where to eat and drink
Stop at the Tittesworth Water Visitor Centre and its light and airy restaurant has great views over the water. It offers a good selection of food options, ranging from a full breakfast to local specialities such as Staffordshire oatcakes, and from hot paninis to afternoon teas with delicious scones and pastries.

What to see
Look out for a couple of unusual experimental areas. There's an engineered 'log jam' near the start which is testing a way of reducing flooding risk in rivers. Towards the end of the walk, Butterfly Beach is designed to encourage breeding butterflies. This 'luxury hotel' for these delightful insects has a sandy beach for a spot of sunbathing on a warm summer day, and thistles, nettles and a host of wild flowers to provide egg-laying sites and food.

While you're there
Visit the Churnet Valley Railway for a magical trip back to the 1950s and 1960s on a preserved steam railway, which meanders along beside the River Churnet and the Caldon Canal. If you're trying to entertain the kids – look out for special children's weekends in summer. These may include offers where those dressing up to match the theme (e.g. Superheroes and Princesses) go free, or close encounters with unusual animals whose handlers come to the stations to bring alive the wonders of the natural world.

8 ALONG MANIFOLD VALLEY

DISTANCE/TIME	5.9 miles (9.5km) / 3hrs 30min
ASCENT/GRADIENT	920ft (280m) / ▲▲
PATHS	Hard surface on Manifold Way, other footpaths can be rough in places and muddy in wet weather, many stiles
LANDSCAPE	Woodland, meadows and valleys
SUGGESTED MAP	OS Explorer OL24 Peak District – White Peak Area
START/FINISH	Grid reference: SK095561
DOG FRIENDLINESS	Keep on lead near livestock, under control at all other times; cattle may be present
PARKING	On Manifold Way near Wetton Mill
PUBLIC TOILETS	At Wetton Mill and beside village hall in Warslow
NOTES	Exercise extreme caution at footpath exit on to B5053 near Warslow

Described by one local as 'A line starting nowhere and ending up at the same place', the narrow gauge Leek and Manifold Valley Light Railway was one of England's most picturesque white elephants. Though it survived a mere 30 years from its first run in June 1904, its legacy is still enjoyed today. It ran for 8 miles (12.9km) from Hulme End to Waterhouses, where passengers and freight had to transfer to the standard-gauge Leek branch of the North Staffordshire Railway. The narrow-gauge railway owed its existence to Leek businessmen who feared that their town would lose out because of the newly opened Buxton-to-Ashbourne line.

Engineer Everard Calthorp, who built the Barsi Railway near Mumbai, used the same techniques and design of locomotive for this line, and as a result it looked more like a miniature Indian railway than a classic English line. The potential success of the line was based on the supposition that the Ecton Copper Mines would re-open and that an extension to Buxton would tap into a lucrative tourist market. But the mines didn't re-open and the extension was never built. To survive, the small railway made a daily collection of milk from local farms and hauled produce from the creamery at Ecton for onward transportation to London. Passenger traffic was light, and when tourists did flock to the area on summer weekends it often caused severe overloading of the carriages. Even with this seasonal upturn the line never made a profit, and when the creamery shut in 1933 it was the end of the road for the miniature trains – the last one ran on 10 March 1934. The track was lifted and the bed presented by the railway company to Staffordshire County Council. They had the remarkable foresight to be one of the first local authorities to take a disused railway line and convert it into a pedestrian path.

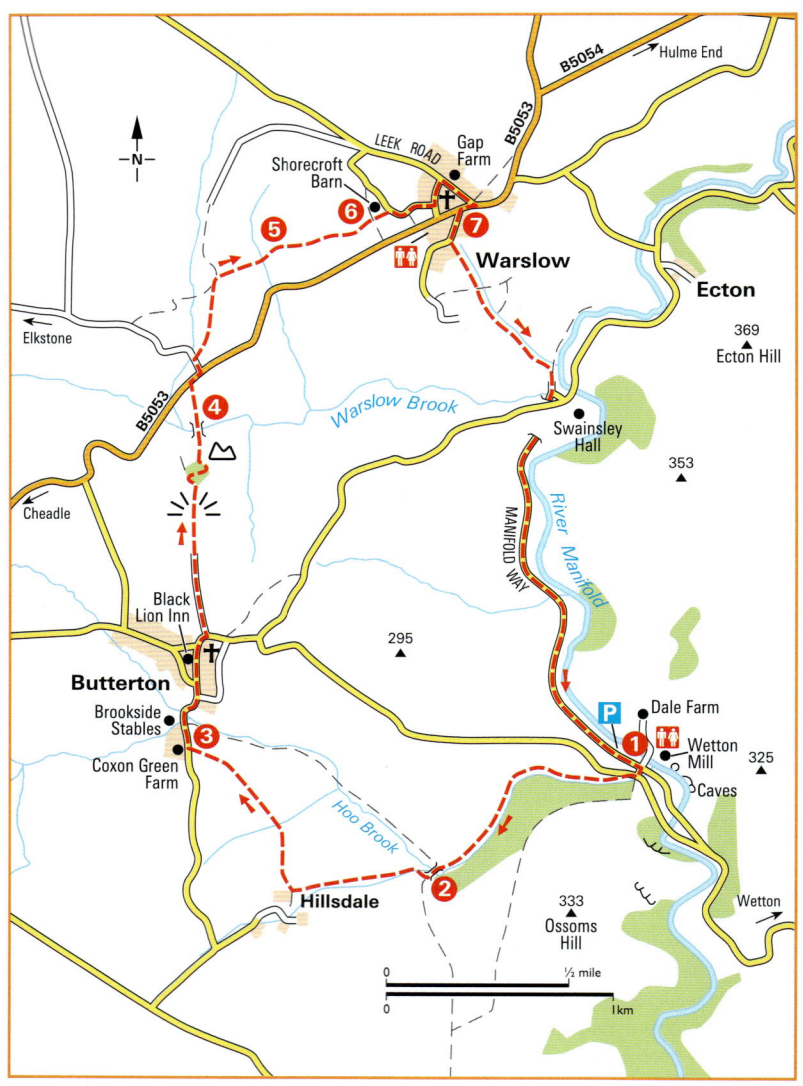

1. Head south down the road then turn right on to the lane towards Butterton. Almost immediately turn right (before the ford) and go through a gate on the left and walk along a valley-bottom track.

2. Two junctions with three footbridges come in quick succession. Follow signs to Hillsdale, going straight ahead then right. Cross a small ford, then bend left at the start of fields. Rise near the field edge, flanking a hill then climbing more steeply to Hillsdale. Turn right, following a footpath over several fields and stiles, aiming roughly for the spire at Butterton. Emerge on to the road opposite Coxon Green Farm.

3. Turn right along the road, cross the long ford and then head uphill. Higher up, fork right away from Pothooks Lane to go past the church and Black Lion

Inn. Turn right at a T-junction on to Waste Lane, then go left on to a track at a white flagpole. Cross a stile into fields, then head beside a row of trees and along a grassy spur. From a fingerpost, descend steeply on a rough and faint path through some trees and down to cross the stream via a shady wooden bridge.

4. Head directly uphill, away from the visible road embankment, then keep a hedge on your left. Cross a stile then exercise extreme caution as you exit directly on to a fast road on a slight but blind bend. Cross over, then fork almost immediately left towards Elkstone. Fork right across a stile on to a footpath, cross a couple of fields, then turn right behind a small derelict building. Follow the line of the wall, cross a stile then a stream and head uphill, keeping the fence on your left.

5. Towards the top of the field, just before the fence meets the wall at a large tree, cross a stile on the right. Head diagonally across the next field, veering left of a line of mature trees. Cross a stile and go through a gap in the next hedgerow. Cross to a gate at the far top corner of the next field, then across boggy ground. Fork diagonally across three small fields to a junction of paths at the next field corner (where a wall meets a hedge).

6. Go through a gate and ahead through the next field to emerge on the road by Shorecroft Barn. Turn right, then at the end, opposite the church, go left. When you reach the T-junction, turn right and pass Gap Farm.

7. At the T-junction with Cheadle Road, cross over on a dog-leg right then left on to School Lane. At a bend right, fork left through a squeeze stile on to a footpath. Descend gently through long narrow fields. Descend through scrub beside a wooded area, then zigzag over a stile and turn right to join the Manifold Way. Follow this easy, well-defined trail through an old railway tunnel, back to the car park.

Where to eat and drink
The Black Lion Inn in Butterton is a good place to relax for an evening after a day's walking (closed on Mondays). Built in 1782, this atmospheric, country hostelry has low beams, roaring open fires and a choice of real ales. Wetton Mill Tea Rooms offers hot and cold drinks, ice creams and snacks.

What to see
The walk passes through a tunnel that served the old railway. This is close to Swainsley Hall, which was the home of the Wardle family at the time of construction. They were shareholders in the company building the railway line, and although happy to take any profits going, they did not want to be troubled by seeing the trains from their house.

While you're there
Visit the old station at Hulme End. Now the Manifold Valley Visitor Centre, it has excellent displays covering the history of the Leek and Manifold Valley Light Railway and the industries and communities it served. There is also a scale model of the line with Hulme End Station as it was in its heyday.

WETTON: A WHITE PEAK VILLAGE

DISTANCE/TIME	8.5 miles (13.7km) / 4hrs 30min
ASCENT/GRADIENT	1771ft (540m) / ▲▲▲
PATHS	Open hillside tracks, some quite steep and rough, field paths and surfaced trail
LANDSCAPE	Walled farmland, open hillside and wooded valley
SUGGESTED MAP	OS Explorer OL24 Peak District – White Peak Area
START/FINISH	Grid reference: SK095561
DOG FRIENDLINESS	On lead around livestock and on Access Land
PARKING	Road side parking near Wetton Mill
PUBLIC TOILETS	Next to Wetton Mill Tea Room, Wetton and Alstonefield

Wetton is an out-of-the way and unspoilt White Peak village, popular with walkers, that sits on the upper eastern edge of the Manifold Valley. Its steep sides are characterised by crags and caves, the latter providing evidence of the very earliest human occupation. But the huge rounded hills that loom above the village also hold clues to the past and in particular how people buried their dead many thousands of years ago.

On the way to Wetton village the walk skirts Wetton Hill, its smooth grassy slopes rising to 1,174ft (358m) and providing a great viewpoint south to Cannock Chase and lowland Staffordshire. Although there's no set path to the summit it's all designated Access Land so you can make your own way to the top – if you have the puff!

Close to the summit of Wetton Hill, and its equally impressive neighbour to the east that the walk visits later on, are the remains of ancient tumuli. Today, they simply look like small grassy mounds, but around 2,500 years ago they marked the last resting places of what were likely to be tribal elders or chiefs. Mostly they were simple chambered cairns, small stone-sided tombs in effect, usually built on prominent locations like hilltops.

Some of these graves contained fragments of pottery and other artefacts, as well as human and animal bones, but virtually all were disturbed by later generations souvenir-hunting or, in the case of several prominent Victorian antiquarians, 'investigating' as many sites as they could find by rather crude excavations and hurriedly carrying away their finds.

There are other prehistoric hilltop burial chambers dotted around the area, including on Narrowdale Hill and Gratton Hill to the northeast of Wetton and Wetton Low just to the south of the village. The place name 'low' comes from the Old English 'hlaw' meaning tumulus or mound and is found at other prominent Peak District sites, including Minninglow and Arbor Low.

If Wetton Hill and Wetton Low demonstrate high level occupation, Wetton Mill characterises human endeavour down in the valley bottom. It's believed that milling has taken place here since the 16th century and a corn mill was certainly operational until the 1850s, but now the former grist buildings house National Trust holiday cottages and a popular tea room. It's a great place to finish a walk, especially on a hot day when the leafy River Manifold provides plenty of shade and the shallow river is ideal for a paddle to cool hot feet.

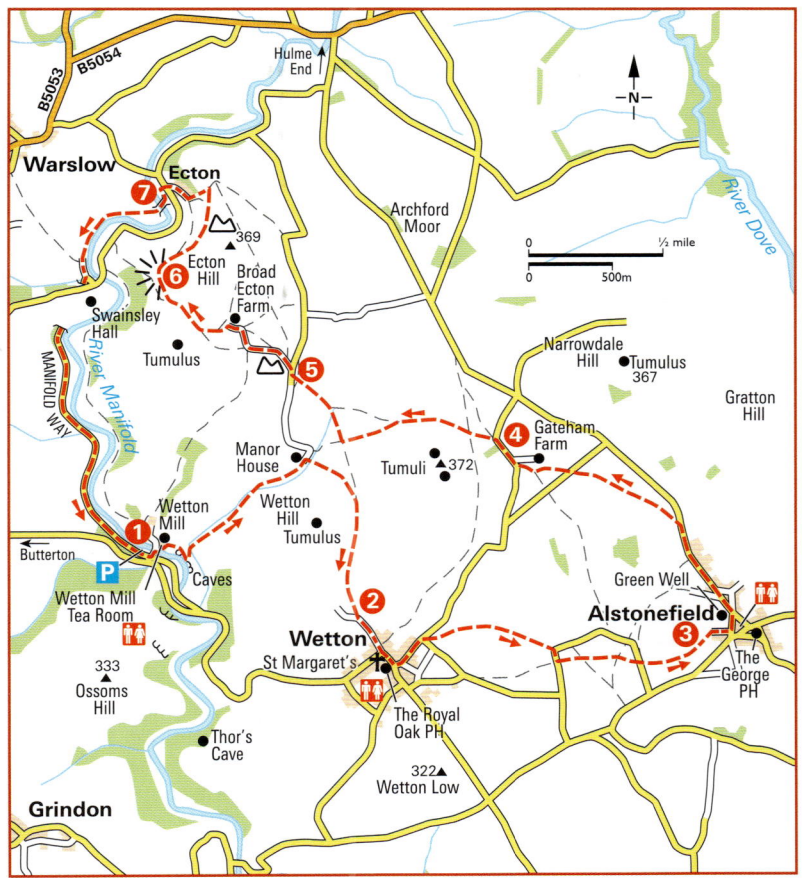

1. Facing the tearoom take the signposted path to the right, between buildings. Go up the grassy hillside and veer left to drop down and join the wide valley bottom route uphill. At Manor House turn right for the route signposted 'Wetton' over a stream and up around Wetton Hill, keeping the wall on your right. Continue ahead through fields to eventually join a lane into Wetton.

2. Turn left on to a road and left again opposite the pub. At the second turning on the right take the footpath diagonally right down through fields. In the far corner go over a wall stile and head right on a walled track. Turn right into a lane, then left for a path across successive fields. Go over a lane and continue uphill to reach Alstonefield via the playing fields.

3. At the road turn left along the pavement and out of the village. Just past the Alstonefield sign go left on a footpath that heads diagonally right through fields (aim to the right of the large hill ahead). Cross a lane and continue to the left of Gateham Farm, then go right along the lane to the first bend.

4. Turn left through the squeeze stile and head half right across the field. The route continues all the way around the lower slopes of the hill until you reach a solitary signpost by a path junction. Turn right to drop down and cross a footbridge, beyond which you head up through a field and copse to reach a lane.

5. Turn left and follow the lane steeply round a hairpin and all the way to Broad Ecton Farm. Here go left, up a field close to the wall, switching sides beyond a gate. At the very top go right, through a gate, and across a field to the corner of a wall. Turn left to reach a gate on the far side.

6. Follow a narrow path around the high and open hillside to the right. Keep to the upper route to reach a crescent of fir trees by an old mine entrance and a former lime kiln beyond. Turn left and zig zag steeply down the grassy slope to a stile partly hidden by gorse bushes at the bottom. Turn right and walk past an odd, green-spired building and down its drive.

7. At the road at the bottom turn right, immediately left and left again to join the Manifold Way. When you meet a lane go through the short tunnel ahead and continue along this to reach the start.

Where to eat and drink

There are two excellent village pubs along the route, The Royal Oak at Wetton and The George at Alstonefield, both walker-friendly with plenty of outside seating and food served daily. Wetton Mill Tea Rooms at the start/finish is open most weekends of the year and daily in summer for snacks and light refreshments.

What to see

As you leave Alstonefield by the road to Hulme End look out for the green well on the left. This was once the main water supply for the village, a valuable source of domestic water for a village built on limestone where surface water very quickly drains away. Together with two small reservoirs, green well was still used until the 1950s when Alstonefield was eventually connected to the mains supply.

While you're there

The annual Manifold Show is organised by the Manifold Valley Agricultural Society, which was formed to bring together the rural communities around the valley. Popular with local people and visitors alike, it's generally held in early August near Castern Hall, south of Wetton, and includes a range of events, displays and different livestock classes.

THE MARKET TOWN OF LEEK

DISTANCE/TIME	4.25 miles (6.8km) / 1hr 45min
ASCENT/GRADIENT	420ft (128m) / ▲▲
PATHS	Meadow track and some road walking, many stiles
LANDSCAPE	Hillside meadow and woodland
SUGGESTED MAP	OS Explorer OL24 Peak District – White Peak Area
START/FINISH	Grid reference: SJ977569
DOG FRIENDLINESS	Must be kept on lead at all times
PARKING	Roadside parking on Abbey Green Road
PUBLIC TOILETS	None on route

Leek is an ancient market town that has long been associated with the textile industry. These days, the silks for which it was once renowned have largely been replaced by synthetic alternatives, although a number of textile manufacturers and factory shops selling brand names direct to the public still remain. But it's a little corn mill on the outskirts of the town, built by an illiterate millwright, that put Leek right at the forefront of the Industrial Revolution.

James Brindley was born at Tunstead, near Buxton in Derbyshire, in 1716, and in 1726 his family moved to Leek. Until the age of 17 he worked as a farm labourer and there is no evidence as to what, if any, formal education he received. He was apprenticed to millwright Abraham Bennett, and after nine years of learning his trade he set up on his own as a millwright in Leek. It was here that he designed and built the water-powered corn mill that today houses a museum to his life and work. However, it wasn't as a millwright that Brindley would make his name, but as a designer and builder of canals. In 1759 the Duke of Bridgewater hired him to devise a system whereby coal could be inexpensively transported from the duke's mines at Worsley to a textile manufacturing centre in Manchester. Brindley's solution was a 10-mile (16.1km) canal that included an underground channel and an aqueduct.

The scale and complexity of the project was unprecedented, and when the Bridgewater Canal was completed in 1765, it revolutionised the way goods were transported in the north of England. In short, the age of the canal had begun. Brindley went on to engineer the Trent and Mersey Canal, the Staffordshire and Worcestershire Canal and many others. In total, he was responsible for 360 miles (579km) of canals, all of which had a huge impact on both the local and national economies. And, as if his career as a millwright and canal engineer wasn't impressive enough, he undertook all of his engineering feats without any written calculations or drawings, preferring instead to do everything in his head.

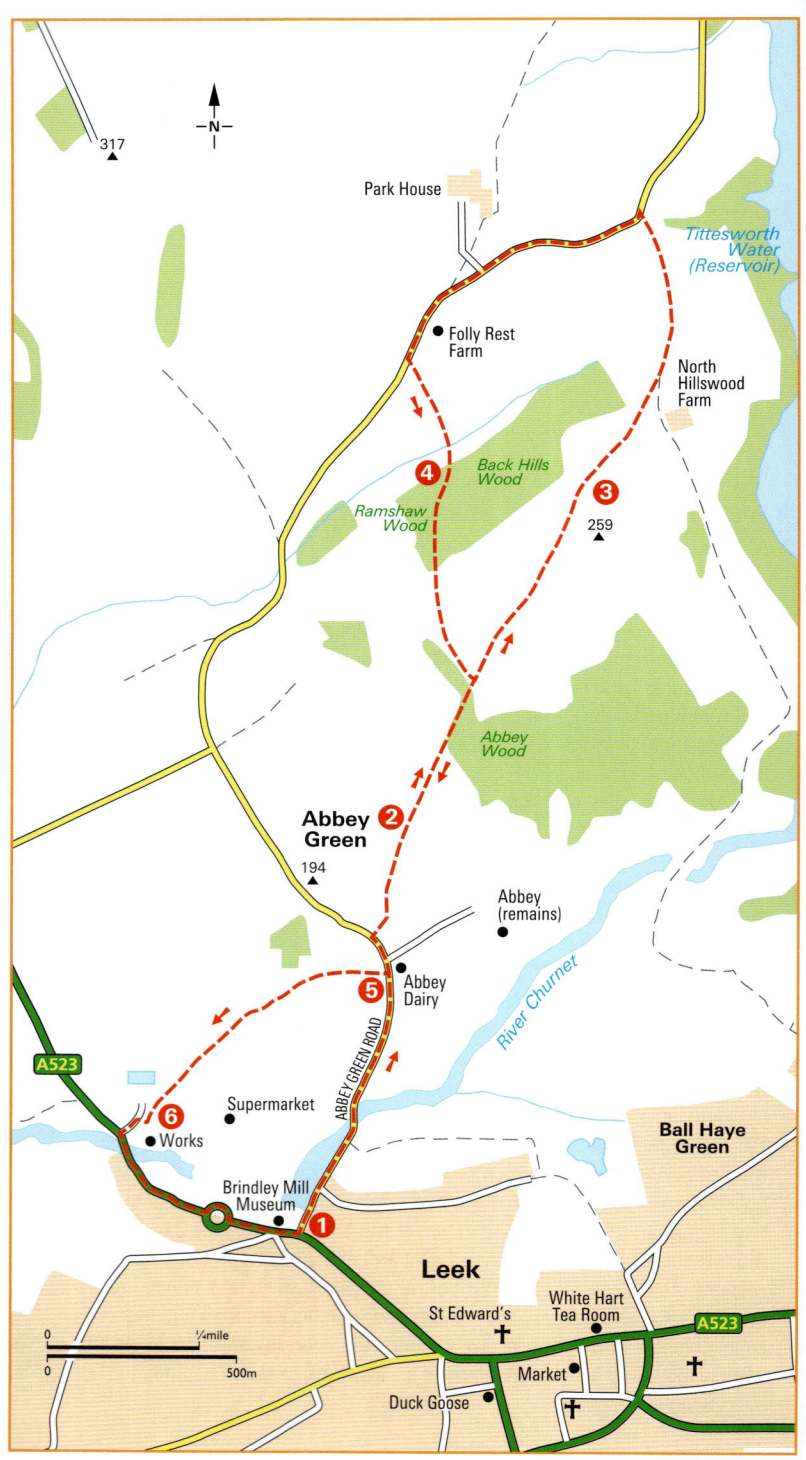

1. From the museum turn left along the A523, and immediately left again along Abbey Green Road. Follow this, bearing left over a bridge, to Abbey Green. At the former Abbey Inn, turn right through the car park and go up the obvious path. After 30 paces, cross a stile and walk diagonally left to the top of the slope.

2. At the top bear right, keeping the fence close to your left. Proceed through a gate into Abbey Wood where the path becomes wider. After another kissing gate carry on up the bridleway until it becomes a grassy track. Aim just to the left of a small copse on the very top of the hill ahead. Continue to a slot in the wall at the corner of Back Hills Wood.

3. Follow the faint track, keeping the dry-stone wall just to your right. At the bottom of the hill go through a gate and join a farm track, keeping North Hillswood Farm to your right. Turn left onto a rough surfaced lane until you reach a metalled road at the end. Turn left and 100yds (91m) after Folly Rest Farm, cross a stile on the left. Descend, keeping the hedge to your left, and via a gate follow the track to the wood.

4. Go over the stile and pick your way along the narrow path through the holly of Ramshaw Wood. At the top right-hand corner, cross the stile and keep going straight, keeping the bank of trees to your right. At the end of these trees go ahead along the bridleway and retrace your steps back to Abbey Green.

5. Opposite Abbey Dairy go right, over a stile, for a waymarked field path and continue in the same direction over a succession of small aluminium gates. After the fifth continue along the field edge, with the fence on your left. At the far top left corner of the next field, cross a stile to your left and descend, now with the hedge and fence to your right.

6. At the bottom, cross the stile and head right past the house. At a metalled road, go left, and then left again along the A523, back to Brindley Mill.

Where to eat and drink
Within Leek there are numerous places to grab something to eat and or drink. Try the White Hart Tea Room, the oldest tea room in the town in a Grade II listed building. Or the Duck Goose bistro where you can enjoy freshly prepared meals or just grab a sandwich, open every day except Tuesday.

What to see
Brindley Mill is a water-powered corn mill with a riverside garden. It illustrates James Brindley's talents as an architect and a millwright and has a small museum dedicated to his life. It is open Sundays from May to early September and Wednesday in June to August, 2pm–5pm.

While you're there
Make sure you take a little time to visit St Edward's Church. It boasts a fine 13th-century roof in which every beam has been hewn from a separate oak tree. Leek's market is held every Wednesday in the Market Place, while the indoor Butter Market is open Friday and Saturday.

ENDON'S SPRINGS

DISTANCE/TIME	3.5 miles (5.7km) / 1hr 30min
ASCENT/GRADIENT	269ft (82m) / ▲
PATHS	Easy meadow paths and some roads, many stiles
LANDSCAPE	Hillside meadow, forest and farmland
SUGGESTED MAP	OS Explorer 258 Stoke-on-Trent & Newcastle-under-Lyme
START/FINISH	Grid reference: SJ928537
DOG FRIENDLINESS	Must be kept on lead at all times
PARKING	Roadside parking on Church Lane
PUBLIC TOILETS	None on route

The name Endon means 'place where lambs are reared', but today the village is best known, not for its mutton, but for its water. The area around Endon, and in fact most of Derbyshire and northern Staffordshire, features an abundance of natural springs. These springs owe their existence to the local geology. The primarily limestone landscape of the Staffordshire moorlands and the rest of the Peak District is intermittently overlaid by a layer of gritstone. As the latter is a non-porous rock, when the water table rises higher than the limestone, water is forced out at the points on the surface where the two rock layers meet. This constant supply of fresh water was doubtless what prompted ancient peoples to settle in the area.

These early settlers began blessing this water supply by adorning local wells with flowers, a ritual known today as well dressing. Its origins are shrouded in mystery: many sources attribute the practice to the period of the Black Death (1348–49) when it's thought that a third of the country's population died of the virus. Some villages remained untouched and, probably quite rightly, attributed this to the clean water supply drawn from their wells. (The plague was borne by rats and their fleas, so dirty water and poor sanitation contributed to the spread of the disease.) However, it's possible that the custom goes back further, perhaps to Celtic times, and the fact that many well dressings have a 'well queen' suggests echoes of ancient fertility rites and rituals.

Today, well dressing is an annual tradition, with a succession of villages dressing their wells between the end of May and early September. Endon's ceremony, which was revived in 1845, traditionally takes place on the Spring Bank Holiday, when two wells are dressed in an elaborate ceremony.

The well dressing itself is usually as intricate as it is elaborate. It is achieved by making a picture, often of a religious theme, out of flowers and petals. The picture is created within a wooden frame filled with soft, wet clay. An outline of the drawing is made using bark, twigs and berries before the spaces are filled in with coloured petals. The picture is made from the bottom upwards so that the petals overlap and rainwater drains off. The finished image is often so ornate it really has to be seen to be believed. Because of the nature of the materials, dressings have to be made in the two or three days just before the ceremony, and they usually only last a week or so. In addition, a well dressing queen is crowned and, on the Bank Holiday Monday, a fair is held in the village, complete with parade, morris dancing and a tossing the sheaf competition.

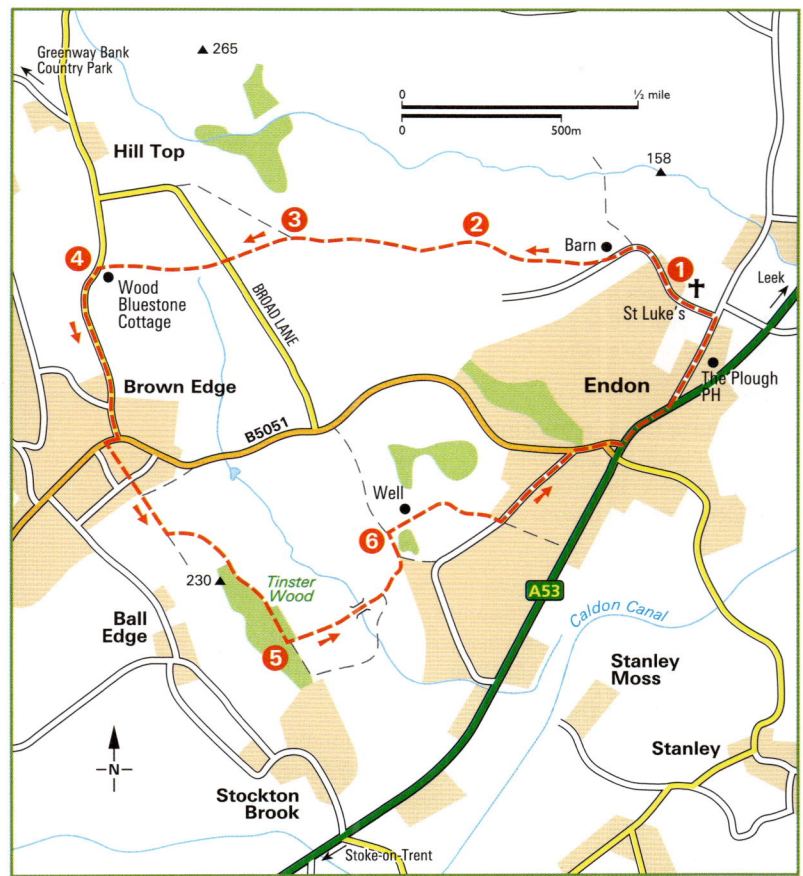

1. From St Luke's Church follow the lane uphill. When the road bends and becomes High View Road, go straight ahead past old farm buildings. Follow the path as it turns left and continue ahead beyond a barn and go through a slot in the wall. Cut off the corner of the field to reach a stile, and maintain this direction to reach a double stile on the far side.

2. Continue in the same direction, keeping a hedge just to your left. Cross the stile at the far side of the field and proceed to another old stile straight ahead. Keep straight on uphill until you reach a well-hidden slot in the top left corner of the wall. Continue up the slope, this time with the hedge to your right.

3. At the top right corner of this field, go straight across the stile and continue along the rough track to a road. Go straight over and across three stiles, following a hedge on the left. Cross yet more stiles, aiming for the far left corner of the field by Wood Bluestone Cottage.

4. Turn left down the road and, at the junction with the B5051, go right, then first left along a signed footpath, over a residential road and up a wide, fenced track. Stay on this as it curves left to the top of the hill and then continues down and along the edge of Tinster Wood. As soon as the track enters the wood proper, head sharp left down a narrow path, somewhat indistinct in places, following it to the bottom left-hand corner.

5. Go through a slot in the wall to your left. Continue straight across a field, keeping the wall to your right, through a pair of wall slots. Cross the small footbridge beneath a tree before crossing a field. At a kissing gate go left up a walled track and left along the road. After 100yds (91m) go right, following the footpath sign beside woodland.

6. At the bottom of this field go through a gate to a surfaced road, following it round to the left. When you reach a proper residential road, go hard left along a rougher track to a surfaced road. Head right and, shortly after, turn left along the A53. Just before you get to The Plough on the left, head left up the road signed to St Luke's Church.

Where to eat and drink
The Plough is conveniently located on the A53 not far from the start/end of the walk. Standard bar snacks and pub food are available seven days a week and a popular carvery is served daily, all year round.

What to see
Despite the reverence in which some wells are clearly held, many are seen only as marks on a map, often existing below the surface. When they do spring up, they're often indicated by little more than a tap, or in some cases, an algae-stained bath tub!

While you're there
Greenway Bank Country Park, just to the northwest of Endon, features an arboretum, picnic sites and 114 acres (46ha) of secluded forest around Serpentine Pool and Knypersley Reservoir. A weekend visitor centre provides more local information.

CHEDDLETON FLINT MILL AND DEEP HAYES

DISTANCE/TIME	3.25 miles (5.3km) / 1hr 30min
ASCENT/GRADIENT	272ft (83m) / ▲
PATHS	Tow path, field and woodland paths (can be muddy), many stiles
LANDSCAPE	Canal, reservoir, forest and farmland
SUGGESTED MAP	OS Explorer OL24 Peak District – White Peak Area
START/FINISH	Grid reference: SJ961533
DOG FRIENDLINESS	On lead in country park, off lead along tow path
PARKING	Deep Hayes Country Park visitor centre (closed at dusk)
PUBLIC TOILETS	Deep Hayes Country Park visitor centre

The walk starts at Deep Hayes Country Park, a recreational area which has been created around a disused reservoir. The reservoir itself was built in 1849 to compensate the River Churnet for the loss of water to several mills further downstream, while at the same time works were completed at nearby Wall Grange to pump 1.5 million gallons (6.8 million litres) of drinking water from Caena's Well. During the 1830s and 1840s thousands died in cholera epidemics because of poor water, so clean water was needed to serve the growing population of the booming Potteries region.

The reservoir at Deep Hayes was formed behind an earth dam 50ft (15m) high and 400ft (122m) long, which was built by hand. It continued to 'top up' the River Churnet until as recently as 1979, when problems with the dam's structure became too costly to repair. The water level was reduced, and three separate pools were made to create the country park you see today, complete with trails, toilets and visitor centre.

The highlight of the walk, though, is undoubtedly the flint mill on the Caldon Canal. Originally a corn mill dating as far back as the 13th century, it was strengthened for flint grinding in 1800. Flint is a hard, nearly pure form of silica; when ground down to a fine powder it's used to harden and whiten pottery (before flint was used, silica was added in the form of fine sand, but the sand was often iron-stained and impure).

The flint arrived by narrow boat. It was heated in kilns at 2,012°F (1,100°C) to make it more brittle, a process known as 'calcining'. The heated flint was then broken up and ground into fine powder by the water-powered, and later steam-driven, millstones. The slip, a mixture of water and fine flint powder, would be dried into blocks called 'cake' and taken to the wharf for dispatch to the potteries.

The mill continued to be worked well into the 20th century. During World War II, George Edwards & Son ground rutile (a black or reddish-brown mineral) for welding rods and, as late as the 1960s, ceramic stains were ground here for potteries overseas (in Saudi Arabia and Finland, for example). The mill finally stopped grinding flint in 1963, but it's open to visitors most weekends and bank holidays.

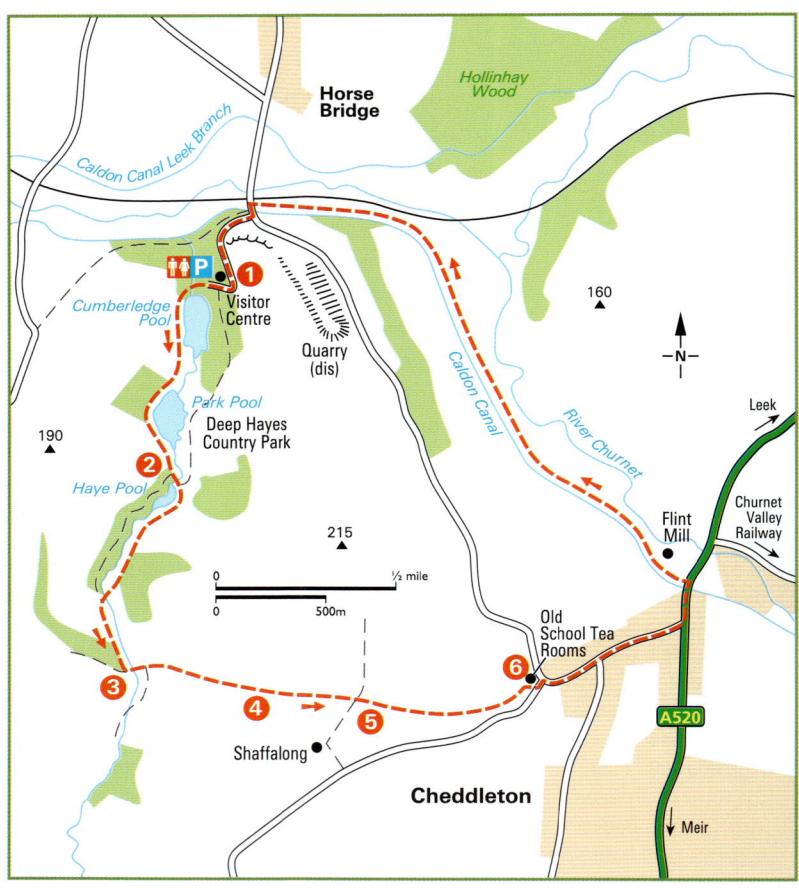

1. From the visitor centre in Deep Hayes Country Park go down to the bottom of the car park and cross the stream before following the shore of the reservoir along a wooded track. Go up some steps and left before the stile, continuing above the shoreline. After the second reservoir and at a fork of two obvious footpaths, go left down some steep steps and across the concrete stepping stones.

2. Once across the stream head right through a fence gap with a sign that says 'Keep dogs on leads'. After a short while this track runs alongside the small stream that fills the reservoirs. When you cross back over the stream, continue to follow it to the left through an aluminium kissing gate, then up some steps beyond a wooden gate ahead.

3. At a path junction (marked by a wooden signpost) head down steps left, back over the stream for the final time, before following the public footpath sign to Cheddleton. After crossing a stile, go right for 30yds (27m) before continuing up the wooded hill on steps. At the top of the wood cross the stile and head straight across the field, aiming left of the farm.

4. In the far corner of the field go along the muddy farm track to a gate. From here follow the obvious, waymarked path over a succession of stiles through a series of small fields to the left of the farm buildings.

5. Beyond a double stile and a plank footbridge, by a wooden public footpath sign, head straight across the field following the line of trees to your left. After the final tree veer right and cross the small stile over a dry-stone wall and drop downhill cross the next field to its far side. Just to the left of a clump of trees is a stile, followed in quick succession by another stile and a slot in the wall, bringing you out onto the road into Cheddleton almost opposite the tea rooms.

6. When you reach the end of this road, head left on the wide pavement of the A520 and, after 100yds (91m), turn left following signs to the flint mill. After exploring the mill museum, keep going along the canal tow path for about 1 mile (1.6km) until you reach a bridge (No. 39) over the canal. Cross over the bridge, before turning right, along the driveway, to return to the visitor centre.

Where to eat and drink
The Old School Tea Rooms offers a fantastic range of food and drinks, from main meals through to snacks and cakes, home-made soup, freshly made sandwiches and baguettes, as well as an all-day brunch. Try the house speciality, Staffordshire oatcakes with a variety of fillings. There is also a small craft centre here, which sells an amazing array of locally produced gifts, including pottery, paintings, photography and needlework. Open Wednesday–Sunday, 10am–4pm, all year round.

What to see
The Caldon Canal, running from Froghall to Etruria Junction on the Trent and Mersey Canal in Stoke-on-Trent, was the brainchild of canal-building genius James Brindley. Flint came from Cheddleton on the Caldon Canal, while high-quality clay came from the West Country, via the River Mersey and the Trent and Mersey Canal.

While you're there
The Churnet Valley Railway runs from Cheddleton to Froghall and back again on various dates throughout the year (up to five days a week in summer). All trips are steam-powered in lovingly restored locomotives, and stop at Consall in addition to Cheddleton and Kingsley and Froghall. Frognall station has a tea room and the others have a nearby places to eat, in addition to other attractions, such as the museum and engine shed at Cheddleton, idyllic canal walking at Consall and the Brindley Mill Museum at Leek. For a timetable, visit Cheddleton Station or www.churnetvalleyrailway.co.uk.

FROM GRINDON TO THOR'S CAVE

DISTANCE/TIME	4.8 miles (7.7km) / 3hrs 30min
ASCENT/GRADIENT	1,020ft (311m) / ▲▲
PATHS	Field paths, some narrow and muddy, hard trail, limestone – may be slippery, several stiles
LANDSCAPE	Hillside, valley, meadows and woodland
SUGGESTED MAP	OS Explorer OL24 Peak District – White Peak Area
START/FINISH	Grid reference: SK084545
DOG FRIENDLINESS	Keep on short lead near livestock and on Manifold Track to prevent tripping other users; under close control at all other times
PARKING	At Grindon church
PUBLIC TOILETS	None on route

Set within the Manifold Valley, whose river rises within a mile of the Dove on Axe Edge, Thor's Cave may be recognisable to you if you've seen Ken Russell's horror film *The Lair of the White Worm* (1988). The opening shot of the film features the famous landmark, and you may, as a result, feel slightly apprehensive when climbing the path up the hillside.

The River Manifold heads south through superb limestone country, twisting and turning and passing some amazing geological features. These include the copper-rich Ecton Hill, the spoils of which made the 5th Duke of Devonshire enough money to build the fashionable and elegant Crescent at Buxton in the 18th century, as well as bustling Beeston Tor.

The awesome Thor's Cave, a gaping void in a 300ft (91m) crag, was the home of prehistoric life forms. Along with nearby Ossom's and Elderbush Caves, it has been excavated and revealed bones and flints from the Stone and Bronze Ages. Formed over thousands of years from the combined effects of wind and rain on the soft limestone, it probably sheltered animals like giant red deer and bears, as well as early humans. Excavations have revealed a Bronze Age burial site, although much of the evidence was lost by somewhat over-zealous 19th-century excavators.

The elegant spire of All Saints church in Grindon is visible from around the valley, earning it the nickname the Cathedral of the Moorlands. The present building is from 1848 but the first church was built in the 11th century as a chapel of ease for St Bartram in Ilam. The War Memorial tablet inside the church shows those of the village who fought in World War I.

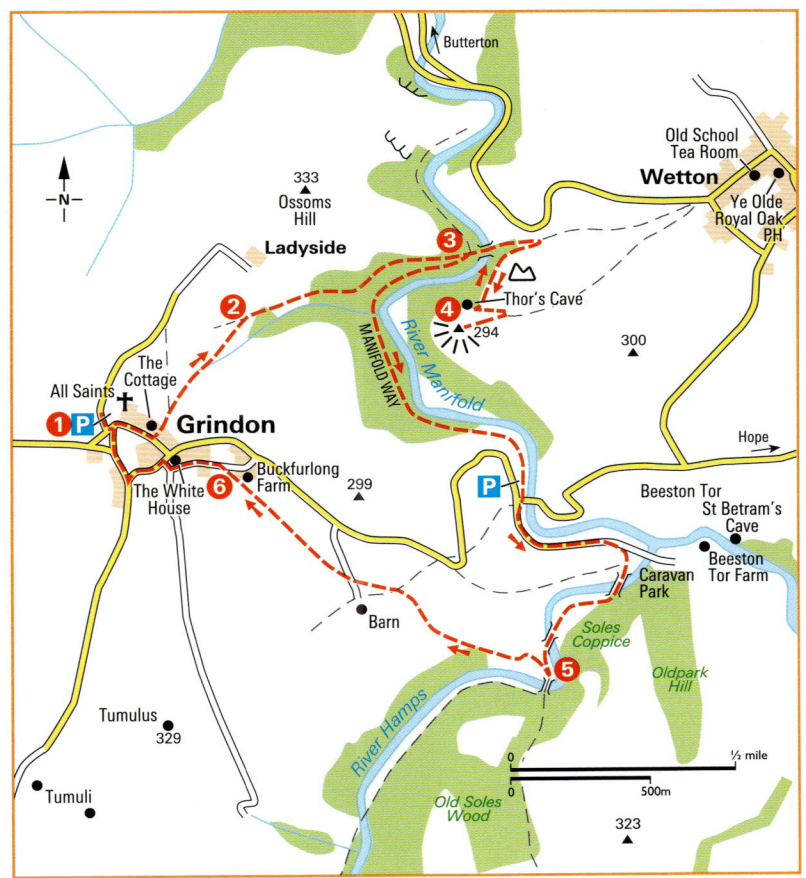

1. From the car park turn left then head downhill past the play area. Immediately past The Cottage fork left on to a track and go through a squeeze stile. Cross a field and head downhill, keeping to the right of two diverging paths. Cross a bridge, go through a gate and head downhill, with the stream and the wood on your right.

2. At the wall at the far end go through a gap stile on your right, continuing downhill into National Trust land at Ladyside. A narrow path runs by a fence into woodland. At a gate fork right and down a field edge then back into scrubbier woodland, descending steeply to a stile by the Manifold Way.

3. Cross the multi-use track, then a bridge, and take the path uphill following the signs for Thor's Cave. Immediately approaching the mouth of the cave, turn left. Continue on a track uphill, curve right before a gate and follow the path to the summit for superb views along the Manifold Valley.

4. Retrace your steps to the Manifold Way and turn left. Continue past a car park, then across a road by a bridge. Of two tarmac tracks, take the far right one ahead (no motor vehicles), and eventually cross two bridges.

5. Immediately before the third bridge, fork right, back on yourself, and cross a stile towards Grindon. Follow the path back, parallel to the road and then curving left and uphill. Go through a gate, then follow the path uphill above a slight valley. Pass through a second gate by a dry dewpond, with a bramble-shrouded wall to your right. Continue rising straight ahead through successive rough pasture fields, passing a barn some distance to the left.

6. Head diagonally left of a farm through a couple of fields. Fork left on to the farm road, which becomes a walled path by a barn. Fork right to join a tarmac track which starts at The White House. Turn right on to the road, then almost immediately take the first left. Follow this road back to the church then turn right for the car park.

Where to eat and drink
From the summit slope of Thor's Cave, a footpath runs eastwards across the fields for just under a mile (1.6km) to Wetton. The Old School Tea Room is open for limited hours (mostly weekends) but is a quirky and excellent café. Alternatively, The Royal Oak in Wetton is a 400-year-old pub located in the centre of the village and has long been popular with walkers. If the weather is fine, you can sit outside in the beer garden.

What to see
Near the church gates in Grindon is an old stone known as the Rindle Stone. It contains the inscription 'The lord of the manor of Grindon established his right to this Rindle at Staffordshire Assizes on March 17th 1862'. A rindle is a brook that only flows in wet weather. Why anyone would want to establish legal right to such a thing is not explained on the stone.

While you're there
The Canopy Walk at RSPB Coombs Valley (5 miles/8km) to the west is a short but pleasant addition to a lovely rugged nature reserve. Take food and drink for a picnic, though, as there isn't a café.

BEESTON TOR

DISTANCE/TIME	9 miles (14.5km) / 5hrs
ASCENT/GRADIENT	2082ft (635m) / ▲▲▲
PATHS	Grassy field paths, farm tracks and surfaced lanes, 10 stiles
LANDSCAPE	Wooded valley bottom and slopes, open hilltop fields
SUGGESTED MAP	OS Explorer OL24 Peak District – White Peak Area
START/FINISH	Grid reference: SK100543
DOG FRIENDLINESS	On lead in fields around livestock, but plenty of enclosed tracks and quiet lanes
PARKING	On Manifold Trail by Weag's Bridge
PUBLIC TOILETS	None on route

Of all the soaring limestone crags of the Manifold valley, Beeston Tor is one of the most impressive as well as probably the most secluded. It's an example of what's known as reef limestone, formed around 350 million years ago when much of the present-day Peak District was a tropical lagoon. Although glimpsed at the start, the full majesty of Beeston Tor is held back for the final stage of the walk, when the huge crag heaves into view from the ridge above Throwley Hall.

At the foot of Beeston Tor is St Bertram's Cave, a small fissure through which the surface water can disappear underground leaving whole sections of the riverbed dry in the summer months. The cave is named after the one-time King of Mercia, whose 8th-century kingdom included what we know today as Staffordshire. Bertram was supposedly born and raised in a cave in the valley, but he renounced his kingship after his wife and child were killed by wolves when he was out hunting. He opted instead for a religious life, building a hermitage near Stafford and becoming a recluse. He's remembered at sites across the county, with a particularly striking modern statue of the saint at Longnor church, but it is said that he spent his last years as a hermit in a Staffordshire cave near Ilam. It's possible that the cave was at the foot of Beeston Tor. St Bertam is buried within Ilam Holy Cross Church where his tomb still regularly attracts pilgrims.

When St Bertam's Cave was properly excavated in the 1920s and '30s there was evidence of prehistoric occupation, plus a hoard of Saxon coins was found. In Edwardian times Beeston Tor was particularly popular with visitors, with the Manifold Valley Light Railway even establishing a special halt just for sightseers. Today, the towering cliffs are a magnet for climbers and there are some testing routes up the fissures and rock chimneys which bear such names as The Beast, The Spider and Beeston Eliminate. A far more sedate attraction lies further down the Manifold Valley, on the walking route and definitely worth a few minutes' inspection. Throwley Old Hall was built on the site of a medieval village, complete with a deer park and ridge and furrow cultivation strips, and although only the ruins of this once imposing Elizabethan building remain it's still possible to appreciate its scale and charm.

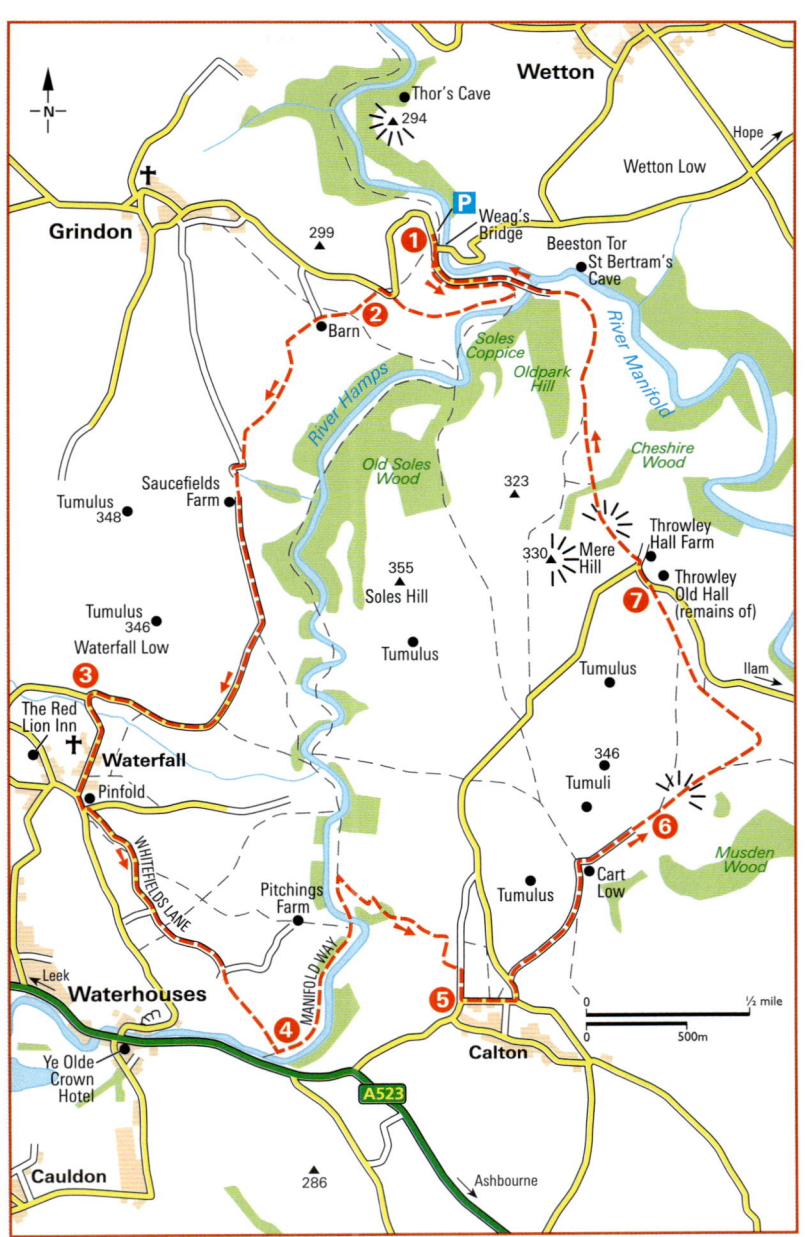

1. From the car park cross the road for the right of two parallel tracks. After 650yds (594m) turn right into Weag's Barn nature reserve for a waymarked bridleway up the slope. At the top keep left and with the wall on your right continue until you meet the corner of a lane. Go up the lane for 50yds (46m) then left on to another bridleway.

2. Drop down and cross a shallow valley, veering right to pass to the right of a large barn. Continue to the far top corner of the field, then go left beside a wall. Where this finally ends go half left to a gate and down to the valley bottom. Now swing left on a waymarked route around Saucefields Farm and along its drive into Waterfall.

3. Turn left to cross the ford and follow the lane up past the church. Turn left at the end, then immediately left and right on to Whitefields Lane. Where it bends sharply left to Pitchings Farm go straight on down a rough walled path that emerges on the Manifold Way near Waterhouses.

4. Turn left and follow the trail for 0.75 mile (1.2km), then go right for a signposted path that slants right, up the hillside. Beyond a gate it zig zags to the top, then swings right towards Calton. Go through a small field on the left to turn right on to a farm track to reach the edge of the village.

5. At a road go left, then left again. Turn right for a walled track which narrows to a path. At Cart Low keep left of the main buildings, then turn right at the signpost to Throwley around the back. Beyond a squeeze stile keep the tumbledown barn on your right and head out across open fields with an old wall on your right.

6. Ignore the signposted left turn and continue straight on downhill. Go through a gate in a crosswall and head half left across a wide field, aiming for Castern Hall on the far hillside. Turn left in the next field and head directly for Throwley Hall, keeping to the slope above the road.

7. Follow the lane through the farm and beyond the gateway between barns turn right and immediately left for a footpath through trees. Head up across a field for a gate at the top beside the farm track. Now walk down the far slope, aiming for Beeston Tor, and join a wide track at a gate that leads down into the valley and back to the car park.

Where to eat and drink
The Red Lion Inn at Waterfall is open weekday evenings and all day at weekends, serving food all day Saturday and lunchtime on Sunday. Further on, Ye Olde Crown Hotel on the A523 at Waterhouses is a family-friendly place that serves meals and snacks every day.

What to see
As you leave Waterfall you pass a restored pinfold on the side of the lane. Most villages had a secure pound like this, usually just a small walled enclosure where stray cattle, sheep, pigs and so on were kept until they were claimed by their owner, usually on payment of a fine.

While you're there
Near Grindon is a memorial to the crew of an RAF plane that crashed trying to drop supplies to the snow-bound villages in 1947.

STOKE-ON-TRENT'S POTTERIES

DISTANCE/TIME	3 miles (4.8km) / 1hr 15min
ASCENT/GRADIENT	262ft (80m) / ▲
PATHS	Pavement and hill trail
LANDSCAPE	Streets and urban parkland
SUGGESTED MAP	OS Explorer 258 Stoke-on-Trent & Newcastle-under-Lyme
START/FINISH	Grid reference: SJ874501
DOG FRIENDLINESS	Must be on lead near roads
PARKING	Ample parking on Moorland Road by Burslem Park
PUBLIC TOILETS	On Market Place in town centre and in Burslem Park

The City of Stoke-on-Trent, known as 'the Potteries,' actually consists of six towns, each with its own sense of history, character and identity: Burslem, Fenton, Hanley, Longton, Tunstall and Stoke itself. All six owe their existence to the rich seams of coal and clay in the area which originally would have been mined at or near the surface. Both coal and clay were mined by the Romans, and excavations at Trent Vale in the 1950s uncovered a pottery kiln and workshop dating from the first century AD. But it was in Burslem in the 16th century that the pottery revolution got under way, thanks largely to the efforts of one man, Josiah Wedgwood.

In addition to being a talented craftsmen and an astute businessman, Wedgwood was also an innovator – he was the first to establish a factory for making fine pots. Until then pottery had been a cottage industry, but Wedgwood's Burslem factory set a new standard, and before long similar buildings were springing up all over Stoke. Today, Burslem still boasts the highest concentration of potteries in the city, several of them visited on this short walk. The first is Moorland Pottery, based on the historic Chelsea Works site, while a little further on near Market Place is the factory shop for Royal Stafford, whose ceramic tableware is still produced locally.

Despite economic downturns and changing markets, Burslem retains its industrial core and a long-standing reputation as the 'Mother Town' of Stoke-on-Trent. This is an urban landscape of period factories, small warehouses and historic canals, as well as grand municipal buildings, some in better shape than others and many now given over to bars and shops. Although a few of the large ceramic producers have gone, many that remain are small in scale but high in value, producing sought-after tableware and collectables. New business parks have been established around the town's fringes to cater for this growing business.

Heading down Nile Street you pass the site of the former Royal Doulton works, where the Staffordshire tradition of china figurines was first established. In 2005, the factory closed when production was switched overseas, and the site is being redeveloped. A little further on is Dudson Factory Outlet, where you can browse a wide range of high-quality but reasonably priced tableware that the firm has been producing for the catering industry for well over a century. Next up is the Moorcroft Factory Shop, while a little further on is their Heritage Visitor Centre, complete with original bottle kiln and open Wednesday to Saturday. Moorcroft has been making fine china for over 100 years and each piece is hand-crafted by skilled craftsmen. The guided factory tour (check times available) allows you to watch the unique processes at first hand, including the application of the design onto the pot which is known as tube lining – they say it's like icing a cake, just a little more difficult.

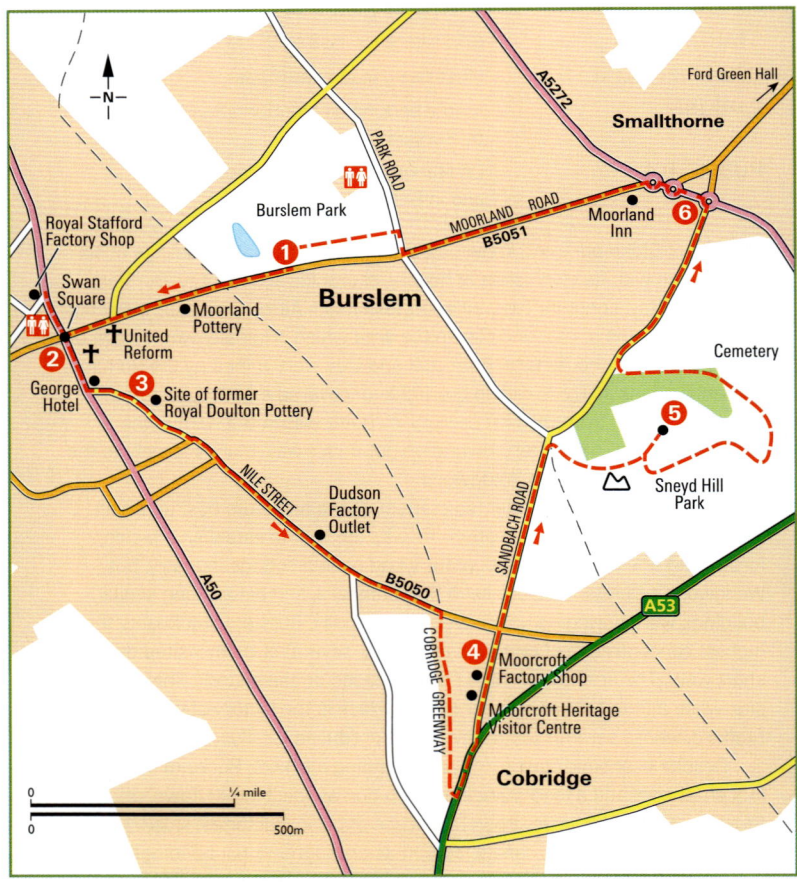

1. From Burslem Park head down Moorland Road past Moorland Pottery into the town centre. At the busy junction at Swan Square turn right and walk uphill for 100 yards (91m) to visit the Royal Stafford factory shop on the left, which includes a small café.

2. Retrace your steps to the junction and keep going straight over, downhill past the war memorial on Swan Bank. Take the second left, just past the imposing George Hotel.

3. Walk down Nile Street, past the site of the former Royal Doulton factory on the left. Go past Dudson Factory Outlet and continue along the road. Just before the bridge go right onto a ramp up to the leafy Cobridge Greenway cycle trail, a former railway line. Turn right and follow this to the end. Turn left, then quickly left again on to Sandbach Road to reach the Moorcroft Heritage Visitor Centre.

4. After visiting the Heritage Centre continue along Sandbach Road and keep going over the traffic lights. After 400yds (366m), just as the road eases round to the right, turn sharp right up the gravel path into Sneyd Hill Park. Immediately take a left fork straight up the hill, following the steep slope to the top for excellent views.

5. From the top of the hill start to walk back down the way you came, but soon bear left on an obvious trail contouring round the hill to the left. Follow this round and down to the bottom, near the cemetery. Turn left and follow the grassy track around the base of the hill until it rejoins the road. Turn right and walk up the broad pavement to the junction at the top of the hill.

6. Turn sharp left, then left again at the final mini-roundabout, past the Moorland Inn and down Moorland Road. After about 500yds (457m) turn right onto Park Road, then immediately left to enter Burslem Park and an excellent spot for a picnic to end the walk.

Where to eat and drink
Although a chain pub, the Moorland Inn offers a varied, good-value menu of traditional pub food mixed with Tex-Mex classics. There are picnic benches at the back and food is served all day long, seven days a week, year-round.

What to see
Take time to soak up the views of Burslem and the rest of Stoke from the vantage point at the top of Sneyd Hill. Burslem Park is Grade 2 listed Victorian park and provides a green oasis amid the urban bustle. Within the park is a café, sculptures, water features and plenty of seating.

While you're there
Ford Green Hall, a mile (1.6km) northeast of Sneyd Hill, is a 17th-century farmhouse with a museum and period Tudor garden. It's been restored and furnished with an outstanding collection of local textiles, ceramics and furniture, while the herb garden shows how plants were once used for medicinal and even cosmetic purposes. Open Sunday to Thursday, 1–4pm, all year.

16 APEDALE COUNTRY PARK

DISTANCE/TIME	4.75 miles (7.7km) / 2hrs
ASCENT/GRADIENT	300ft (91m) / ▲▲
PATHS	Wide gravel tracks, roads and dirt trails, many stiles
LANDSCAPE	Ancient woodland, farmland and hilltop
SUGGESTED MAP	OS Explorer 258 Stoke-on-Trent & Newcastle-under-Lyme
START/FINISH	Grid reference: SJ823484
DOG FRIENDLINESS	Under close control in the country park
PARKING	Car park opposite Heritage Centre, gates close at dusk
PUBLIC TOILETS	At Heritage Centre, when open

Apedale Community Country Park, just to the west of Newcastle-under-Lyme, has a rich and varied history. The name itself has two possible meanings: one suggests that the word ape comes from the Latin apis meaning bee; the other is that ape is short for apple. Whichever you prefer, it seems probable that Apedale was once an ancient rural landscape, although for the last 2,000 years, it has been anything but...

Iron smelting in Apedale probably goes back at least to Roman times, if not before, but the impact on the landscape would have been negligible compared to what came later. Mining in the region is known to date back as far as the 1200s. This was made possible in the early days thanks to large deposits of coal lying at or very near the surface. Of the four main Staffordshire deposits, the Potteries Coalfield was by far the biggest, comprising an area of 100sq miles (259sq km). The Potteries, though, were doubly blessed. Not only was there coal to be mined and sold, but there were rich seams of high-quality clays that could be used to make pots. As the pottery industry developed, so the demand for coal increased, and the Apedale collieries would have played a major role in meeting that demand. The arrival of the first canals in 1777, thanks partly to the vision of people like Josiah Wedgwood, precipitated a boom in business throughout the region, and the emergence of the railways 60 years later proved to be another catalyst to productivity and prosperity.

With the Industrial Revolution well under way, iron mining and smelting enjoyed its own boom thanks to the invention of the blast furnace in the late 18th century. Apedale was a major centre of production, at one point providing employment for more than 3,000 men. Rising costs, however, sent local industry into decline by the 1920s, and when the owners lost their fortune in the Wall Street Crash, it ended altogether. Coal mining in the area, however, continued until 1998, when the last deep mine was closed at Silverdale, just a mile or two to the south of Apedale.

For much of the 20th century Apedale remained a barren and desolate place but today little evidence of the area's industrial heritage remains. Nature has reclaimed the spoil heaps with luxurious ferns (see Fern Bank, on the map), and trees are recolonising the land, creating 455 acres (184ha) of woodland, meadows and pools that everyone can enjoy. Active reclamation work began in 1995 and continued efforts to improve and develop the park and its facilities reflect a triumph of nature over industry. Apedale Community Country Park is probably as green now as it's been in the last 300 years, an ancient rural landscape reborn.

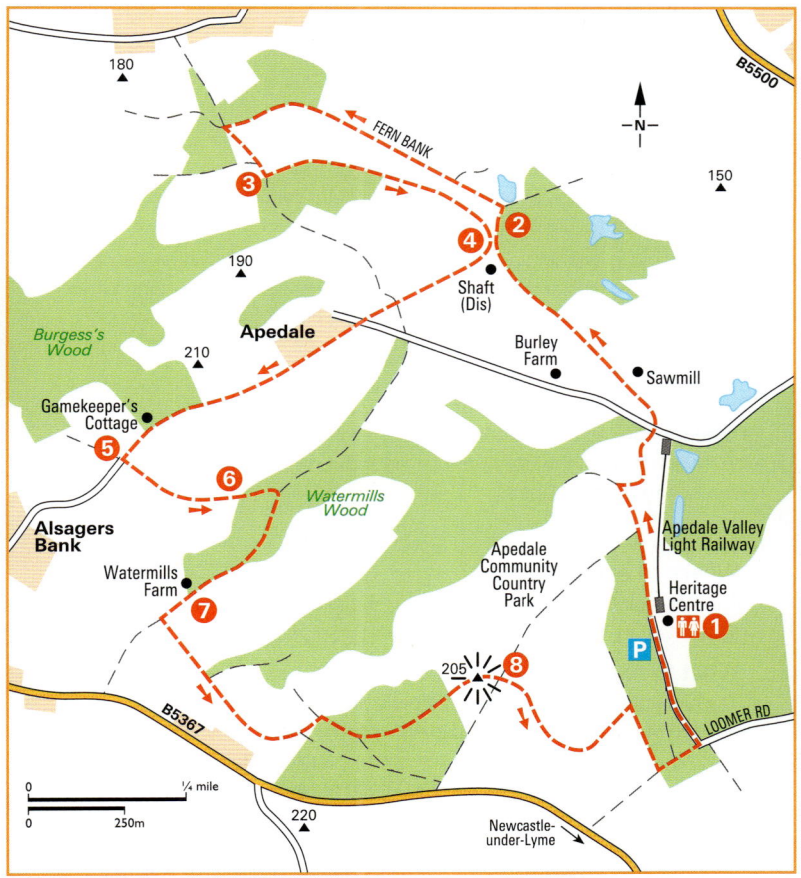

1. From the Heritage Centre in Apedale Community Country Park take a path to go right, through a gate. After 400yds (366m) turn right down to a corner of the park, then continue straight ahead, passing to the left of the sawmill. At a fork in the path, head right down a short hill to reach the corner of a lake.

2. Ignoring the stile, turn left along the narrow path into the woods. Stay on the main path, go over a plank footbridge, then go right at a fork to emerge into Fern Bank, containing giant, head-high ferns. Follow this path to reach a junction, with a clearing to your left. Walk through the clearing to reach the main gravel track.

3. Turn left and continue for 600yds (549m) to a gate and the turn-off for the lake, Point 2. About 30 paces after the gate, head right up a signed footpath along the edge of a small copse, keeping the fence to your right. At the top of this wood, 30 paces off the track to your left is a disused mineshaft.

4. Continue up the track and straight ahead to the village of Apedale, a former mining community. On the right, just after the track veers to the left, is Gamekeeper's Cottage, once the site of a colliery.

5. About 100yds (91m) beyond the cottage turn left and go over a stile by a gate. Cross the field ahead to reach another stile. Go left to yet another stile, head right following a fence to the bottom of the hill, then skirt left to reach another stile.

6. Cross into Watermills Wood and follow the trail to another stile, then come to a junction of two paths. Head right here and, after 10 paces, fork right again. You'll shortly come to a succession of stiles before continuing up to Watermills Farm.

7. Go over a stile and continue for 100yds (91m) before following a footpath left over a series of fields and stiles to some farm buildings on your right. When the fence veers round to the left, follow it to the edge of a young plantation. At the wide gravel track, head right and at a fork go left to reach the summit and the preserved pit wheel and wagon.

8. From the summit drop down the other side, continuing over a crossroads for a gently curving track to a T-junction. Head right here, and then take the wide track left down the hill. At the tarmac road head left and continue back towards the Heritage Centre.

Where to eat and drink
The Heritage Centre café, conveniently situated at the start of the walk, sells a variety of drinks and snacks and is open daily 10.30am–4pm.

What to see
The highlight of the walk is undoubtedly the view from the hilltop at Point 8, where a wide circle of carved wooden posts indicates the position of various distant landmarks on the horizon, such as Mow Cop Castle, 6 miles (9.7km) to the north, and Pye Green Mast, 25 miles (40km) to the south on Cannock Chase. The scene is relatively pollution-free today, and it's hard to imagine that the view to the east was once shrouded in smog, or that 'smoky postcards' were once very popular as a souvenir of the times when plenty of smoke meant plenty of work.

While you're there
By the Heritage Centre at the start of the walk is Apedale Valley Light Railway, with plans to extend the current line to 1.2miles (1.9km) stretching into the Country Park. The narrow-gauge line has steam trains and diesels running throughout the year – see www.avlr.org.uk.

ILAM AND THE RIVER MANIFOLD

17

DISTANCE/TIME	5.2 miles (8.4km) / 2hrs 45min
ASCENT/GRADIENT	820ft (250m) / ▲▲
PATHS	Tarmac roads, parkland, open hillside and shady woodland (may be muddy), many stiles
LANDSCAPE	Parkland, woodland and hillside
SUGGESTED MAP	OS Explorer OL24 Peak District – White Peak Area
START/FINISH	Grid reference: SK131507
DOG FRIENDLINESS	Keep on lead unless threatened by cattle
PARKING	At Ilam Hall National Trust pay car park
PUBLIC TOILETS	At Ilam Hall

The Manifold and Dove Rivers were both fished by Izaak Walton, known as the 'Father of Angling', and the author of *The Compleat Angler*, or *The Contemplative Man's Recreation*. Since the first edition appeared in 1653 it has never been out of print. Born in Stafford in 1593, Izaak Walton moved to London as an apprentice ironmonger, becoming a craftsman and guild member when he was 25 years old. For most of his working life he owned an ironmongers shop in Fleet Street and lived in a house in Chancery Lane.

A keen angler, he spent much of his spare time fishing on the Thames, but it was not until retirement that he was able to devote himself to his hobby completely. 'I have laid aside business, and gone a-fishing.'

The view we have of Walton from his book is of a genial older man strolling along river banks in pastoral England. But nothing could be further from the truth. Walton lived during a period of political upheaval and unrest. In 1649 he saw the execution of Charles I and left London for Staffordshire, where he stayed during the Civil War. A staunch Royalist, he is mentioned among the supporters of Charles II after the Battle of Worcester in 1651. Following the battle he visited a friend who had been imprisoned in Stafford. From this friend Walton received the king's ring, which he delivered to Colonel Blague, then a prisoner in the Tower of London. The colonel escaped, made his way to France and returned the ring to the king. If Walton had been caught, he would have been executed. Just two years after 'the only known adventure' in his life he published his famous book.

The Compleat Angler is the story of three sportsmen – Viator, a huntsman, Auceps, a fowler, and Piscator, the fisherman – who walk the River Lea on May Day, debating the finer points of their sport. The fifth edition in 1676 contained an addition by Walton's friend, Charles Cotton, who lived at Beresford Hall near Hartington. Cotton built a fishing house on the banks of the Dove near his home, which still stands today. This 'holy shrine for all anglers' has the interlacing initials of both men and the inscription 'Piscatoribus Scarum 1674'.

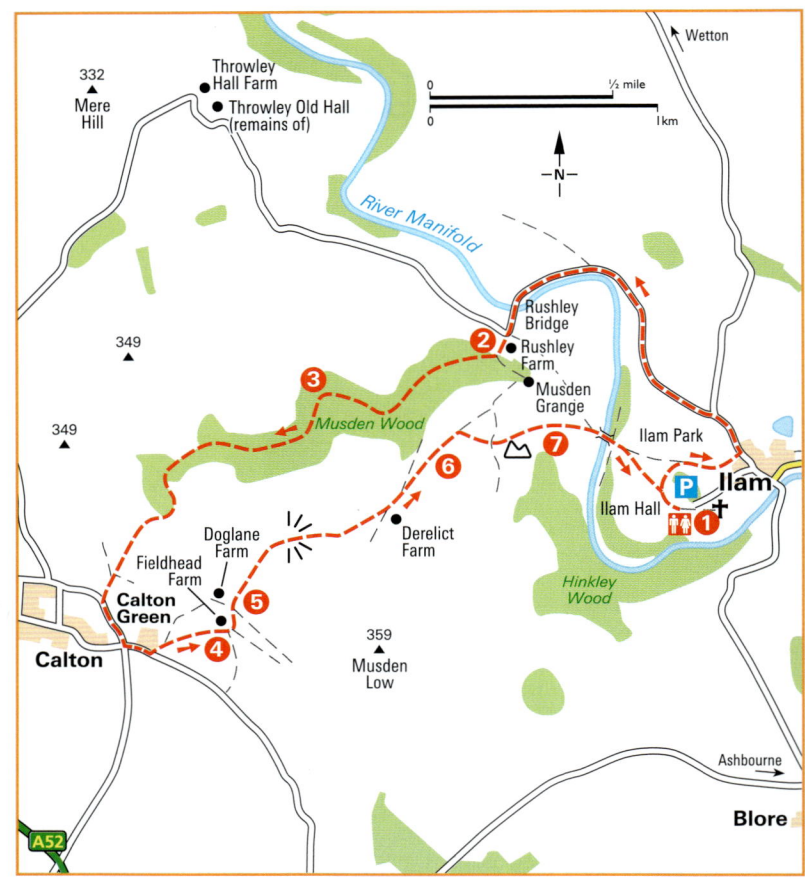

1. Leave the car park from the corner by the information panel (pedestrian exit) and turn right through a black iron gate. Follow the 'Circular Walk' on a faint track through the park around to the right. Cross a stile and turn left on to the road out of Ilam village. Go uphill, then turn left on to the Castern and Throwley Road. Fork left with the road towards The Orchards, then across Rushley Bridge.

2. Go through Rushley Farm, then turn right through an easily missed walkers' gate. It's beside sheep pens and before the drive up to Musden Grange. A second gate leads into hilly pasture. Bend left into a valley bottom, continuing through woodland then several fields.

3. Go over a series of stiles and gates and, at the final one, turn left on to a country lane. At the crossroads turn left towards Ashbourne. Go left through a gate at the next public footpath sign, and cross the field diagonally to a double stile. Maintain your direction diagonally across six fields, passing just to the left of a farm and crossing a tall and wide stile through a holly hedge.

4. At a gate in the hedge to the right of Fieldhead Farm turn left on to the gravel track. Follow this round the boundary of the farm then, at the second bend left, take the easily missed second footpath on the right (just to the right of a metal gate).

5. Follow the field edge path uphill. In the next field, pass a small depression in the ground then follow the left wall down the field. Join a farm road, pass a derelict farmstead, then veer right of the track. Head beside the field wall then through a gap stile in the far corner.

6. Follow the direction pointer past a redundant gap stile to a fallen down waymarker where fields to your right come to a corner at a tumbledown section of wall. Go right and follow the new wall on your right at the top of a sloping field. Go through a collapsed gap and veer diagonally left downhill, aiming just to the left of the pointed hill (Thorpe Cloud) ahead. After crossing both a clear then a faint vehicle track, the path through the grass becomes clearer.

7. Go across two fields, a stile and then a bridge and into Ilam Park. Turn right on to a track then at a gate fork left and uphill on a broad track that crosses the grounds back to the car park. Note that where the track fades, you should stay left of an apparent waymarker – it's just an orienteering post.

Where to eat and drink
The National Trust's Manifold Tea Room, located above the shop and overlooking the terraced gardens of Ilam Hall, provides welcome refreshment. It's open at weekends throughout the year and daily in the summer. There is a large area of outside seating that allows terrific views across the park.

What to see
As you cross Ilam Park, try to pick out the well-preserved remains of medieval ridge and furrow fields on the right-hand side. Look for the track that runs across them. It was once used by local tradesmen and servants at Ilam Hall who were forbidden to use the main drive.

While you're there
In the grounds of the hall, kids (of all ages) can enjoy a game of Pooh Sticks on St Bertram's Bridge then continue on to the 'natural play' area of Hinkley Hollow, where den building and log balancing are encouraged. Alternatively, try the family-friendly orienteering course. Those wishing for more sedate entertainment may enjoy visiting the ruins of Throwley Old Hall, the imposing remnants of a former medieval manor house standing proud above the Manifold Valley.

AROUND CALDON LOW

DISTANCE/TIME	6 miles (9.7km) / 2hrs 30min
ASCENT/GRADIENT	480ft (146m) / ▲▲
PATHS	Field and woodland paths, can be muddy, many stiles
LANDSCAPE	Farmland, quarry and hilltop
SUGGESTED MAP	OS Explorer 259 Derby & OS Explorer OL24 Peak District – White Peak Area
START/FINISH	Grid reference: SK086494
DOG FRIENDLINESS	Must be kept on lead near livestock
PARKING	Roadside parking near cement works
PUBLIC TOILETS	None on route

The story of Caldon Low begins around 350 million years ago. Thanks to the whims of continental drift, the North Staffordshire moorlands and the Peak District of Derbyshire were much further south than they are today, and the region was covered by a shallow tropical sea. Over millions of years, a layer of shells and coral slowly built up on the seabed, both formed from the calcium carbonate secretions of a variety of marine animals.

As there was little current to disturb these deposits, this layer was slowly compacted by additional layers of sediment, again over millions of years, to create limestone. Chalk, marble and limestone are all calcium carbonate, each made under different conditions. Limestone is in fact almost pure calcium carbonate and as a result is very light in colour (hence the name White Peak, as opposed to the gritstone areas of the Dark Peak further north).

In places like the White Peak, subsequent weathering, erosion and the ice age scoured away the softer topsoil leaving the limestone outcrops at or near the surface, which could then be readily quarried. This is what happened at Caldon Low Quarry, which at the height of the Industrial Revolution yielded some 6,000 tons a week. The limestone was transported on a tramway to the terminus of the Caldon Canal at Froghall, 3 miles (4.8km) west, and from there it was taken by barge to Stoke, Macclesfield and other canal-fed towns across the Midlands.

High-quality stone was used directly for building, while aggregate (crushed stone) was used for making roads. When calcium carbonate is heated, it leaves a deposit of calcium oxide or quicklime. Quicklime is even more useful than limestone. As a fertiliser it improves crop yields by reducing the acidity of soil, and it also reacts with the main impurities in iron ore to make iron and calcium silicate (or slag), which floats on top of the molten iron and is removed for use in road building.

At Froghall, the limestone was fired in kilns to produce quicklime. The wharf and the kilns are long abandoned and the quarry is much quieter. It's now a designated geological Site of Special Scientific Interest and is dominated by the massive cement works at the start of the walk.

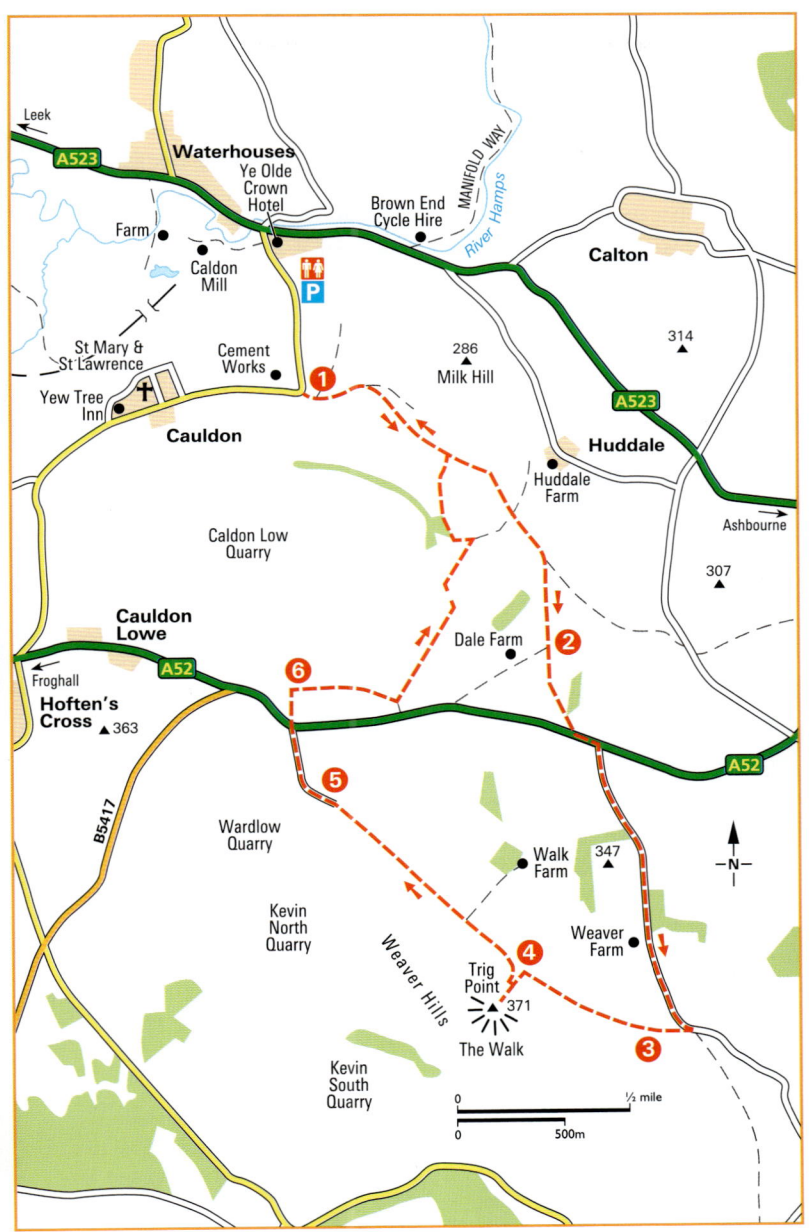

1. From the road corner head east along the gravel track, walking away from Cauldon. At the first corner go straight on for a track along a small valley. Pass a barn on your right, go through a slot or swing gate and then take the right fork along a wide dirt track. Go through the second gate ahead of you and after 25 paces go right, through an overgrown area, for a small stile into a wide, sloping field. Carry on straight up the hill.

2. At the far top corner of the field, go through a gate and straight across the next field to a gap in the wall ahead. After the gap, head for the far left-hand corner of the next field and cross a stile onto the A52. Bear left for 100yds (91m), then turn right along the narrow metalled road past Weaver Farm. As the road veers to the left it meets a fence. Go right, back on yourself, up the hill towards a gate in the dry-stone wall.

3. After crossing the stile here keep following the dry-stone wall to your right. At the next gate continue in the same direction, with the wall to your left. At the end of this wall bear slightly right to join another wall on the right and follow it to the gate.

4. Before crossing the dry-stone wall ahead, go left for 100yds (91m) and then right over a stile, before making straight for the trig point. From the trig point retrace your steps to the stile, but instead of crossing it, head left across the field, making for the dry-stone wall at the bottom. Follow this wall northwest and alongside the Wardlow quarry.

5. Continue as far as the A52 and go straight across, following a public footpath sign. Continue over the thistly plateau of this field to a stile.

6. Turn right, go over another stile and along a waymarked route through the narrow belt of trees. At the far end go ahead through young trees. Cross the stile in the far right corner and go left between the fence and wall. At the second stile turn right and go down the field edge to a stile. Go left for 100yds (91m) and then right along a trail through a narrow valley. At the bottom of the valley rejoin the main track to return to the start point.

Where to eat and drink
Near to the start is the Ye Olde Crown Hotel, which serves meals and real ales. Also close by is the Yew Tree Inn, which has a very eclectic interior but only serves food at the weekends.

What to see
The trig point on the summit has expansive views out over South Staffordshire. The ancient mound here indicates that this may have been used as a beacon for sending warning messages by bonfire in medieval times.

While you're there
Take a short bike ride along the Manifold Way (see Walk 8). Mountain bikes and tandems can be hired from Brown End Farm Cycle Hire just to the east of Waterhouses. Bikes can be hired by the day or half day and cycle helmets can be provided.

ONECOTE

DISTANCE/TIME	8.25 miles (13.3km) / 5hrs
ASCENT/GRADIENT	1443ft (440xm) / ▲▲▲
PATHS	Field paths, lanes and rough moorland tracks, some potentially boggy, 24 stiles
LANDSCAPE	Rolling farmland, rough pasture and open moors
SUGGESTED MAP	OS Explorer OL24 Peak District – White Peak Area
START/FINISH	Grid reference: SK049552
DOG FRIENDLINESS	Plenty of livestock in fields, so on lead for most of the time
PARKING	Roadside on Douse Lane, Onecote
PUBLIC TOILETS	None on route

The Staffordshire Moorlands occupy the southwest corner of the Peak District National Park, but compared to the crowds in nearby Hartington or Dovedale the high, rounded moors west of the River Manifold are sparsely populated and relatively little visited. This is rugged hillfarming country, typified by a few small villages like Onecote (pronounced 'Oncut') and dozens of isolated farmsteads, where cattle and sheep graze the rough pasture. Although farming is the main livelihood today, in the late 1700s there was a copper mine at Mixon, which is passed towards the end of the walk. Packhorses took the ore to copper works at Cheadle, but there was little profit in the business and the mine lasted barely 50 years.

With little tree cover the open moorland can be an exposed place in bad weather, but choose a decent day and you will be rewarded with far-reaching views both across Staffordshire and the Potteries and into the heart of the Peak District. The sound of skylarks and pipits fill the air and the wet meadows and flushes are home to curlew, lapwing and snipe.

The River Hamps, which the walk shadows at its beginning and end, is also a valuable wildlife corridor. However, this diminutive tributary of the Manifold that rises high on the moors often disappears completely in hot weather, hence its Old English name 'Hanespe' meaning 'summer dry'.

Onecote Lane End, a late 18th-century farmhouse (and private property) on the edge of the village of Onecote, might seem an unremarkable place today, but its previous residents once provided one of our greatest novelists with a plot line. It was home to the Cook family and in the 1840s Joseph Cook spent four years and nearly £900 on a lawsuit to try and obtain £300 bequeathed to him by his late father, Thomas, that was due to be paid when his wife passed away. A solicitor from Leek who was involved in the case produced a pamphlet protesting at the injustice and sent a copy to Charles Dickens, who had just published the first of what was to be 20 instalments of *Bleak House*. The novelist promptly used the case, with little in the way of embellishment, in subsequent chapters to describe a long and drawn-out litigation that's at the heart of what is one of his finest novels. Also drawing on his personal experience as a law clerk, it's a withering criticism of the British judicial system and in particular the slow and unwieldy Chancery law that was subsequently reformed.

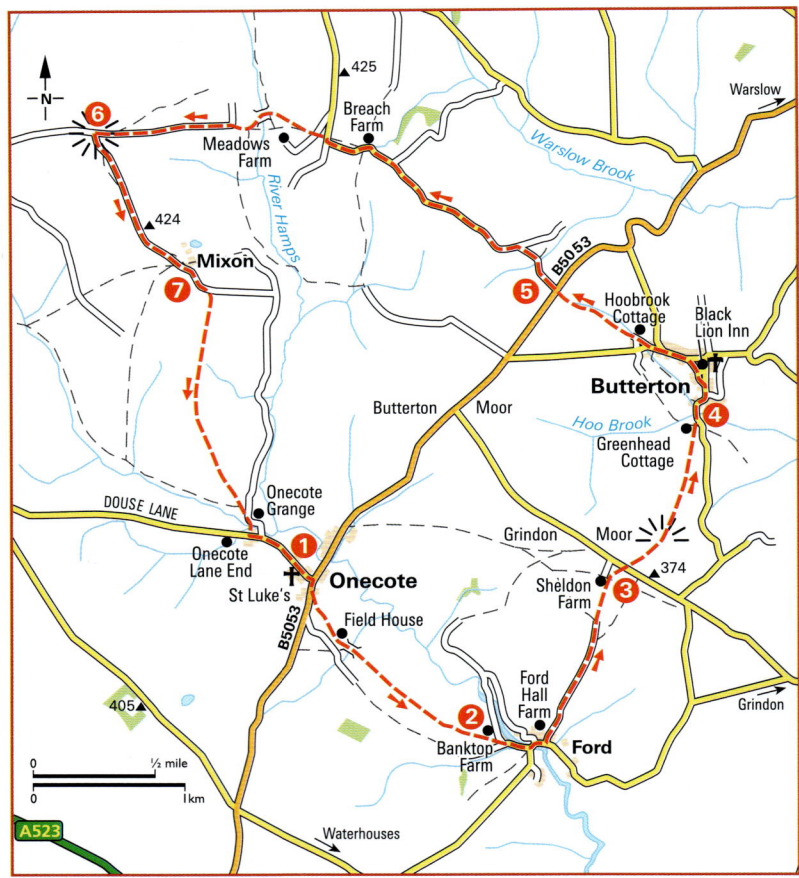

1. Turn right out of Douse Lane along the B5053 for 100yds (91m). Cross over for the footpath through a field, turn right on to a track and follow waymarks to the right of Field House. Follow the path through undergrowth and after a footbridge go up a bank. Follow the signpost to Ford, straight ahead through successive fields, before dropping down left to the hamlet.

2. Walk through the farmyard of Banktop, turn left on to the lane and left again over a bridge. Just past Ford Hall Farm take the footpath on the left, following the waymarked path around The Old Hall. At the back swing right, up through fields, to join a rough track. Nearing the top ignore a right fork and cross a stile to pass to the right of Sheldon Farm then half right to reach a gate.

3. Cross the road for a footpath through a bumpy field. Beyond a gate go over a stile on the right, then head left downhill. Approaching a barn go left through a squeeze stile and straight down fields towards Butterton. At the bottom go over steps by Greenhead Cottage and turn right to follow its driveway to the road.

4. Turn left and walk through Butterton, swinging west to join the Onecote/Warslow road. Leaving the village go right before the hill on a surfaced drive. Just past Hoobrook Cottage go straight on at the bend for a waymarked path out across fields above a stream. Continue this all the way to the road and cross it for the gated lane opposite.

5. Follow this quiet lane for about a mile (1.6km). At Breach Farm it ascends steeply via hairpins, then as it reaches the top turn left on a signposted footpath. Cross a farm drive and go down through fields. Nearing the bottom cross a stile and head down left to cross the River Hamps via a footbridge. Climb back up the far side and join a wide track past a farm and all the way up to the top of the hill.

6. Cross the cattle grid and turn immediately left, over a stile, to join a rough track beside the field edge. Entering a wide open field head half left, then beyond the brow of the hill go along the right-hand side of a wall. Cross some waste ground for a wall stile in the far corner and turn right through the next field to reach Mixon.

7. Go up steps on the right, signposted 'Onecote'. Keep to the top of the fields and where the farm drive bends left downhill, go straight on for a field edge path. Beyond a cross wall go half left through a wide field, join a track in the next, then head right for a stile by a cattle trough. Turn half left down through fields, passing to the right of Onecote Grange, for footbridges to a lane. Turn left to return to Onecote.

Where to eat and drink
For a half way stop try the Black Lion Inn at Butterton, a long-time walkers' favourite with open fires, games rooms and a selection of real ales. The pub welcomes families and serves food every lunchtime and evening (Tuesday to Saturday) and lunchtime (Sunday), closed on Mondays.

What to see
In the church at Butterton there's a photo of local men who fought in World War I. What's remarkable about it is that they all returned safely. Sadly this was very uncommon, and indeed Butterton is the only 'Thankful Village' (as they were known) in Staffordshire, and one of only 53 parishes in the whole of England and Wales without any such casualties.

CONSALL NATURE PARK

DISTANCE/TIME	3.5 miles (5.7km) / 1hr 30min
ASCENT/GRADIENT	360ft (110m) / ▲▲
PATHS	Gravel tracks, tow paths and roads, can be muddy, many stiles and steps
LANDSCAPE	Canal, meadow and woodland
SUGGESTED MAP	OS Explorers 258 Stoke-on-Trent & Newcastle-under-Lyme; OS Explorer 259 Derby
START/FINISH	Grid reference: SJ994483
DOG FRIENDLINESS	Must be kept on lead in nature park
PARKING	Consall Nature Park visitor centre
PUBLIC TOILETS	At visitor centre

Consall Nature Park, like Dimmings Dale near Alton, is a part of the Churnet Valley and has a long industrial history. Iron working is known to have taken place here as early as the 13th century, when vast tracts of woodland were felled to provide charcoal for smelting. Later, towards the end of the 18th century, the place was mined for ironstone, and the arrival of the Caldon Canal and the Churnet Valley Railway meant it was once again stripped of trees to make way for progress. At its peak, 1,500 men worked here, filling 30 barges a day with iron ore.

Today this region has been largely reclaimed by nature, but many landmarks remain. The railway, for example, was built in 1849 to link Manchester and Macclesfield with the rest of the Midlands, transporting iron ore, coal and limestone all over the district. Although it stopped operating commercially in the 1960s, it has been given a new lease of life as a tourist attraction, and the once-derelict Consall Station has been lovingly restored. Before the arrival of the railway, the Caldon Canal served a similar purpose, and there are still giant lime kilns where the canal and the river meet. These kilns were used to burn limestone from the vast Caldonlow quarries near by to produce quicklime, which could then be used in fertiliser or mortar. Even The Black Lion pub was built in the early 1800s specially to serve the men who lived and worked in the area. To this day it's still not accessible by road. Back then, it could be reached only by a cart track, by the steep steps running up beside the kilns, by canal and, later, by rail.

At the top of the steps beside the kilns are the remnants of spoil heaps, but the further you go from the river, the harder it is to find evidence of the damage done in the name of progress. In 1994 the Consall Nature Park was designated as a Site of Special Scientific Interest, as the largest area of semi-natural woodland in Staffordshire. Today this region is dominated by birch trees, which are often the first to recover after deforestation. There are no large trees since these were felled when the original forest was cleared for charcoal, mining and railways, although there are signs that oak trees may be starting to establish themselves, protected in their youth by the silver birches.

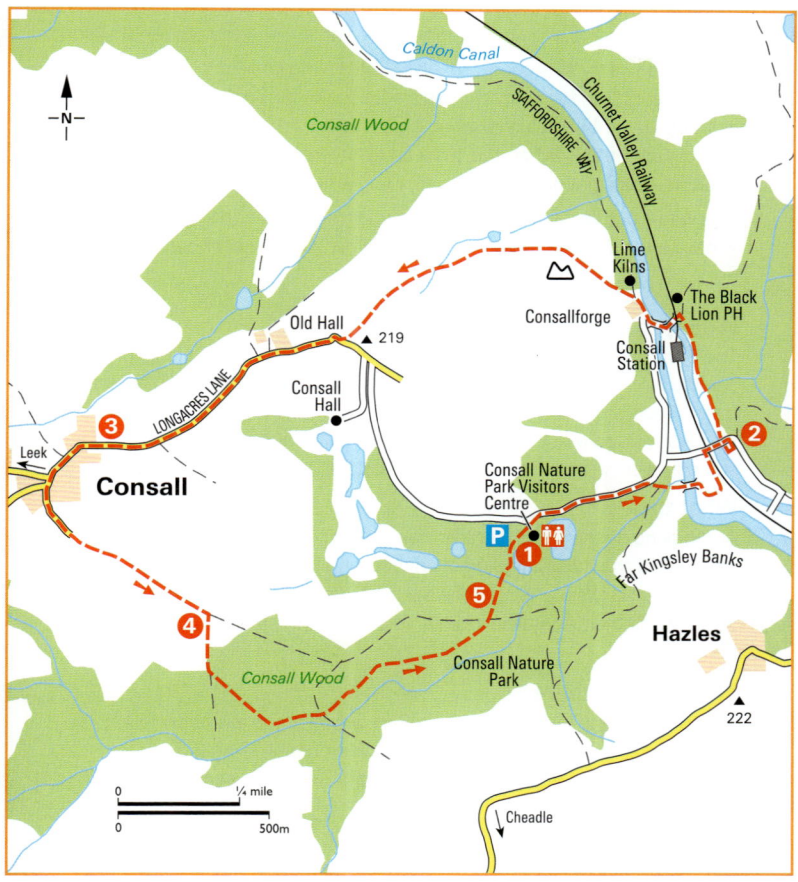

1. From the car park head to the left of the visitor centre to join a road. Go right and, at the far bottom of the road, bear diagonally right over a field to cross a footbridge. Follow the path right and then left to reach the corner of a bridge across a railway. Cross the railway and the canal and go right down a set of steps.

2. Turn right and walk along the tow path. Soon after you pass Consall Station on your left, walk under the railway opposite The Black Lion pub and cross the canal and then the river. Just to the left of the lime kiln go up 204 steep steps and, at the top, walk right, along a grass track. At the brow of the hill follow the path to a gate and two little mounds. After picking your way through these mounds, cross the stile in the corner of the field and, after 30 paces, walk right via a stile. Head diagonally left across this field to cross a stile and continue on the track. At the metalled road go right and follow it towards Consall.

3. After 600yds (549m) reach a black-and-white timbered farmhouse on your right in the village of Consall. Just after a T-junction (signposted to Leek) go left across a farmyard following a signed public footpath. Cross a stile, continue along the wide track to another stile, then follow a line of trees just to your left-hand side. Carry on through a series of stiles to the corner of a wood.

4. In the wood carry straight on, ignoring the trail to your left. When the path you're on bears left, follow it to cross a stile back into Consall Nature Park. Go straight down the hill, again ignoring a path to the left. At the bottom, head left along the wider track. When this joins an even wider grassy track, bear right and continue straight on, ignoring paths to the left and right.

5. By a water outpipe, follow the track round to the right, then go left at the fork, pass a fishing lake to your right and return to the visitor centre.

Where to eat and drink
The Black Lion, in the heart of the Churnet Valley, is a great place for a pie and pint. It does the usual bar snacks and has an extensive restaurant menu. Food is served daily in summer. As we went to press The Black Lion was closed due to a fire in September 2023, although the outside bar still offers service on Saturdays and Sundays.

What to see
At the pond by the visitor centre, look out for resident water voles. They're not the most outgoing of animals and their burrow – a nest made of rushes and grass – is often below the surface. You should be able to see signs of their existence, from tracks in the mud to the nibbled tops of pond plants.

While you're there
Spend some time in Consall Nature Park Visitor Centre: it has a touch table, interactive displays, and information on both the industrial and natural history of the area. It also sells cold drinks and snacks.

FROGHALL WHARF AND THE CHURNET VALLEY

DISTANCE/TIME	4.5 miles (7.2km) / 2hrs 15min
ASCENT/GRADIENT	650ft (198m) / ▲▲
PATHS	Grass paths and dirt tracks may be muddy and slippery in very wet weather; many stiles and steep steps
LANDSCAPE	Forest and farmland
SUGGESTED MAP	OS Explorer 259 Derby
START/FINISH	Grid reference: SK027477
DOG FRIENDLINESS	Keep on lead near livestock
PARKING	Froghall Wharf car park
PUBLIC TOILETS	At Froghall Wharf

These days Froghall Wharf is a very pleasant and secluded picnic site at the heart of North Staffordshire's Churnet Valley, but this hasn't always been the case. In 1777 the Caldon Canal from Stoke-on-Trent to Froghall was completed by engineering whizz James Brindley. Froghall was chosen as the site for the eastern terminus of the canal because of its proximity to the limestone quarries situated at Caldon Low, just 3 miles (4.8km) to the east.

In theory, the limestone could have been taken from the quarry to Froghall on a basic tramway and then loaded onto barges bound for Stoke-on-Trent. In practice however, the quarries were some 680ft (207m) higher than the canal, which meant building the tramway was almost as difficult as building the canal. The first version, with rails of wood topped by an iron strip, was built in 1778, but soon proved to be inadequate. A replacement, completed in 1785, fared little better. A few years later, though, a third line was built and this was made more efficient by an ingenious device called a brake drum. Full wagons at the top of the incline were attached to empty wagons at the bottom via a large wooden drum; when these loaded wagons were rolled to the bottom, the empty wagons were pulled to the top, letting gravity do all the hard work.

By the start of the 19th century, the tramway was delivering thousands of tons of limestone a week to Froghall Wharf. In the 1840s, a fourth tramway was built, which followed a virtually straight line to the quarry, and this line remained in use right up until 1920. When the limestone reached the wharf it was either loaded directly onto barges to be taken to Stoke for use in construction, or it was fed into the tops of the enormous lime kilns that can still be seen at the wharf today. Layers of coal were added and then the mixture was fired to reduce the limestone to quicklime. This was then collected at the bottom and taken to nearby farms for use as a fertiliser; quicklime was also used in mortar and as an ingredient in smelting iron from iron ore.

Froghall Wharf has now been designated a Site of Special Scientific Interest (SSSI), thanks to its flower meadows and large areas of woodland, which support 50 species of birds, plus many more species of insects dependent on over-mature trees.

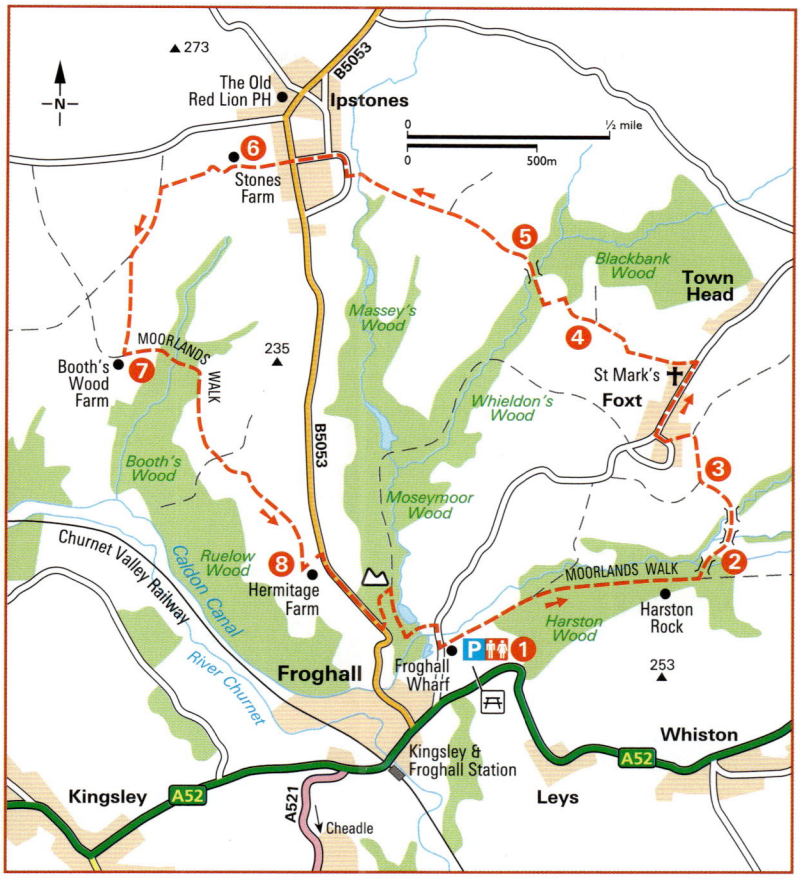

1. From the car park go up a short ramp and along the gravel track ahead. At the fork head right and, just after Harston Rock, go left down a trail signed 'Moorlands Walk'. At the bottom cross a footbridge.

2. Shortly after the footbridge, cross a stile and the bottom of a field. Once back in the woods again, cross another footbridge and go through a narrow stone slot. Continue across a field to a stile and another footbridge. Cross another stile and follow a dry-stone wall up the hill.

3. At the top bear right and continue round, following the curve of the wall. After a wall gap, go down a gravel track to a surfaced road, then head right to the wide fork. Go right through Foxt, and after the church go hard left down a lane.

4. Just before a private drive go left and then at the end right, following the path along a fence. After crossing the stile continue through the wood to a small stream. Cross and shortly after go through a kissing gate and follow the path to a farm road.

5. Turn right to Ipstones. At the end, follow the footpath round to the left and then immediately up stone steps to the road. Follow the road right and then round to the left and, at the next corner, continue between the houses and along a road. At the main road go right then left along the footpath (signed) to Stones Farm.

6. Bear slightly to the left of the farm and, just past it, go over a stile on your right and then continue left along the track. Go through a gate and carry on to another. In the next field cross diagonally left to a gap in a hedge. Continue down the field to cross a stile in the far right corner. Keep on down the left-hand edge of this field to a track to Booth's Wood Farm, going left before the buildings into the field.

7. Cross a stile and head left, following the Moorlands Walk into Booth's Wood, and follow a stepped footpath down to a footbridge. At the top of the wood go over the stile and across the field to the corner of a dry-stone wall. Follow this wall and track to reach Hermitage Farm.

8. Go right on the main road and, after 400yds (366m), follow the footpath sign into the woods on the left. Follow this steep path down to a T-junction, then turn right to the canal. At the canal turn left towards the bridge, then cross it to reach the car park.

Where to eat and drink
If you want to stop halfway try The Old Red Lion in Ipstones. It serves hot and cold food in the evenings, Monday to Friday, and all day at weekends, and has a range of real ales.

What to see
As you leave the car park behind at the start you're actually walking along the line of the fourth and final tramway built between Froghall and Caldon Low. It followed an almost straight line between the two, and the cuttings and embankments that made this possible can still be seen higher up the track.

22 ELLASTONE AND CALWICH ABBEY

DISTANCE/TIME	4 miles (6.4km) / 1hr 30min
ASCENT/GRADIENT	360ft (110m) / ▲▲
PATHS	Gravel tracks, roads and grass trails, many stiles
LANDSCAPE	Farmland
SUGGESTED MAP	OS Explorer 259 Derby
START/FINISH	Grid reference: SK118426
DOG FRIENDLINESS	Must be kept on lead
PARKING	Ample parking along village roads
PUBLIC TOILETS	None on route

Ellastone, near the Derbyshire border to the southwest of Ashbourne, is known for its literary and musical associations, both of which involve people named George, or so it would seem. The first is George Eliot, author of – among others – *Silas Marner* (1861) and *Middlemarch* (1871). Eliot's first novel *Adam Bede* is based on the village of Ellastone; in the book it is referred to as Hayslope, while Staffordshire is named Loamshire. When it was first published in 1859, by a completely unknown author, a number of impostors tried to claim authorship of the book. Only then was it revealed that George Elliot was a pen name for Marian Evans, who wrote for the prestigious Westminster Review.

The scandal that broke when it was discovered that George Eliot was a woman was exacerbated by the fact that she was also having an extramarital affair with George Henry Lewis, her editor. Unable to divorce his faithless wife, George Henry entered into a common-law marriage with George Eliot. Polite Victorian society was far too conservative for such sordid behaviour, and the author was ostracised by her family and friends. This rejection became one of the themes of her next novel, *The Mill on the Floss*, published in 1860.

As for *Adam Bede*, its success then, as now, lay in Eliot's ability to reflect everyday life in her characters and the worlds they inhabited. Shunning the romanticism prevalent in the first half of the 19th century, she was one of the first writers to insist on realism, believing that novels should reflect not only the real world, but also some underlying moral purpose above and beyond the entertainment to be had from a good read. In *Adam Bede*, the hero is thought to have been based heavily on Marian's own father, and in amongst a tragic love story – interlaced with rich descriptions of rural life – lies the novel's central theme, that selflessness is the secret of happiness.

The second George to find inspiration in Ellastone was George Frideric Handel (1685–1759), who was later described by Beethoven as the 'the greatest composer who ever lived'. Handel's most famous work is arguably *The Messiah*, which he composed in a furious 24 days while staying with friends at Calwich Abbey in 1741 (Calwich Abbey is passed in the early stages of the walk). *The Messiah* was first performed, in aid of charity, in Dublin a year later, where it was met with rapturous applause. Some years later, King George II was so moved on hearing the *Hallelujah Chorus* that he rose to his feet; the audience duly followed his example and the tradition remains today, even in the absence of royalty.

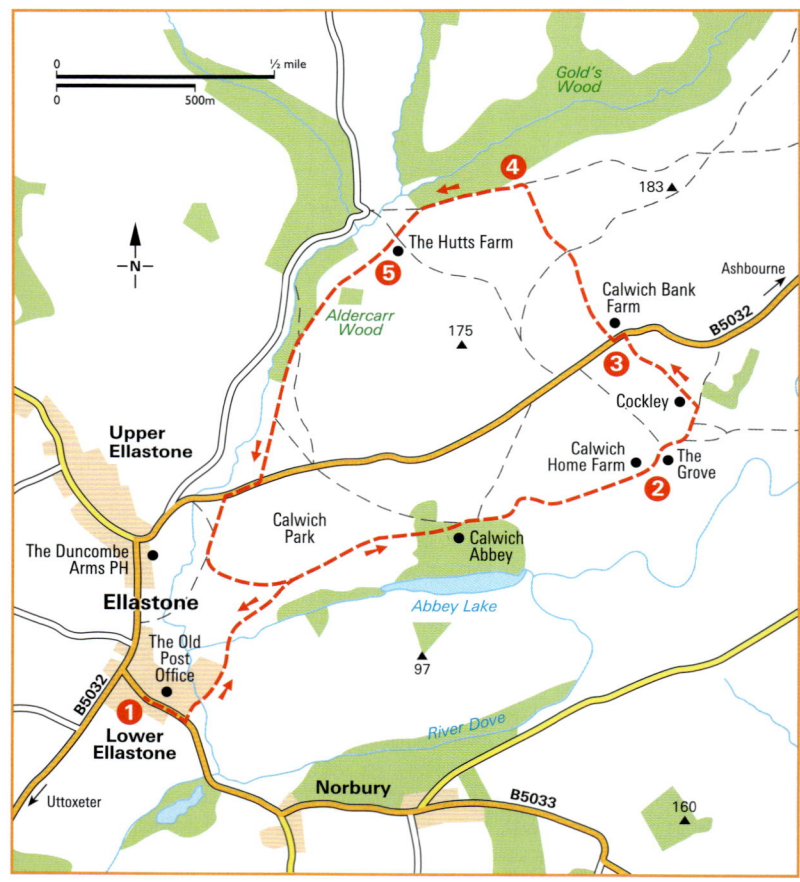

1. From the former post office, opposite the red post box, go left and then take the first left down an obvious gravel track. Keep going straight to Calwich Abbey. Follow the track left of the abbey and along the metalled road as far as Calwich Home Farm.

2. Pass the farm and follow the track round to the left of The Grove and through a gate. At the fork go left, through another gate and down a slope and, after 50yds (46m), veer left off the track up a short hill to a stile in front of Cockley farm. Cross the stile and head just to the right of Cockley, following a dirt and grass track all the way to the B5032.

3. At the road go left and then first right, through Calwich Bank Farm and up a gravel track. When the track bears round to the right, keep going straight into a field, making for a gap in the hedge at the top right-hand corner. Go through the gap, over a stile on the left and then follow the hedge left, down the field.

4. At the bottom follow the hedge round to the left and cut diagonally right across the field to a stile. After crossing the stile, skirt round the top of the wood to another stile and continue as far as The Hutts Farm. After a stile take the gravel track up the hill to a gate into the farmyard and head straight on to another stile into a field.

5. Continue straight across, making for the corner of Aldercarr Wood ahead to the left. Keep going straight on and down to the far bottom corner of the field, and carry on along the right-hand edge of the next field. At the far end cross another stile and continue straight on (not diagonally left) to the B5032. Turn right along the road and, after 100yds (91m), take the path to the left. Head diagonally right across the field to a double stile and then left round the bottom of a small mound with trees. Keep going as far as the junction of the two bridleways, between Point 1 and Point 2, and from here retrace your steps back to the start.

Where to eat and drink
The Duncombe Arms in Ellastone serves a range of meals and snacks, plus traditional beers, at lunchtime and evenings throughout the week.

What to see
Sadly, little remains of the abbey – founded in 1148 – where Handel once penned his greatest work, and not much remains of Calwich Hall, which was built in its place. All that can be seen today is a disused stable block and a fishing temple by the lake.

While you're there
Ashbourne is a picturesque and predominantly Georgian market town near the edge of the Peak District, and is well worth a visit. Market days are Thursday and Saturday, but its best tradition is surely the Royal Shrovetide Football Match, when the Up'ards (those from north of the Henmore Brook) play the Down'ards (those from the south) using a pitch where the goals are 3 miles (4.8km) apart. The game is played with a specially made and painted ball, and is played over two days and can last until 10pm, flowing back and forth through the town.

AROUND ALTON

DISTANCE/TIME	5 miles (8km) / 2hrs
ASCENT/GRADIENT	361ft (110m) / ▲▲
PATHS	Roads, gravel tracks and dirt trails
LANDSCAPE	Forest and farmland
SUGGESTED MAP	OS Explorer 259 Derby
START/FINISH	Grid reference: SK073423
DOG FRIENDLINESS	Can be off lead in woods
PARKING	Parking on Alton village roads
PUBLIC TOILETS	None on route

For its size, the village of Alton has more than its fair share of history, not to mention a name that's practically synonymous with stomach-churning, roller-coaster rides. The first recorded settlement in the area was an Iron Age fort on Bunbury Hill – the site of the present-day Alton Towers – built before 1000 BC. In the eighth century AD it became a fortress for the Saxon king Coelred, and in the 12th century it was given to a soldier by the name of Bertram de Verdun, as thanks for the part he played in the Crusades.

In 1176 de Verdun built a castle high above the Churnet Valley, on the opposite side to the original fort. The castle remains are at the start of the walk but they're on the site of a children's centre, so you can only glimpse the ruined tower and walls. A sheer cliff lies below the north side, and on the east and south sides is a deep ditch. The lower parts of a wall remain, as does most of a rectangular tower and the base of a round tower. The castle is thought to have been in a state of neglect at the time of Verdun's death, and subsequent centuries did little to stop the rot. It was held for King Charles I in the Civil War but later dismantled by Parliament to stop it being used by Royalists.

Opposite the castle is the present-day Catholic Youth Centre, begun in 1847 to a design by A W Pugin, who was partly responsible for the Houses of Parliament. Pugin was at the vanguard of the Gothic revival, when every landowner wanted a mock castle on his land, hence the battlemented cornices. Originally a private home, it was used as a boarding school from 1919 until 1989; and has been a youth centre since 1995.

While Pugin was rebuilding the estate, successive generations of the Talbot family began to rebuild the landscape, especially the area of Dimmings Dale to the west of Alton. Ore smelting had flourished in the valley for 150 years but by 1850 the industry was gone. Hillsides had been stripped of trees to fire smelting furnaces, spoil heaps littered the valley and the stream had been dammed to provide water to operate the smelting mill. Today, thanks to the Talbot family, the forest has been restored and the spoil heaps are gone, but the lakes and the original mill still remain as part of a peaceful forest walk.

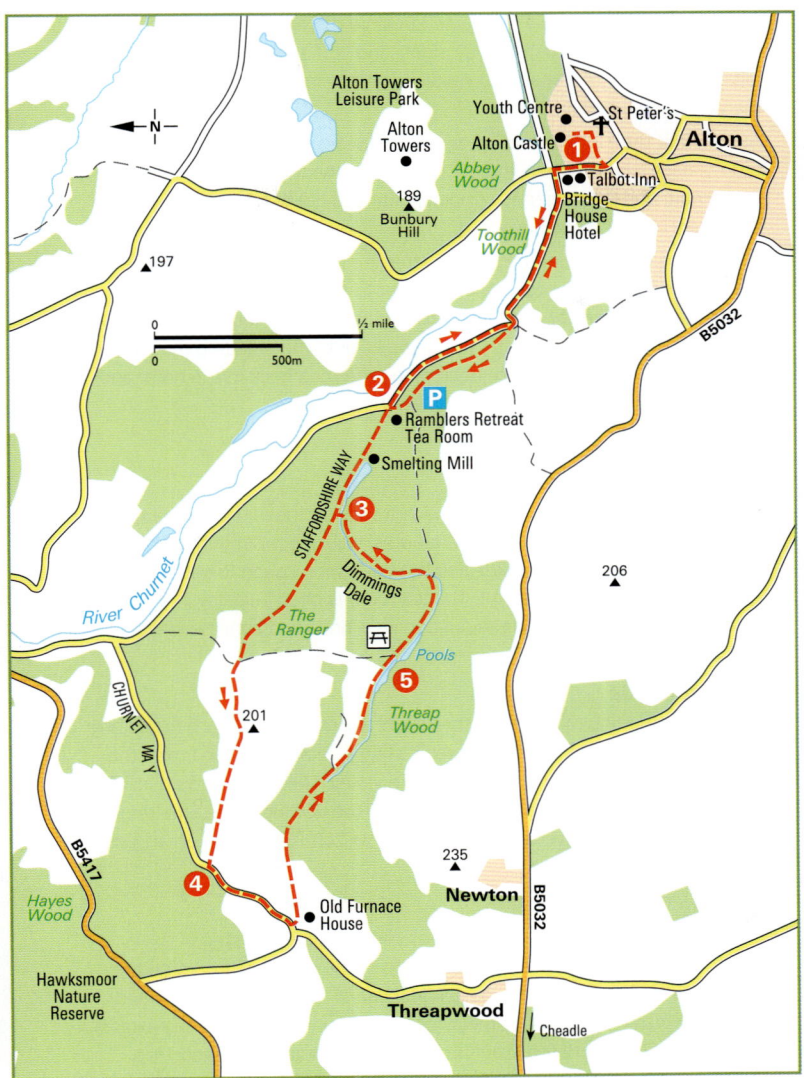

1. At the castle gate, head straight down the track to the right of St Peter's Church. At the main road, head right, down the hill to the river and the Bridge House Hotel. Head left along a metalled road, past the hotel, going straight ahead where the road goes round to the left, along the base of Toothill Wood. Just after the road goes round an obvious hairpin bend, follow a wide track into the woods on the left, shown by a public bridleway sign. After 400yds (366m) go right off the track down a less obvious trail which will bring you out at Dimmings Dale car park and the Ramblers Retreat Tea Room.

2. Go through the car park to the right of the tea room and then continue straight on following signs for the Staffordshire Way. Pass the smelting mill and lake on your left, and continue straight on at the end of the lake, staying to the right of the impressive stone house.

3. When you climb up to a path junction amid the open woods, go straight over, following more Staffordshire Way signs, and still ascending. At the top of the hill go right along the metalled road, over a cattle grid and follow this road all the way to a T-junction.

4. Go left at the junction and, after 400yds (366m), go left again just before Old Furnace House. When you get to a fork in the track, head right, close to the stream and past a series of pools, until you get to a picnic table and a causeway between two pools.

5. Continue to the left of the stream after the final pool, staying on the left at the first wooden footbridge. When you get to a dry-stone wall barring the way straight ahead, go right over a wooden footbridge and continue to follow the river left. This path will shortly bring you back to the smelting mill and the Ramblers Retreat. From there head along the road back to the hotel and then retrace your steps back to St Peter's Church.

Where to eat and drink
The Ramblers Retreat Tea Room is in a very secluded spot in the heart of the Churnet Valley, just a few minutes' walk from Dimmings Dale. The food, ranging from cakes and snacks right through to substantial meals, is invariably excellent. The tea room is open Tuesday 11am–3pm, Wednesday to Friday 10am–4pm and weekends and bank holidays 9.30am–4.30pm.

What to see
The old smelting mill is now a private residence and it's hard to see any detail, but the original waterwheel is still there and you can't miss the necklace of pools that stretches up the valley. The mill was built in 1741 and was used for smelting lead ore. After the decline of the smelting industry, it was converted to a corn mill, its 20ft (6m) wheel driving three pairs of grinding stones.

While you're there
The Hawksmoor Nature Reserve has been in the ownership of the National Trust since 1927. It was originally the site of an iron-smelting furnace, and at Gibridding you can still see the remains of an inclined plane which was once a tramway used for hauling coal from the extensive mines at Cheadle to the Froghall-to-Uttoxeter canal. The wood is a haven for insects and birds, including spotted flycatchers in summer and occasional buzzards in the winter.

THE CHURNET VALLEY

DISTANCE/TIME	7 miles (11.3km) / 2hrs 15min
ASCENT/GRADIENT	262ft (80m) / ▲▲
PATHS	Field paths and tracks, one steep woodland descent, firm railway trackbed
LANDSCAPE	Steep wooded valley and open hillside pasture
SUGGESTED MAP	OS Explorer 259 Derby
START/FINISH	Grid reference: SK073423
DOG FRIENDLINESS	Good on trail and Saltersford Lane, but on lead in livestock fields
PARKING	High Street, Alton
PUBLIC TOILETS	None on route

It's easy to forget that many of the paths we walk for pleasure today were once important trading routes, used for centuries to transport goods and commodities around the country. The second half of this walk, a long and gentle ascent out of the Churnet Valley from Denstone, is along a route called Saltersford Lane. There are great views of the Weaver Hills and the distant edge of the Peak District to the north, but look closer to hand and you will notice that this wide, unsurfaced hedged track is slightly sunken and contains a continuous line of old stone sets or causeway.

The clue to the origin of Saltersford Lane is in its name. It was once a so-called saltway, a route used since medieval times by traders to transport salt. Leading packhorses or ox carts they would typically bring this precious commodity, used to preserve food long before the age of artificial additives and refridgerators, from salt-producing Cheshire to communities across the Midlands. Although the precise routes are unclear, Saltersford Lane would probably have linked the likes of Nantwich, Newcastle-under-Lyme, Cheadle and Derby. But it wasn't just salt that was transported, of course. Other products like coal, textiles and food were shipped across the region by this means and the paths were also regularly used for taking animals to market and other local journeys.

As at nearby Consall and Froghall, there is evidence of more modern transport routes through the Churnet Valley. Large quantities of ironstone and limestone were shipped out first by canal barges and later railway wagons. Built in 1811, the Uttoxeter Canal ran for 13 miles from a junction with the Caldon Canal at Froghall along the Churnet Valley via Alton and Denstone to finish at Uttoxeter. However, by 1850 it was rendered redundant by the new North Staffordshire Railway, which even appropriated some of the canal for its route. Today, you can still make out short sections of the canal, shallow and overgrown, especially as you approach Crumpwood Weir where the canal originally crossed the River Churnet. There's even one surviving bridge on the canal, its stones now green and overgrown, which you can inspect just off the walk. The railway fared a little better, surviving until Dr Beeching's cuts in 1965. Originally there wasn't a station at Denstone, but this was added following the opening of Denstone College in 1873 which still remains a day boarding school for boys and girls

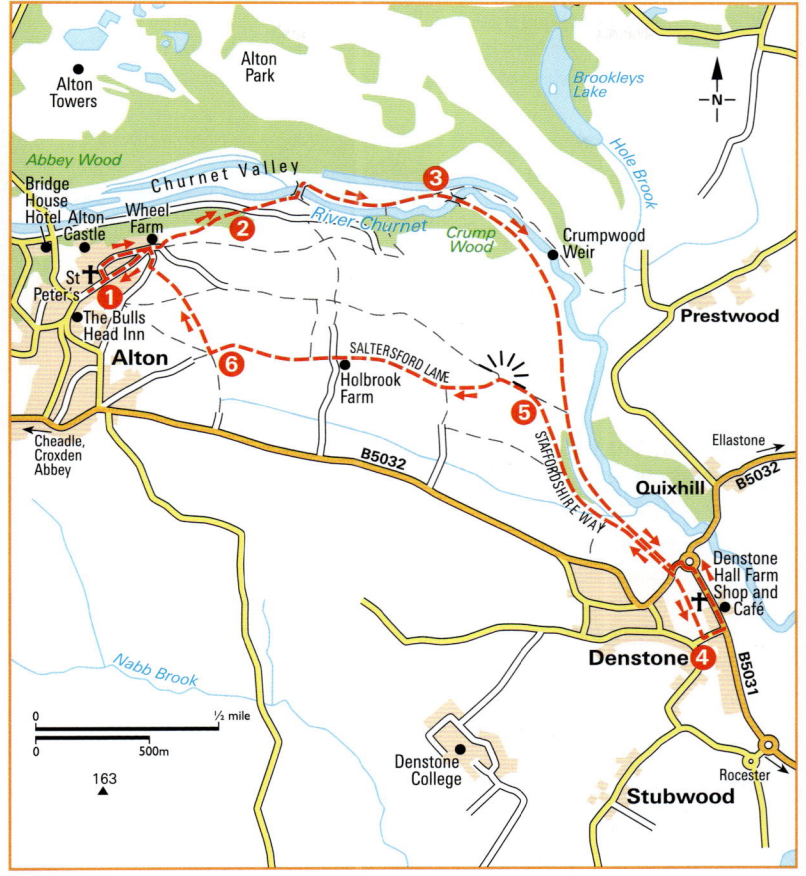

1. Walk up Alton High Street and turn left on Castle Hill Road past the church. Bear right in front of Alton Castle and at the bend at the far end of the lane continue ahead past Wheel Farm. Go through a gate and head half left across a field. Look for the wall gap on the left, beyond which is a path down the wooded hillside.

2. Turn right at the bottom and cross a driveway for the stile opposite. Now go down to the river and along the bank until you reach a footbridge. Cross to the far bank and turn right to continue through a meadow downstream. Before you reach an old railway bridge drift left for a gate on to the former track.

3. Turn right and follow this multi-user route along the course of the old railway, swinging gently southwards beside the meandering River Churnet past Crumpwood Weir. The valley broadens out and becomes less wooded, and the trail eventually ends between the platforms of the former Denstone Station.

4. Turn left on to the road and left again past Denstone Hall Farm Shop & Café. At the roundabout go left over the railway bridge, then turn immediately right for a public footpath along the edge of fields above the railway trail. Follow Staffordshire Way signs up across fields until a gate leads on to Saltersford Lane.

5. Follow this wide hedged track gently uphill, going through a gate at Holbrook Farm. Beyond here it can get a little boggy, but the line of stone slabs keeps you out of the worst of it. About 650yds (594m) on you reach a point with stiles either side.

6. Still following waymarks for the Staffordshire Way, turn right and walk up the right side of two fields. At the far end go half left for a stile in the hedge, then the same direction across further fields to reach the lane on the edge of Alton. Turn right then left into Town Head to return to the start.

Where to eat and drink
The Bulls Head Inn on Alton's High Street is open all day Friday to Sunday and 5pm–10pm on Monday to Thursday. Alternatively head down to the Bridge House Hotel below the village which has a pleasant riverside beer garden. Half way along the route is Denstone Hall Farm Shop & Café, open every day for a tasty range of snacks and light meals. There's outdoor seating and walkers are welcome.

What to see
Depending on when you visit, it's likely you will hear the distant strains of the crowds enjoying (if that's the right term) the rides at Alton Towers. The former seat of the Earl of Shrewsbury has been turned into a hugely popular theme park, with the remains of the neo-Gothic house now host to over two million thrill-seeking visitors every year.

While you're there
Founded at the end of the 12th century, Croxden Abbey, a mile south of Alton, was one of the last Cistercian abbeys to be built in England, and its architecture is more elaborate than earlier monasteries built by this strict order. The east end was unusually ornate, consisting of five chapels radiating from an ambulatory, of which only fragments now remain. Today, the massive west front dominates the ruins, with rich mouldings around the middle doorway and three slender windows.

DUNSTALL HALL

DISTANCE/TIME	3.5 miles (5.7km) / 2hrs
ASCENT/GRADIENT	344ft (105m) / ▲
PATHS	Grassy field paths, dirt tracks and lanes, several stiles
LANDSCAPE	Woods, parkland and fields
SUGGESTED MAP	OS Explorer 245 The National Forest
START/FINISH	Grid reference: SK186187
DOG FRIENDLINESS	Keep on lead around livestock
PARKING	Public car park by village hall, Barton-under-Needwood
PUBLIC TOILETS	By car park

The centrepiece of this walk is Dunstall Hall, dating from the 1800s but replacing a much earlier building that once stood on the site of nearby Old Hall farm. Still privately owned, the hall and 1,000-acre (405ha) estate have passed through many different pairs of hands over the centuries, including those of Sir Richard Arkwright, son of the famous inventor of the world's first water-powered cotton spinning mill. After his father died he sold most of the family's mills, invested in landed property like Dunstall, and made his own personal fortune, so much so that on his death in 1842 he left over £3 million in his will (around £300 million in today's money).

In 2001, the owners of Dunstall Estate, began a tree-planting scheme as part of the wider National Forest programme. In recent years more than 180,000 trees have been planted and a series of new permissive paths has been established for visitors to enjoy. You will walk through the young woodland early on in the walk after leaving Barton-under-Needwood; and also part of the newly created Douglas Wood beyond Old Hall farm. The National Forest covers over 200sq miles (518sq km) of Staffordshire, Derbyshire and Leicestershire and has increased tree cover by 12 per cent in just 20 years. The plan is ultimately to plant 30 million trees and cover a third of the forest area. However, alongside the new planting, the National Forest also incorporates the little that remains of the ancient woodland of Staffordshire's Needwood Forest (which once spread to Barton). There are walks galore and events throughout the year for all the family, see www.nationalforest.org.

Near Dunstall Hall you pass the home of Dunstall Cricket Club and one of the most picturesque cricket grounds in the county. The club was founded in the late 1870s and, despite its rural setting, boasts many sides and some real talent. The first team play in the county's League Division 1, and past club professionals have included former England legends Derek Randall and Devon Malcolm. If a match is under way, why not call in and enjoy some quintessential English village sport?

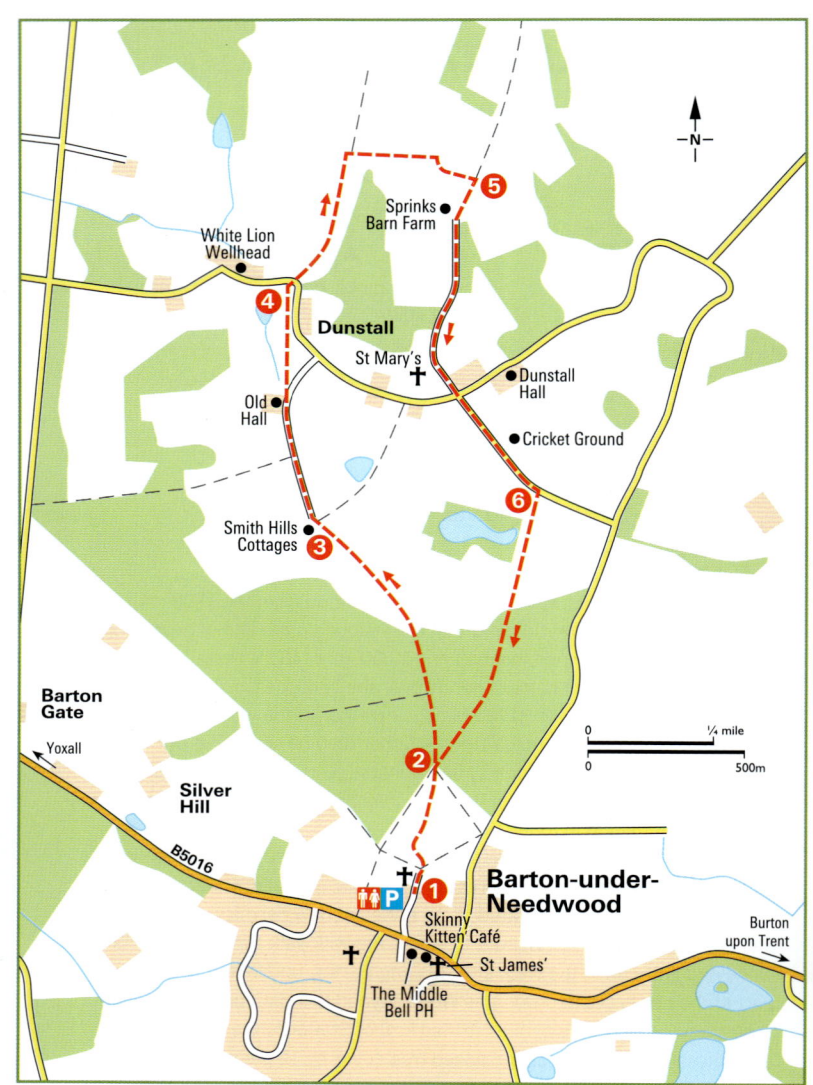

1. From the car park turn left along Crowberry Lane, past the Methodist Church. Go through a gate onto a wide farm track, then over a stile and ahead to an information panel. Go through the gate and straight ahead through the field to reach a solitary post.

2. Veer half left to go through a gate into woodland. Stay on the main path, ignoring permissive routes off left and right, then via another gate walk out across a wide field. Bear slightly left to reach Smith Hills Cottages.

3. Go through two gates and across a lane for a track into a field. Where it meets a surfaced lane go straight on. With the entrance to Old Hall on your left go over a stile ahead and through a meadow, aiming for the gate in the far right corner. Continue on a path to reach a road.

4. Cross the road carefully for a stile opposite. Walk along the right edge of the field for 440yds (402m) until you get to a waymarker post. Turn right and walk down across the field, through a belt of trees and up across another field towards farm buildings. Aim for the metal gate between large sheds and go through this to cross the farmyard. Go through a gate for a double stile onto a lane.

5. Turn right and follow the lane past Sprinks Barn Farm (Landrover and 4x4 servicing specialists) as it becomes a surfaced drive. At the crossroads at the bottom of the hill, with the church on your right, go straight over, past the cricket ground and as far as a bend.

6. Turn right over a stile for a fenced path past an overgrown old pool. Continue through woodland to the gate at the far end. Go ahead through the field to the solitary post, then veer slightly left on the route back to the start.

Where to eat and drink
The Middle Bell is located near the start of the walk in Barton-under-Needwood. Food is served at lunchtimes and evenings and all day at weekends. For lighter snacks try the equally excellent Skinny Kitten Café also on Main Street.

What to see
At Point 4 you can deviate from the route by heading left up the lane for 200yds (190m) to visit the White Lion. Despite its name this isn't a pub, but an ornate stone wellhead carved to celebrate Queen Victoria's Jubilee and which for many years provided local people with drinking water. The Wellhead sits down a narrow pathway at a gap in the hedge just beyond White Lion Cottage. The Arkwright family's wealth paid for St Mary's Church in Dunstall. The pulpit is built from Caen stone, but the chancel is much more local, lined with alabaster from nearby Hanbury.

While you're there
A few miles to the south, off the A38 near Alrewas, is the National Memorial Arboretum. Opened in 2001, it's the UK's permanent centre of remembrance where more than 25,000 trees have been planted, 400 memorials established and over 16,000 names carved on stone walls to commemorate members of the armed forces and civil services. The arboretum is free to enter and open year-round.

LOGGERHEADS

DISTANCE/TIME	5.5 miles (8.8km) / 2hrs
ASCENT/GRADIENT	240ft (73m) / ▲
PATHS	Gravel tracks, roads and grass trails, many stiles
LANDSCAPE	Woodland and farmland
SUGGESTED MAP	OS Explorer 243 Market Drayton
START/FINISH	Grid reference: SJ738359
DOG FRIENDLINESS	Keep on lead near livestock
PARKING	Ample parking in Loggerheads village
PUBLIC TOILETS	None on route

Loggerhead, meaning 'blockhead' or 'fool,' is believed to be derived from the word 'logger', which was used colloquially to refer to a block of wood for hobbling horses. Loggerheads itself takes its name from the Loggerheads pub, formerly known as the Three Loggerheads, whose sign featured two fools' heads and a third, that of an onlooker.

But it was at Bloreheath, just to the west of the village, where history was made, for it was there that the first major battle of the Wars of the Roses was fought. This involved an ongoing dispute between the House of Lancaster, led by King Henry VI, and the House of York, led by Richard, Duke of York. As an experienced soldier and leader, Richard believed he had a better claim to the throne than Henry and duly expected to inherit the crown; when the King sired a son and heir, however, Richard realised that he would have to resort to force.

The year is 1459: Richard's allies are fragmented all over England, and to consolidate his forces he orders Neville, Earl of Salisbury, to march from his castle in Yorkshire to his own pile in Ludlow, about 40 miles (64km) south of Bloreheath. Aware of this march, Queen Margaret directs James Touchet, Lord Audley, to intercept Salisbury's army. Knowing that the road to Ludlow will take Salisbury through a defile near Bloreheath, Audley assembles 10,000 soldiers on the heath overlooking the road. On Sunday 23 September, the two sides oppose each other across the valley, Salisbury on the slopes where Audley's Cross now stands and Audley on the other side. Salisbury has nothing in the way of firearms, and is heavily outnumbered. And so, the scene is set for a rout.

But Salisbury has other ideas. He senses that Audley is over-confident and that he may be tempted into a glorious cavalry charge, to impress Queen Margaret and to destroy his enemy. To make it even more tempting, Salisbury feigns a retreat by withdrawing his pikemen from the front, leaving an opening for a charge. Seizing this opportunity, Audley orders his cavalry down the hill but underestimates the difficulty of ascending the steep, muddy slope of the brook at the bottom. Exposed and vulnerable, the horses are no match for Salisbury's archers who have been waiting in the wings. The result is unequivocal. Twice Audley's forces charge and twice they are mown down. A third assault involves more than 4,000 infantry. Audley is slain in the bitter hand-to-hand fighting which ensues, and today Audley's Cross still marks the spot where he died. The battle lasted all day. By nightfall, more than 2,000 Lancastrians lay dead or dying on the blood-soaked battlefield, while Yorkist casualties numbered just 56. But ultimately it was to no avail; after 30 years of war the Lancastrians kept the throne.

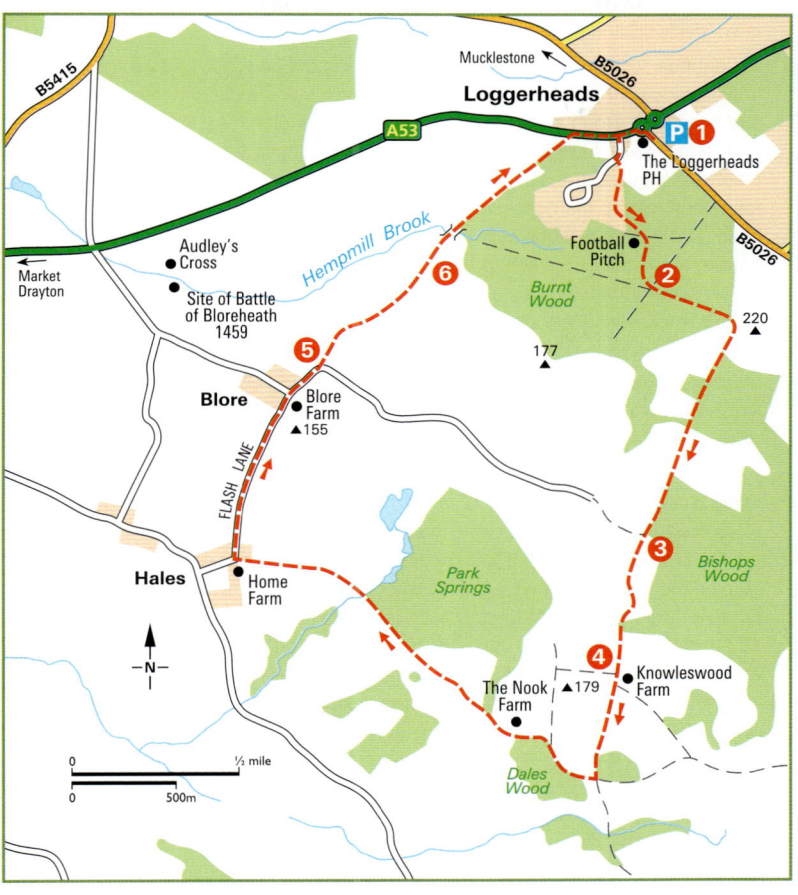

1. Head along the A53 in the direction of Market Drayton and take the first left along Kestrel Drive. Just after The Robins head left along a woodland track down the back of some houses keeping the high panel fence to your right. When you reach the end of a cul-de-sac, go left on a woodland track with roofs of bungalows visible to your left turn onto the track to the right. After 219 yards (200m) with the Loggerheads Football Club buildings on your left bear left across the clearing and past an iron bar across a wide track and, at the fork, go right, past the football pitch, then turn left uphill take the track uphill. Where this forks go right along the edge of the football pitch and at the end of the pitch turn left uphill to reach a major path junction.

2. Take the fourth path on your left and where this bends left at the far end, follow a narrow path through the undergrowth ahead right to reach a wide gravel track. Turn right through the gate and continue for 0.5 miles (800m), until the main track goes right.

3. Head over a stile and along the footpath with a hedge to your right-hand side. At the bottom of the field bear right towards the right-hand corner of the bank of trees. Go through the gate and head left up track to Knowleswood farm (derelict) and another gate.

4. Continue straight ahead and, at the bottom of the field, go right over a stile and drop down through a small dip. At the bottom of the dip go through a gate and head right along a concrete track. At a fork go left to The Nook Farm and, after a mile (1.6km) reach Home Farm. Turn right along the semi-surfaced Flash Lane and up the gentle hill to Blore Farm. When you get to a junction follow the road to the right-hand side of the farmhouse, after 200yds (183m), head left through a hedge over a stile. Follow this hedge right to a stile in the bottom of the field. This stile probably provides the best vantage point from which to view the main battlefield, now private farm land, which was centred on the shallow valley to your left.

5. Continue to the bottom right-hand corner of the next field before bearing diagonally right across another field to the right-hand end of a bank of trees. Cross the small stile and follow the faint track straight across the middle of the next field to another stile.

6. Follow the path through a young plantation, keeping left at the fork, to a fence ahead and cross a stile. Keep following the faint track alongside a wood to your right and, when you come to a clearing, continue around the edge of the field to a series of small footbridges. At the corner of this field, cross a stile and footbridge to a wide grassy track, which you follow right and up the hill to a large, lone oak at the top. Turn left here to cross a stile back onto the A53 to return to the start. Follow the path around the edge of the new housing estate to emerge on to the A53 and go left along the main road to the turn of Kestrel Drive. As we went to press there was a temporary fencing here to divert walkers around a construction site.

Where to eat and drink
The Loggerheads is located at the start of the walk and in the centre of the village and is a popular pub that welcomes families. Food is served daily, including a Sunday carvery.

What to see
Although it's difficult to actually walk across the battlefield today, is considered especially important because it's one of only a handful of medieval battlefields to have escaped modern development.

While you're there
It's said that Queen Margaret watched the defeat of the Lancastrian forces from the church tower at Mucklestone. Fearing for her safety, she made plans to flee, instructing the local blacksmith to put the shoes on her horse the wrong way round to disguise her escape.

HANCHURCH HILLS

DISTANCE/TIME	7 miles (11.3km) / 2hrs 30min
ASCENT/GRADIENT	420ft (128m) / ▲▲
PATHS	Gravel tracks, field paths and roads
LANDSCAPE	Woodland, farmland and village
SUGGESTED MAP	OS Explorer 243 Market Drayton
START/FINISH	Grid reference: SJ839399
DOG FRIENDLINESS	Off-lead opportunities in woods and on fenced tracks
PARKING	Hanchurch Hills Picnic Place car park
PUBLIC TOILETS	None on route

The walk begins in Swynnerton Old Park, near the first of this walk's water towers. Of course, it's not just coincidence that there are so many water towers in the area; the sandstone strata of Meecebrook Valley, formed during the Triassic period, is capable of providing 1.5 million gallons (7 million litres) of clean water a day.

At the end of the 19th century, in response to an increase in demand for high-quality water, thanks in part to the new fashion for indoor baths, the Staffordshire Potteries Water Board built the Hatton Water Works, a project which took the best part of 20 years to complete. Water was pumped directly to Hanchurch Reservoir (now Hanchurch Pools), which then supplied water to Newcastle, Stoke and the Trent Valley.

Today, water is still pumped at Hatton, but electricity has now replaced steam and the Grade II listed, yellow- and red-brick buildings have been converted into various luxury apartments. The carefully restored water tower just north of Swynnerton, however, gives an idea of quite how impressive these Italianate-style buildings must once have been, with their red-brick columns, circular windows and triumphal archways superimposed on warm, yellow-brick façades. The Swynnerton tower itself has been ingeniously rebuilt as a house, with its vast windows and spiral staircase in the middle, up to the first floor.

Swynnerton, meanwhile, has more than its fair share of historic buildings for a village so small. The oldest of these is 13th-century St Mary's Church. Apart from the statue of Christ (see What to See), the feature of most interest is undoubtedly the simple Norman doorway, which nonetheless has a detailed beakhead moulding. Over the road is a Roman Catholic church dedicated to Our Lady of the Assumption and built from local stone by Gilbert Blount, who tried to imbue his designs with a distinctly Gothic feel.

The chapel itself is attached to Swynnerton Hall which, though not obvious from the village, dominates the Swynnerton skyline from the south. The hall was built in 1725 to replace an earlier manor house demolished by Cromwell in the Civil War. Its owner, Sir John Fitzherbert, supported the Royalist cause. His grandson Basil built the hall seen today.

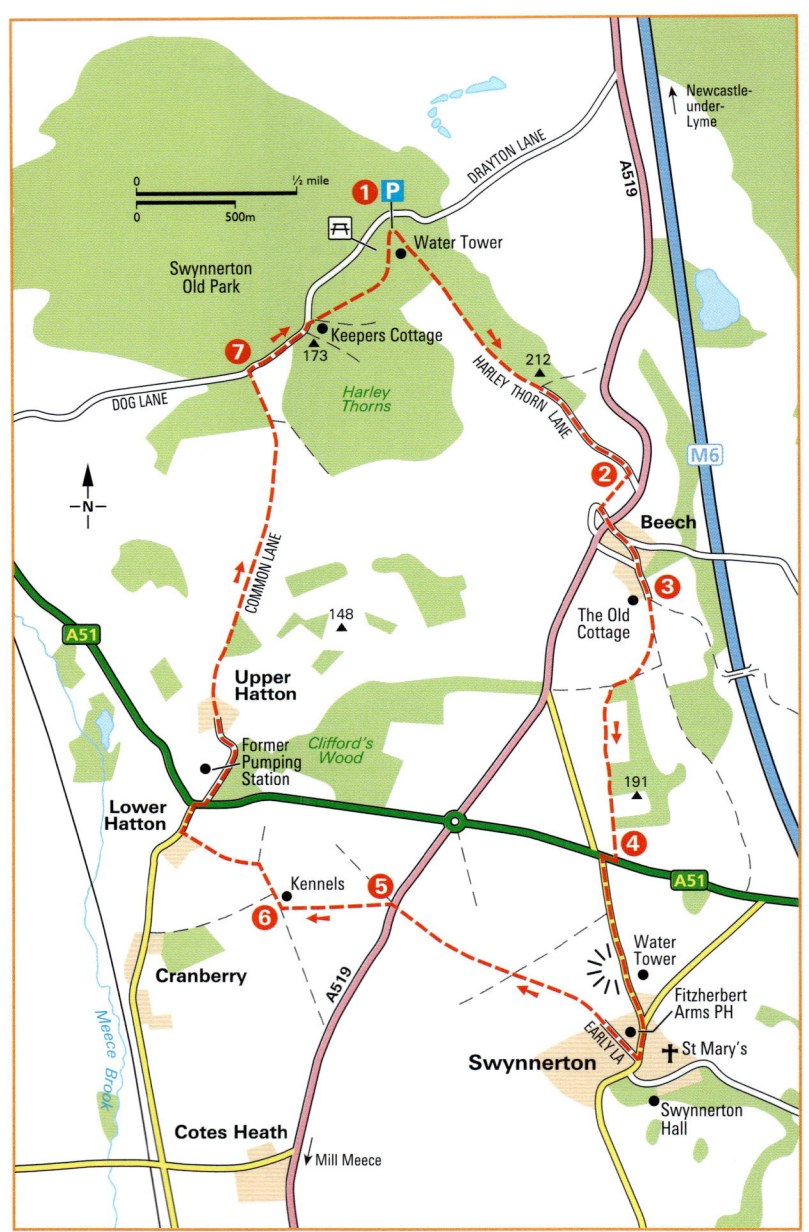

1. From the car park take the left fork along a gravel track, which is Harley Thorn Lane. Then veer left again at the next fork past a derelict water tower and covered reservoir on your right. After 650yds (594m) go through a gate and continue ahead along the metalled road.

2. Just before the A519 go right up a gravel track and, shortly after, at a hairpin in another road, head left, going downhill. At the next fork go right. At the road junction turn left and follow the road until you come to a fork just after The Old Cottage on your right.

3. Go right here and keep following the main path, ignoring the public footpath signs to the left. Where the obvious gravel bridleway veers left, head straight on and up into the woods. At the top of the woods, carry straight on, following the track to the A51.

4. Turn right, then take the first left, following the minor road towards Swynnerton. Just past the Fitzherbert Arms on the right, turn right along Early Lane. At the end of the road, keep going straight along a signed footpath. At the far end, go straight on, in the same direction, across the middle of a wide field. Continue on this public footpath through three more fields to the A519.

5. Cross the road with care and then carry on by going left in the next field, beside the hedge. Continue to the end of the field, go through some trees and then right to the stile and a gravel drive.

6. Turn right past the kennels and, at Lower Hatton Stables, turn right along the road to the A51. Take care crossing this road, heading right then taking the first left, past Lower Hatton Pumping Station, now private residences. Follow this road to Upper Hatton and then carry on straight along Common Lane all the way back to Swynnerton Old Park.

7. At Dog Lane turn right and, after 400yds (366m), just beyond Keepers Cottage, turn right up a woodland path. Head left at the fork immediately after the start of the track. When you reach a clearing with a car park and picnic site, make for the left of the water tower, continuing along the track back to the start.

Where to eat and drink
The Fitzherbert Arms at Swynnerton is open at lunchtimes and evenings in the week and all day at weekends, and serves a range of meals and snacks. A little further afield try Slater's Country Inn on the A51 at Hill Chorlton.

What to see
The viewpoint in front of Swynnerton water tower has a good view over the Millbrook Valley and beyond. Also worth a look, if it's open, is St Mary's Church, which features an impressive statue of Christ dating from c.1260–80.

While you're there
The Mill Meece Pumping Station has supplied water to the Potteries since 1914. Preserved steam engines are fired up on steaming days and rally events. Open most Sundays 11am-3pm (free admission). Check their website for other times and dates.

BARLASTON AND WEDGWOOD COUNTRY

DISTANCE/TIME	3.25 miles (5.3km) / 1hr 15min
ASCENT/GRADIENT	180ft (55m) / ▲
PATHS	Roads, gravel tracks and tow paths, several stiles
LANDSCAPE	Village, farmland and canal
SUGGESTED MAP	OS Explorer 258 Stoke-on-Trent & Newcastle-under-Lyme
START/FINISH	Grid reference: SJ889395
DOG FRIENDLINESS	Must be kept on lead near livestock
PARKING	Roadside parking near Wedgwood visitor centre entrance
PUBLIC TOILETS	Wedgwood visitor centre (customers only)

During the 18th and 19th centuries white stoneware was all the rage in polite society, thanks in part to an influx of expensive white china from the Orient. In the quest for a cheaper alternative, potters spent decades experimenting with powdered flint from the local mills. Flint, when mixed with clay, helps to whiten it, but there were so many problems with the process and such a high level of wastage that for a time English china was more expensive than silver. In the 1760s, however, Josiah Wedgwood perfected creamware and a few years later, when Queen Charlotte purchased an entire tea set, marketing genius Josiah cannily changed the name to Queen's Ware. The rest, as they say, is pottery.

The Wedgwood family came from Burslem, a district of what is now Stoke-on-Trent. Craftsman Gilbert Wedgwood was recorded as the first Master Potter in the family in 1640 – and his most famous descendant, Josiah, was born in 1730. Josiah worked in his father's pottery from the age of nine, and in 1744 he was apprenticed to his older brother Thomas. An attack of smallpox seriously reduced Josiah's output (his right leg later had to be amputated as a result of the illness) but the time it gave him to research and experiment in his chosen craft stood him in good stead in later years.

After a number of partnerships Josiah set up his own pottery in Burslem in 1759. Until then pottery had been something of a cottage industry, but Wedgwood broke the mould, building – for the first time ever – a pottery factory. And rather than rely on family members, his idea was to pay people to work in the factory, with materials and tools he supplied. This made the whole production process so much more efficient and, ultimately, more lucrative.

A decade later, with business booming, Josiah Wedgwood built a bigger factory in Burslem which he called Etruria (at the time, Greek vases were believed to be Etruscan in origin). This became a model for other pottery manufacturers. Here, he applied rigorous, scientific techniques to producing new, innovative pottery. The results of his efforts can still be purchased today and include Jasperware (characterised by unglazed, pale blue stoneware with white relief portraits or classical scenes) and black basalt ware, also known as Egyptian ware, a hard stone-like material used for vases and busts of historical figures. But of course, when Josiah Wedgwood died in Etruria in 1795 his legacy wasn't just limited to porcelain. His success, vision and innovative business practices made him a leading figure of the Industrial Revolution and his impact on the local countryside was immense, not least because of the hundreds of miles of canals that he was – at least in part – responsible for, including the Trent and Mersey and the Caldon canals.

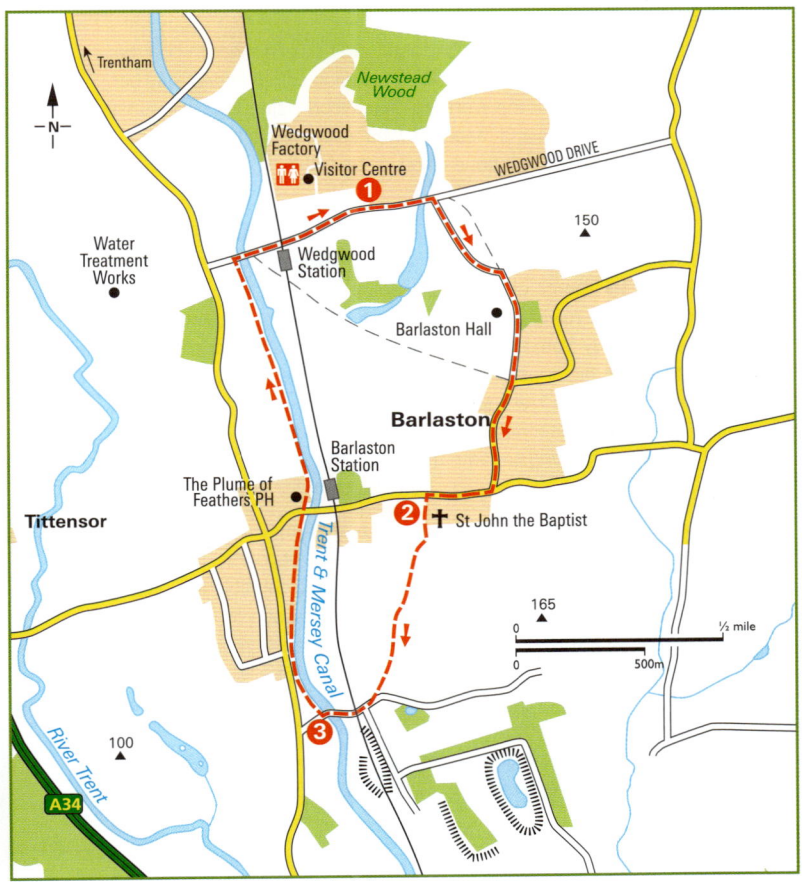

1. From the visitor centre drive, head left across the lake and then right up the drive towards Barlaston Hall. Go past this hall and continue along the metalled road as far as the T-junction in Barlaston. Turn right and after 250yds (229m), just past the Church of St John the Baptist on your left, head left along a wide gravel track.

2. The track passes through a broad expanse of open farmland, with sweeping (if not altogether dramatic) views of the Trent and Mersey Canal to the right. After about 800yds (732m), before the third gate, go right on a less obvious but waymarked path around the edge of the field to reach a stile. After crossing the stile head right along a wide track, then cross the railway via an underpass, before bearing right to a bridge over the canal. Go over the bridge and take the steps down to the left.

3. At the bottom of the steps head left and then follow the canal all the way to the first bridge (at Barlaston) and then the second (at Wedgwood Station). Head left here, up to the metalled road, and then right, back towards the visitor centre.

Where to eat and drink
The Plume of Feathers pub by Barlaston Station is a modern pub that offers a wide-ranging menu, including morning coffee and all-day bar food. The restaurant at the World of Wedgwood visitor centre also has a variety of light snacks and meals, as well as elegant afternoon tea – all served on Wedgwood fine bone china, of course.

What to see
The Trent and Mersey Canal, completed in 1777, linked the River Trent at Derwent Mouth near Derby with the Bridgewater Canal at Preston Brook, near the mouth of the River Mersey. This effectively meant the country could be navigated all the way from the west coast to the east, and that fine clay from the West Country could be shipped to the doorstep of Wedgwood's factories. James Brindley designed and built both the Bridgewater and the Trent and Mersey, the latter comprising some 93 miles (150km) of waterway and 76 locks, not to mention a tunnel almost 1.75 miles (2.8km) long beneath the heart of Stoke-on-Trent.

While you're there
The World of Wedgwood visitor centre is a multi-million pound attraction featuring a museum, shop, two restaurants and, of course, the Wedgwood factory itself. As well as a fine display of rare and valuable exhibits, the museum also traces the rich history of the Wedgwood company and visitors can walk the factory floor to see the production process, from throwing to firing. You can take your turn at the potter's wheel, try your painting skills or talk to Wedgwood's craftspeople in the demonstration area. If you still have any energy for shopping, take time to browse for souvenirs, ornaments and tableware, including some exclusive lines. The centre is open Wednesday to Sunday 10am-5pm and on Bank Holiday Mondays.

DOWNS BANKS

DISTANCE/TIME	2 miles (3.2km) / 1hr 15mins
ASCENT/GRADIENT	311ft (95m) / ▲
PATHS	Unsurfaced paths and tracks, mostly firm, 1 stile
LANDSCAPE	Wooded valley with open grassy slopes and heath
SUGGESTED MAP	OS Explorer 258 Stoke-on-Trent
START/FINISH	Grid reference: SJ901365
DOG FRIENDLINESS	Dogs are welcome throughout the site
PARKING	Main visitor car park, off Washdale Lane
PUBLIC TOILETS	None on route

For many first-time visitors, Downs Banks comes as something of a surprise. Amid the more open farmland of north Staffordshire, with its rugged pasture and ridges, this enclosed little valley centred on Downs Banks Brook is, to use the National Trust's own description, a little wilderness of woodland and heath.

Downs Banks were once crossed by an ancient packhorse trail from the East Midlands to Chester. It remained common land until the end of the 18th century, when it was enclosed by hedges for farming, traces of which can still be seen, particularly near the picnic sites. Until the 1940s the land was used to grow hops bound for the nearby Joules brewery. In 1950, when the area was threatened with industrialisation from Meaford Power Station, 160 acres (65ha) were purchased by John Joules & Sons, endowed by public subscription and given to the National Trust so that the public could enjoy the area forever. Today, a memorial stone of Cornish granite stands near the south corner of the park to commemorate this presentation, and to serve as a tribute to those who lost their lives during World War II.

Another monument in Downs Banks is the Millennium Viewpoint, a small stone pillar erected by Barlaston and Stone rural parish councils at the highest point of the estate. Depending on the weather, of course, there are far-off views of such landmarks as the Wrekin and Long Mynd far to the south and Mow Cop Castle and Axe Edge to the north.

Since taking on Downs Banks, the National Trust has tried to maintain the heath and woods in the face of encroaching scrub and invasive vegetation like bracken. It not only helps retain the landscape character, in particular preserving the relatively scarce acidic grassland and encouraging the native heather and bilberry, but also benefits rare wildlife like lizards and snakes traditionally associated with sandy heaths. One of the ways they do this is by grazing cattle on fenced areas during the summer and you will probably encounter this roaming but docile beef herd on your walk.

There is a real mix of woodland across Downs Banks, from birch and native oak to even a small pine plantation half way down a slope. At the foot of the valley are shady, marshy areas beside the brook where alders, willow and marsh marigolds grow. Together with the heath and open grassy slopes, Downs Banks really is a wonderful mix of habitat all concentrated into an unassuming little valley just a stone's throw from the Potteries.

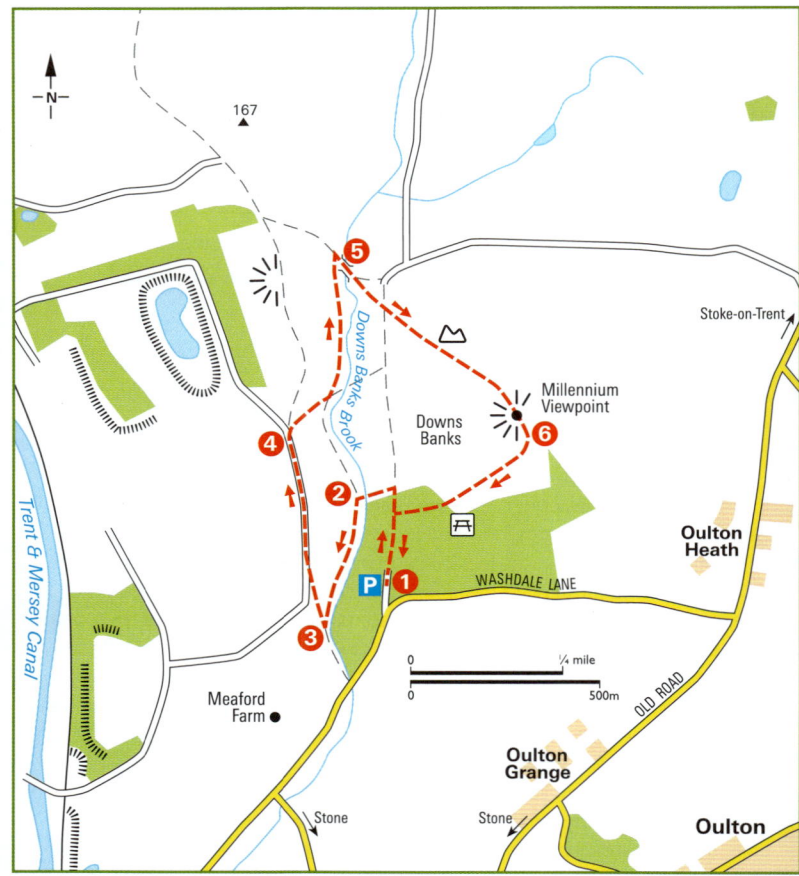

1. With your back to the car park turn left on to the wide bridleway into the centre of Downs Banks. Just before you reach gates ahead and right go left on a grassy path. Ignore the route uphill and instead swing left and down to cross Downs Banks Brook via a couple of stepping stones.

2. Cross the stile and turn left on to the firm path. Go through a gate and continue along the hillside path, with the stream below on your left. The path gradually drops down and when you reach a section of stone banking beside the stream go right, up a stepped path.

3. Follow this rising path around the western boundary of the estate, with good views both across Downs Banks and west to the Hanchurch Hills. Continue through a gate and on until a broad track branches off to the right down the slope.

4. Walk down this waymarked bridleway and at the bottom, in front of a gate and the stream, go left on the wide track. Ignore a left fork uphill beyond a bench and turn right, alongside the stream, to cross it via a footbridge.

5. On the far bank fork right, up some shallow steps, and at the path junction go straight over for a broad track up the spur of the hill. Steadily climb the semi-open hillside until you reach the Millennium Viewpoint on the open hilltop.

6. Continue along the main path. In 150yds (137m) turn right well before you reach a gate for a wide track out across and then down the open hillside. Beyond a gate continue downhill through pine trees until you reach a broad track. Turn left to return to the car park.

Where to eat and drink
For refreshments head to Stone, a mile away to the south, where The Swan Inn on Stafford Street is a handsome Grade II listed building and serves a great selection of local beers and ciders. For an original and high quality meal visit The Wayfarer country pub and restaurant, on the A34 on the other side of the town.

What to see
Among the native shrubs benefiting from the heathland restoration at Downs Banks is gorse. This prickly evergreen has distinctive bright yellow flowers, said to smell a little like coconut, which are an important source of nectar for insects. Gorse also provides an important shelter and nest site for small birds, like yellowhammers and stonechats. However, gorse itself can spread quickly and needs to be carefully managed.

While you're there
Stone has been a brewing town for almost a thousand years and today the small, family-run Lymestone Brewery is continuing that tradition. You can visit the brewery and see how real ale is made, perhaps sampling one of the latest mouth-watering brews or taking home one of their bottled beers. See www.lymestonebrewery.net for more details.

AROUND TUTBURY

DISTANCE/TIME	2.75 miles (4.4km) / 1hr
ASCENT/GRADIENT	88ft (27m) / ▲
PATHS	Road and field track, many stiles
LANDSCAPE	Town, farmland and riverside
SUGGESTED MAP	OS Explorer 245 The National Forest
START/FINISH	Grid reference: SK213294
DOG FRIENDLINESS	Keep on lead at all times
PARKING	Tutbury Mill picnic site
PUBLIC TOILETS	At town car park in Tutbury

The village of Tutbury, just across the border from neighbouring Derbyshire, boasts a long history of making – and finding – money, and nowhere is this more obvious than at the picnic site near the start of the walk. In 1781, a five-storey mill was built here on the Mill Fleam, an artificial braid of the River Dove. Originally it was a cotton mill employing more than 300 workers, with two 14ft (4.3m) waterwheels powering an astonishing 7,000 spindles. Mill Farm, across the road, was originally a warehouse.

After more than 100 years the cotton mill closed, but in 1890 Henry Newton acquired it for making plaster of Paris from gypsum, mined in the Fauld Hills 2 miles (3.2km) west of Tutbury. In its purest form, gypsum is known as alabaster and because it is relatively soft it is ideal for ornamental carving. Gypsum is also used for brewing pale ale, which accounts for the flourishing beer industry in Burton upon Trent, 5 miles (8km) to the south. Production of plaster continued until 1968, when the mill was demolished, but British Gypsum still mines in the Fauld Hills.

Despite all this hard work and industry over the centuries, there were easier ways to find your fortune in Tutbury. In 1831, men excavating the river to improve the flow of water to the mill found several hundred medieval coins (The Tutbury Hoard). The river was quarantined to prevent looting, and a major dig was conducted. Remarkably, more than 100,000 silver coins were recovered, some of which can still be seen at the The Potteries Museum & Art Gallery in Hanley. The question was, where had the cash come from? The answer lay in a battle fought and lost over 500 years before by Thomas, Duke of Lancaster and Lord of Tutbury Castle. Thomas sided with the Scots against his cousin Edward II in the early 1300s, so the King attacked the castle to teach him a lesson. Thomas lay in wait at Burton Bridge, but was outflanked and duly defeated by Edward in 1322. His fortune was smuggled out of the castle, but the horses floundered crossing the river. When it was found again in 1831, it was claimed by the Crown.

These days Tutbury is known more for its fine Georgian crystal than its bloody medieval heritage. The first glassworks were founded at the height of the Industrial Revolution, and today you can still purchase Tutbury Crystal within the village.

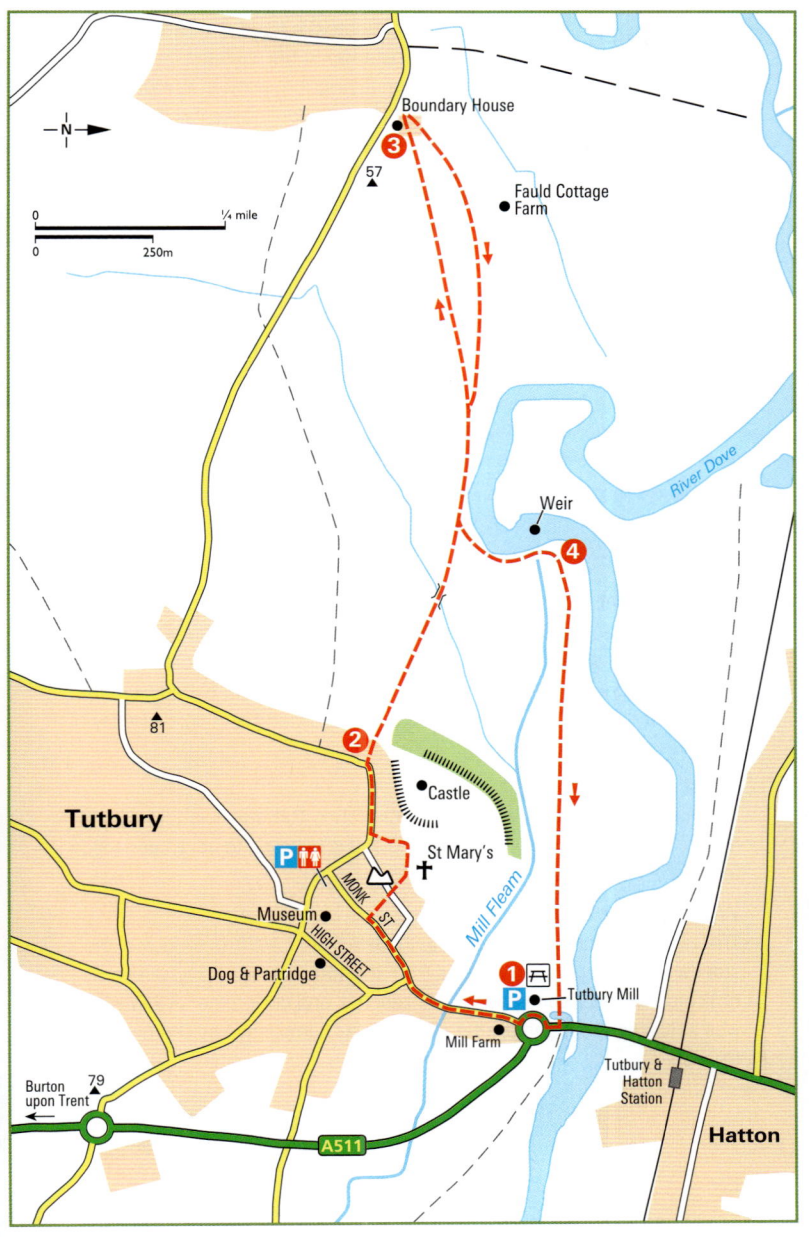

1. From the picnic site, head right at the roundabout into the town. Stay right at the first fork onto Monk Street and, after 150yds (137m), head right at Castle Court up a footpath to St Mary's Church. Pass the church and the castle entrance to reach the road. Go right here and, at the top of a short hill, follow the footpath signs to the right.

2. Go down this footpath, veering half right onto the flood plain. In the far corner of the field go through the open gateway to the next and cross the stile a few paces away on the left. Head diagonally right to another obvious stile-footbridge-stile. Cut off the left corner of the field, aiming for the middle of the left-hand hedge. Cross the stile here and walk straight across the long meadow, heading for the left of some farmhouses in the distance. After 600yds (549m), at the meeting of two hedges, cross a double stile and continue with a hedge to your left. Cross another double stile at the end of this field and keep following the hedge to your left.

3. As you reach Boundary House, to your left, go right along the obvious concrete track back towards Fauld Cottage Farm. Head to the right of the farm gate, off the concrete, to a stile. Over the stile, head straight across the middle of the field to an obvious gate on the far side. After the gate, head straight towards the castle, back the way you came. At the far left corner of the meadow, very close to the river, cross the stile and skirt left around the bank beneath a line of trees. Cross Mill Fleam near to the weir.

4. Now head sharp right into an open meadow. Follow the faint path along Mill Fleam back to the picnic site and the car park on the far side.

Where to eat and drink
There are several good cafés along the length of the High Street, try one for a hot drink and quick snack. For something a bit more substantial, the Dog & Partridge is one of England's oldest coaching inns, dating from the 15th century. It has a beer garden, is dog friendly and is open every day of the week.

What to see
The elaborate west door of St Mary's Church in Tutbury, built c.1160, is a fine example of Norman craftsmanship and is believed to have been made from local alabaster.

While you're there
The vast earthworks of Tutbury Castle date from c.1070, but much of the stonework that exists today dates from the 15th century. Mary, Queen of Scots, was imprisoned here by Elizabeth I, and during the Civil War it was a Royalist stronghold, after which it was demolished by Cromwell's troops.

31 HANBURY AND ITS CRATER

DISTANCE/TIME	4.75 miles (7.7km) / 2hrs
ASCENT/GRADIENT	240ft (73m) / ▲
PATHS	Meadow tracks and bridleways, many stiles
LANDSCAPE	Farmland and bomb crater
SUGGESTED MAP	OS Explorer 245 The National Forest
START/FINISH	Grid reference: SK171279
DOG FRIENDLINESS	Must be kept on lead near livestock
PARKING	St Werburgh's Church car park
PUBLIC TOILETS	None on route

The history of Hanbury starts with the legend of St Werburgh. During the seventh century AD Werburgh, daughter of pagan King Wulfere of Mercia, founded nunneries at Repton, Trentham, Weedon and Hanbury, the latter believed to have been situated to the east of what is now St Werburgh's Church.

Legend has it that when Werburgh died she was buried at Trentham, but her body was stolen back by the people of Hanbury and buried in a new shrine near the nunnery. As a direct result Hanbury became a major centre for Christianity for well over a century. When the Danes invaded in AD 875, Werburgh's body was again moved, this time to Chester for safe keeping, and it was there, in the cathedral, that she was finally laid to rest.

Today, however, Hanbury is known for a much more recent tragedy. At 11am on 27 November 1944, the village witnessed the largest explosion caused by a conventional weapon in either World War; only the atomic bombs at Hiroshima and Nagasaki were bigger. In all, 70 people were killed in the blast, and 18 bodies were never recovered.

The reason for the explosion is unclear, although the site is hard to miss, marked as it is by a crater more than 0.25 miles (400m) across and 100yds (91m) deep. The area around Hanbury is rich in gypsum and alabaster and a number of exhausted mine shafts became convenient storage depots for high explosives during the war. RAF personnel and Italian prisoners of war dispatched this arsenal with heightening urgency as the Allied offensive in Europe got under way, and it's thought that carelessness, inexperience and cost-cutting all had a part to play on that fateful November morning. The first the villagers knew about it was a distant rumble before the explosion proper, which blackened the sky as tens of thousands of tons of soil and rocks were blasted into the surrounding landscape. An entire farm, including its occupants and livestock, disappeared completely, and dozens of underground munitions workers – both British and Italian – were killed. A reservoir for the nearby plaster works burst its dam, unleashing 6 million gallons (27 million litres) of water, boulders, mud and trees onto the factory below, killing 27 workers. The explosion could be heard from London, and was recorded as an earth tremor as far away as Geneva.

Today, nature has healed the scars on the landscape as hawthorn, larch and silver birch have re-colonised both the crater and the surrounding area, providing a habitat for – among other things – a vast colony of rabbits. There's still a gypsum works to the north, below which is an extensive system of mines spread over 10sq miles (26sq km).

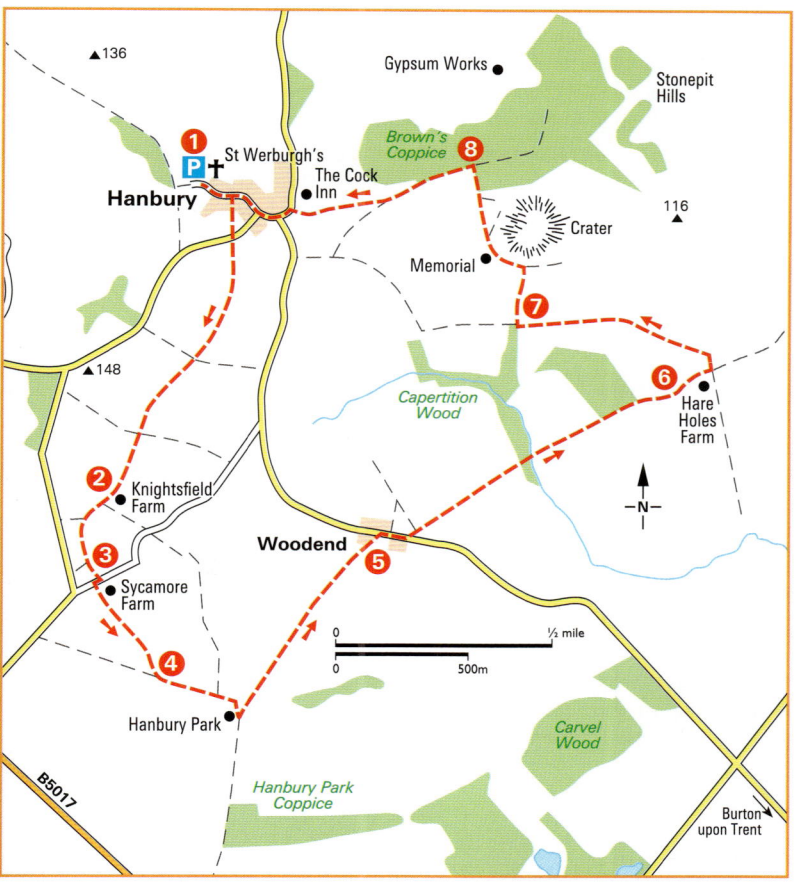

1. From the car park, go back along Church Lane and after 150yds (137m), go right down a drive between houses and through a gate. Cross the field to a pair of stiles over a road and continue across the field to a gate, then to the corner of a hedge. Keeping this hedge to your right, head for Knightsfield Farm.

2. Go through the farm courtyard and along a rough surfaced track. As it bears to the right, follow a footpath sign, left, across stiles, keeping the hedge to your left. At a turning circle on a driveway go straight across to a footbridge before continuing, with the hedge to your left, to reach the road.

3. Turn right, then after 80yds (73m) go left at the footpath sign beside the building. Cross the yard into the field ahead to reach the stile at the bottom. Continue up the next field, crossing the stile at the top.

4. Where the hedge goes left, follow it across another stile and, via fields, aim for the imposing brick buildings of Hanbury Park. Go through a series of metal swing gates into the farm courtyard, then left past the open barn and through a wide gate away from the farm. Continue on the bridleway to Woodend.

5. At the road head right for 100yds (91m), then go left over a stile, making for a stile in the fence ahead and to the right. Head diagonally left across a field to a stile, then continue straight across the next field to a stile. Cross Capertition Wood to an open field, continuing with a hedge to the left, up a hill, across stiles, then down to another. At the end of the field cross one more.

6. Skirting to the left of the farm, climb over a succession of stiles before turning sharp left immediately after an iron gate. Once across the stile in the corner, go ahead through three more fields, following waymarkers past a small pond. Drop down to the right-hand end of a bank of trees.

7. At a path junction turn right up a short hill via kissing gates, towards trees. Head round to the left to see the crater, now re-colonised by nature. Follow the path round to the left, past the memorial stone, to a bridleway leading away from it.

8. At the end of this bridleway, head left across a field, keeping the hedge to your right. Go through a kissing gate in the hedge ahead and continue straight ahead to a gate at the top. When you reach the end of the hedge on your left, go through a gate and a stile to return to Hanbury.

Where to eat and drink
The Cock Inn is a charming little pub with picnic tables and good views. It also has newspaper reports of the tragedy lining the walls for those who are interested in finding out more. Open every day of the week from noon until 10-11pm, traditional pub meals available daily and in the choice of a roast on Sunday.

What to see
The memorial just to the southwest of the crater is made of fine white granite, a gift from the Commandant of the Italian Air Force Supply Depot at Novara, in northwest Italy. The stone lists the names of the people killed, including those whose bodies were never recovered. It is a poignant reminder of the tragedy.

While you're there
Apart from the core of the west tower and the 13th-century arcades with round piers, St Werburgh's Church is of little interest architecturally, having been almost entirely rebuilt in the late 19th century. But if the church is open (and it usually is), look for the window in the south aisle featuring a memorial to those who died in the explosion, made using fragments of 14th-century stained glass.

STAFFORD CASTLE

DISTANCE/TIME	4 miles (6.4km) / 1hr 30min
ASCENT/GRADIENT	240ft (73m) / ▲
PATHS	Pavement, gravel tracks and grass trails
LANDSCAPE	Town, golf course, hilltop and farmland
SUGGESTED MAP	OS Explorer 244 Cannock Chase & Chasewater
START/FINISH	Grid reference: SJ918233
DOG FRIENDLINESS	Keep on lead near livestock
PARKING	Doxey Road pay-and-display at start; also at the castle
PUBLIC TOILETS	Stafford Castle visitor centre and in town centre

In the 11th century, a castle was built on the hill to the west of Stafford by William the Conqueror to keep rebellious Saxons in check. It was at this time that the substantial earthworks you can see around the present-day castle were built. They involved a series of avenues, deep ditches, steep slopes and an impressive motte, or steep-sided earth mound, at the centre of the castle complex. Today, it's possible to take a tour of these earthworks by following a series of excellent information panels around the site, and with the help of sketches it's not hard to imagine how the castle may have looked.

Initially the site was more of a hilltop settlement, with wooden ramparts built in concentric rings behind a series of deep ditches. The castle proper would have been a three-storey timber keep on the motte, which doubled as the lord's residence and his military headquarters. The timber may have been plastered and painted to look like stone, to fool any approaching enemies as well as to resist fire.

It wasn't until the middle of the 14th century that Ralph, Lord Stafford, built the first stone castle on the site. It stayed in the family until 1521, when Henry VIII had Edward Stafford executed on a dubious charge of treason (he actually had a distant claim to the throne). The Staffords recovered their property and titles 25 years later but failed to recover their fortune. By the end of the 16th century the castle was in ruins, and remained so until the Civil War broke out in 1642. Isabel, Lady Stafford, was requested by Charles I to defend the castle against Parliamentary forces, and successfully resisted months of siege. The castle continued to be neglected until Sir George Jerningham had the ruin cleared of debris in the early 19th century and rebuilt the eastern towers in what was an early example of Gothic revival architecture. The lords and ladies of the mid-19th century were a romantic bunch and liked nothing better than to dress up their summer piles as Gothic follies complete with pointed arches and mock battlements.

Alas, Sir George never got around to the rest of the renovation and the castle has been more or less neglected ever since. In 1961, a boy playing on the remaining stonework was tragically killed by a collapsing window. The reaction of the local council was to demolish the upper part of the building, although they resisted calls to demolish the entire thing on the basis that it might still contain some of the original 14th-century masonry. Indeed, excavations begun in 1974 have shown this to be the case. The castle is preserved now, with a visitor centre providing a useful insight into the chronicle of the castle, and in particular its Norman founders.

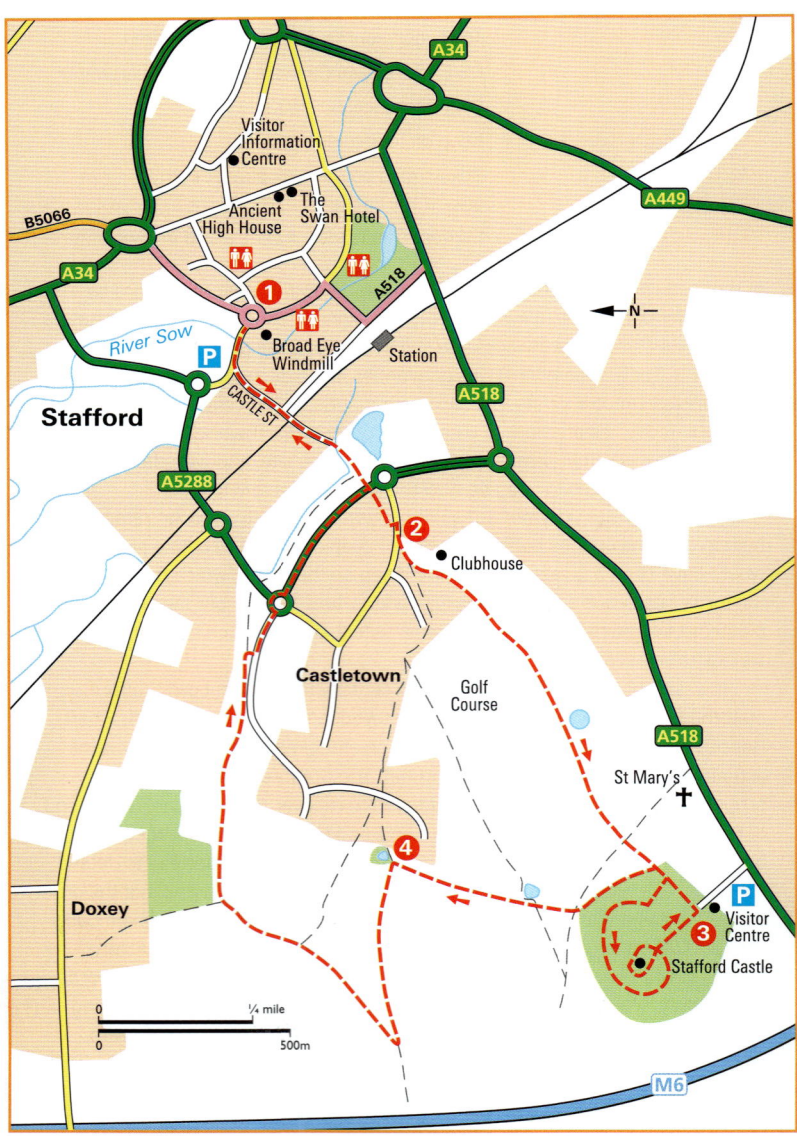

1. From the roundabout by Broad Eye Windmill head away from the town, over the river. After 100yds (91m) turn left along Castle Street, over the railway, and continue ahead on a cycle path to a roundabout. Cross and walk along the path, which soon joins the road on its left.

2. Cross over, turn right, then bear left by a line of trees, going left again at a footpath sign. Bear left here, keeping the houses to your right. Follow the gravel track up the middle of the golf course and, at the very top, keep going straight across the field ahead, following a faint grass path to the bottom left corner of the woods below the castle. A gap leads into the woods.

3. The path left leads to the visitor centre, but first, keep up ahead for the castle's self-guided walk (0.75 miles/1.2km) following signboards in a spiral up to the stone keep. Descend the tarmac track to the visitor centre. This is packed with information on the Norman Conquest and features a short film on the history of the castle. There's also a shop selling snacks, souvenirs and guides. From the visitor centre head uphill a few steps, then turn right on the wide path above the bottom of the wood to the gap (Point 3), then skirt left around the outside of the wood. At the corner of the wood, go through a hedge and turn right down the field-edge path, with the hedge on your right. Descending through these fields serves to illustrate how tough it must have been for Saxon forces to charge in the opposite direction; even assuming they survived the onslaught of arrows from Norman longbows, by the time they got anywhere near the castle they'd have been absolutely spent.

4. At the foot of the field, with a pond just ahead, turn left above a tall ivy hedge, then cross a field. Cross a second field with a hedge on your left, then turn hard right on a wide track. Follow this downhill, then round to the right (you can use an old railbed alongside on the left here). When the track runs out, bear right onto a road and keep left across a roundabout. Just before the next roundabout head left on the cycle path, retracing your steps back into Stafford.

Where to eat and drink
There are numerous tea shops, bakeries, restaurants and bars to choose from in the town centre, but you can't go wrong with The Swan, dating from 1750. The brasserie serves an extensive and varied menu, throughout the day and evening (pre booking is advisable).

What to see
Although the castle is barely 200ft (60m) higher than the surrounding countryside, it commands surprisingly good views in every direction. From the top, looking out over the earthworks, it's easy to see how enemy forces could be spotted approaching from miles away, and how easy it must have been to defend.

While you're there
Built in 1595 The Ancient High House is the largest timber-framed town house in England. Open Tue–Sat 10am–4pm.

SHUGBOROUGH ESTATE

DISTANCE/TIME	5.5 miles (8.8km) / 2hrs 15min
ASCENT/GRADIENT	180ft (55m) / ▲
PATHS	Gravel tracks, roads and tow paths
LANDSCAPE	Forest, country park and canal
SUGGESTED MAP	OS Explorer 244 Cannock Chase & Chasewater
START/FINISH	Grid reference: SK004205
DOG FRIENDLINESS	Must be kept on lead near main roads and in park
PARKING	Seven Springs car park
PUBLIC TOILETS	None on route

Shugborough, a 900-acre (365ha) estate on the edge of Cannock Chase, is without doubt the grandest stately home in Staffordshire. As the ancestral pile of the Earls of Lichfield for more than 300 years, it was home to Thomas Patrick Anson, Fifth Earl of Lichfield, until his death in 2005. He was better known as the world-famous photographer Patrick Lichfield, who was a second cousin the late Queen Elizabeth II.

Originally built in 1693 as a small country manor, it has been altered and added to by successive generations of the Anson family, and by two people in particular: Thomas Anson (1695–1773) and his brother George (1697–1762). Thomas, well-travelled and well-educated, inherited the house in 1720, and made major changes over the next 50 years. The most significant alteration – or at least the one most apparent from the outside – was the addition of a magnificent eight-columned ionic portico designed by Samuel Wyatt in 1794. Much of this work was paid for out of George's own fortune: during his lifetime he had earned considerable fame and riches as a naval officer by capturing a Spanish treasure galleon. He later went on to become an admiral.

As a well-travelled man, Thomas would have been very aware of what was considered good taste throughout his dealings with architects, and the house as we see it today is testimony to his ideals and what was considered the height of fashion for much of the 18th century. This, it's important to remember, was the age of reason, when industry and science were starting to take over the world; architects and their employers were keen to reflect this idea in their country piles, and the geometric simplicity of ancient Greek and Roman architecture seemed like a logical choice. It embodied the ideals of man being at the centre of the universe, taming nature with his new-found knowledge.

The gardens, too, were ordered and regimented, set out in a formal geometric pattern with the house at the centre of the estate, and, by implication, the universe. It was the same ideal that made classical motifs on Wedgwood pottery so enduring, and it's no surprise that Thomas Anson was a patron of the famous potter. Almost as a direct consequence of this insistence on law and order in gardens and architecture, the architects of the 19th century instigated a backlash against reason: romance was king, disorder was beauty, and the so-called 'Gothic' style enjoyed a revival in mansions and follies across England.

From the outside, the mansion today is much the same as it must have been during Thomas Anson's day. In 1966, following the death of the Fourth Earl of Lichfield, the estate was given to the National Trust. The house isn't open all year, but as the route of the walk is on either a public bridleway or established rights of way it can be completed at any time of year.

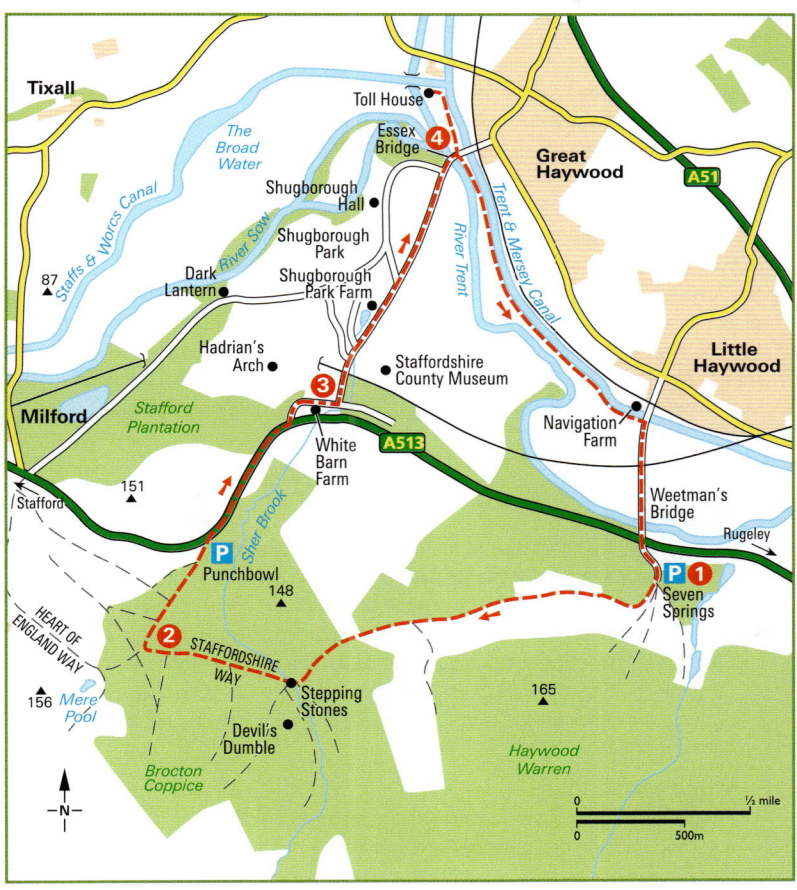

1. At the end of the Seven Springs car park take the right-hand path, past a barrier, and at a junction in 130yds (119m) continue to the right. Follow a wide gravel track, ignoring all paths to the left or right, for 0.75 miles (1.2km) to Stepping Stones. Cross the stream here and turn right for 0.5 miles (800m) to reach a major junction of paths.

2. Head right here, following the Staffordshire Way bridleway sign. Continue along a wide gravel track, again ignoring less obvious paths to the left or right, as far as the A513. Cross the road carefully and follow it right for 400yds (366m) before turning left at a road entrance to Shugborough Estate.

3. Follow the metalled road past the Staffordshire County Museum and the Hall's main car park and ticket office. Here you will also find the Craft Workshops and the Walled Garden. The garden was established in 1805 as a horticultural centre of excellence; and completely restored in 2007 to its original state (they are even growing historic varieties of fruit and vegetables that are quite rare today). Bear left to pass Shugborough Park Farm, then ignore the driveway bending left to the house itself, and instead keep ahead onto a tarmac bridleway. It's worth pausing to take a closer look at the façade. From close range it's interesting to note that the columns aren't made of stone at all, but are instead made of wood which has been clad with slate and painted to look like stone, a solution that would have been considerably cheaper. Follow the lane to the long, narrow Essex Bridge, and cross it to the canal beyond.

4. The route continues along the tow path to your right. By way of a short diversion, head under the canal bridge onto the tow path to the left. In just 350yds (320m) is the junction of the Trent and Mersey Canal with the Staffordshire and Worcestershire Canal. The toll-keeper's cottage has disappeared, but a toll house with arched windows and a kiosk still remain on the south side of the S & W. Continue on the tow path (canal on your left) for a mile (1.6km). At Navigation Farm head right on the metalled road. Carry on over Weetman's Bridge, cross the A513 carefully, and continue up a short drive back to the car park.

What to see

There are no fewer than eight monuments of national importance to be seen in the 900 acres (365ha) of parkland around Shugborough, but the most obvious of these en route are the Dark Lantern and the Triumphal Arch. These follies were designed by, among others, James 'Athenian' Stuart, a classicist whose popularity reflected the tastes of the time. Originally built by the Earl of Essex to gain access to Cannock Chase for hunting, the Essex Bridge is the longest packhorse bridge in England, and has never been widened.

While you're there

In addition to the house itself, the estate features a working farm in a second building designed by Samuel Wyatt, with demonstrations of farmhouse cooking, milking, and bread-, butter- and cheese-making by guides in period dress. The old servants' quarters, meanwhile, house the County Museum, where costumed actors recreate what life was like on the estate a hundred years ago.

GREAT HAYWOOD

DISTANCE/TIME	4.5 miles (7.2km) / 2hrs
ASCENT/GRADIENT	114ft (35m) / ▲
PATHS	Surfaced drive, canal towpath and pavement, no stiles
LANDSCAPE	Woods, parkland, canal and common
SUGGESTED MAP	OS Explorer 244 Cannock Chase & Chasewater
START/FINISH	Grid reference: SJ974209
DOG FRIENDLINESS	On lead in Shugborough Estate, but off lead on towpath and enclosed tracks
PARKING	Milford Common pay-and-display car park
PUBLIC TOILETS	By Milford Common

James Brindley was the foremost canal-builder of his age and in the 1760s he developed an ambitious plan. Dubbed the Grand Cross, his idea was to link England's four main estuaries – the Mersey, Severn, Thames and Humber – by a series of new inland waterways. These would be the trunk routes, off which would be smaller local canals. Great Haywood, just to the north of Cannock Chase, was an important junction in that new network.

The main route in Brindley's scheme was the 93-mile (150km) Trent & Mersey Canal, sometimes called the 'Grand Trunk'. It was finished in 1777 and linked the two key ports of Liverpool and Hull via Stoke and the Potteries, connecting with the navigable River Trent in Derbyshire. Great Haywood was the point where it met another of Brindley's arterial routes, also built by him at about the same time. The Staffordshire & Worcestershire Canal was shorter, at 46 miles (74km), and from Great Haywood headed southwest via Wolverhampton to meet the River Severn at Stourport. The other two canals in Brindley's Grand Cross were the Oxford Canal and Coventry Canal, which together connected with the Thames and the other Midlands' waterways.

Although the canals were soon superseded by the railways, which in turn were eclipsed by road traffic (including a motorway network in some ways mirroring Brindley's canals masterplan), Britain's inland waterways have seen something of a renaissance in the last few decades. Haywood Junction is now home to a smart marina and including a chandlery, workshop and boat repair service. Throughout the year this is a bustling and colourful location, with boats constantly manoeuvring and plenty of comings and goings along the towpath. A popular cruising route from Great Haywood is the 'Four Counties Ring', a 110-mile (176km) journey connecting the Trent & Mersey, Staffordshire & Worcestershire and the Shropshire Union Canal, taking most boats between 1–2 weeks to complete.

As you leave the Shugborough Estate you first have to cross the River Trent before reaching the canal. You do this via Essex Bridge, built in the 1550s by the Earl of Essex, it is said so that Queen Elizabeth I could visit him at nearby Chartley Castle. The elegant bridge once had 40 arches (it now has 14) and extended all the way into Shugborough Park, but it remains the longest packhorse bridge in England and a scheduled ancient monument.

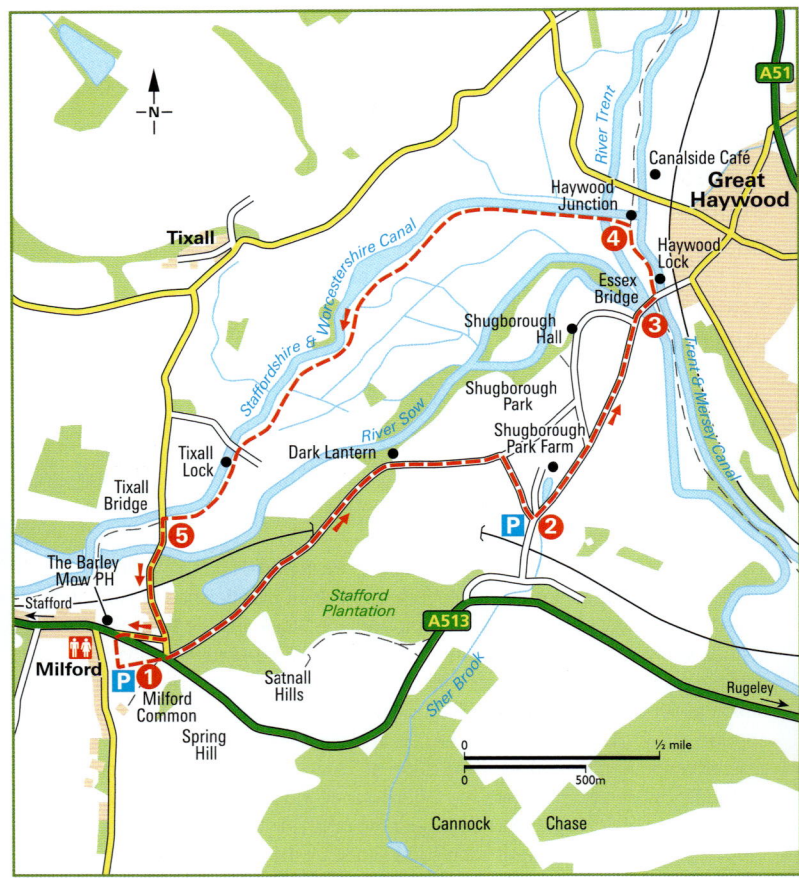

1. From the car park walk eastwards across the open green towards the main entrance of Shugborough and cross the A513 with care. Enter the estate through the gates and follow the drive for a mile (1.6km), first among the woods then out into the open grounds. At a broad fork go right to reach the car park near the farm.

2. Turn left and walk along the main drive, past Shugborough Park Farm. Where it branches left to the Hall go straight on along a fenced, surfaced track. At the far end continue across the narrow Essex Bridge.

3. If you want to visit Great Haywood go straight on under the railway, otherwise go right on the far side of Essex Bridge to join the canal towpath. Turn left, go under Bridge 73 and past the lock to head north beside the Trent & Mersey Canal.

4. At Haywood Junction don't cross the old brick bridge, but go right of it in order to pass underneath, now heading left on the Staffordshire & Worcestershire Canal, signposted 'Wolverhampton'. Go over the River Trent and continue along the towpath for 1.5 miles (2.4km), via Tixall Lock.

5. Go under Tixall Bridge (number 106) and immediately turn left up to the road. Turn right and join the road to cross the river. Now follow the pavement back to Milford Common and the start of the walk.

Where to eat and drink

The Barley Mow, overlooking Milford Common, is a popular choice with families. There's an outdoor play area and food is served all day, every day. About halfway around is the Canalside Café, where you sit inside or out and enjoy a slice of cake or a sandwich with your tea or coffee or something substantial, open from 9am to 4pm.

What to see

As you leave Haywood Junction and head west towards Milford you might notice that the canal becomes unusually broad and almost meanders for a short section. This is supposedly because when the canal was being built the owner of nearby Tixall Hall complained that a man-made waterway would ruin his view, so they compromised and fashioned a stretch of canal that more resembled a lake or a natural river.

While you're there

If you want to combine the walk with a proper visit to Shugborough (see Walk 33), decide in advance what you want to see – because there's a lot to choose from! Apart from the stunning Georgian mansion house, one-time home of celebrated photographer Patrick Lichfield and with changing exhibitions, there's also a working farm, riverside gardens and arboretum, and walled kitchen garden.

35 THE SHROPSHIRE UNION CANAL

DISTANCE/TIME	2.75 miles (4.4km) / 1hr
ASCENT/GRADIENT	75ft (23m) / ▲
PATHS	Roads, dirt tracks and canal tow paths
LANDSCAPE	Farmland, woodland and canal
SUGGESTED MAP	OS Explorer 243 Market Drayton
START/FINISH	Grid reference: SJ793229
DOG FRIENDLINESS	Keep on lead on road
PARKING	Roadside parking at Norbury Junction
PUBLIC TOILETS	None on route

The Shropshire Union Canal, or 'Shroppie', runs 60 miles (96km) from the edge of Wolverhampton to the Mersey at Ellesmere Port, north of Chester. The canal is named after the Shropshire Union Railways and Canal Company, which was an amalgamation of several local canal companies.

The canal almost wasn't one. The intention was to build a railway using canal foundations, as it was believed – quite rightly – that railways were a viable alternative to canals. However, Welsh resistance to railways meant that a canal was built instead using railway foundations, or, to be more precise, the foundations of railway engineering techniques. Instead of following a river, the canal took a direct route across country, through cuttings and on embankments, ostensibly to shorten journey times. The embankments, in particular, were major undertakings, as it was considerably harder to raise a wide watertight channel 60ft (18m) above the surroundings than it was to lay a railway line in the same way. Local landowner Lord Anson wanted to keep his wood unmolested for pheasant shooting, so he refused permission for the canal to pass through. The diversion involved building a vast embankment over a mile (1.6km) long and 60ft (18m) high.

The man responsible for the embankment, along with the rest of the canal, was Thomas Telford. Today, Telford is remembered more as a bridge engineer than a canal builder, counting the Menai Suspension Bridge among his many achievements. But the Shelmore Embankment caused him more than its fair share of problems. Even after moving millions of tons of earth from nearby Woodseaves to build it, he had to cope with collapse after collapse. It took six years to build this embankment, and it was only made sound in 1835, a year after Telford's death.

The Shroppie remained in use until World War I. At the beginning of the 20th century chocolate maker John Cadbury used it to pick up milk from farms between Norbury Junction and his factory at Knighton. Farmers would leave churns at collecting points along the tow path and they would be returned empty at the end of the day.

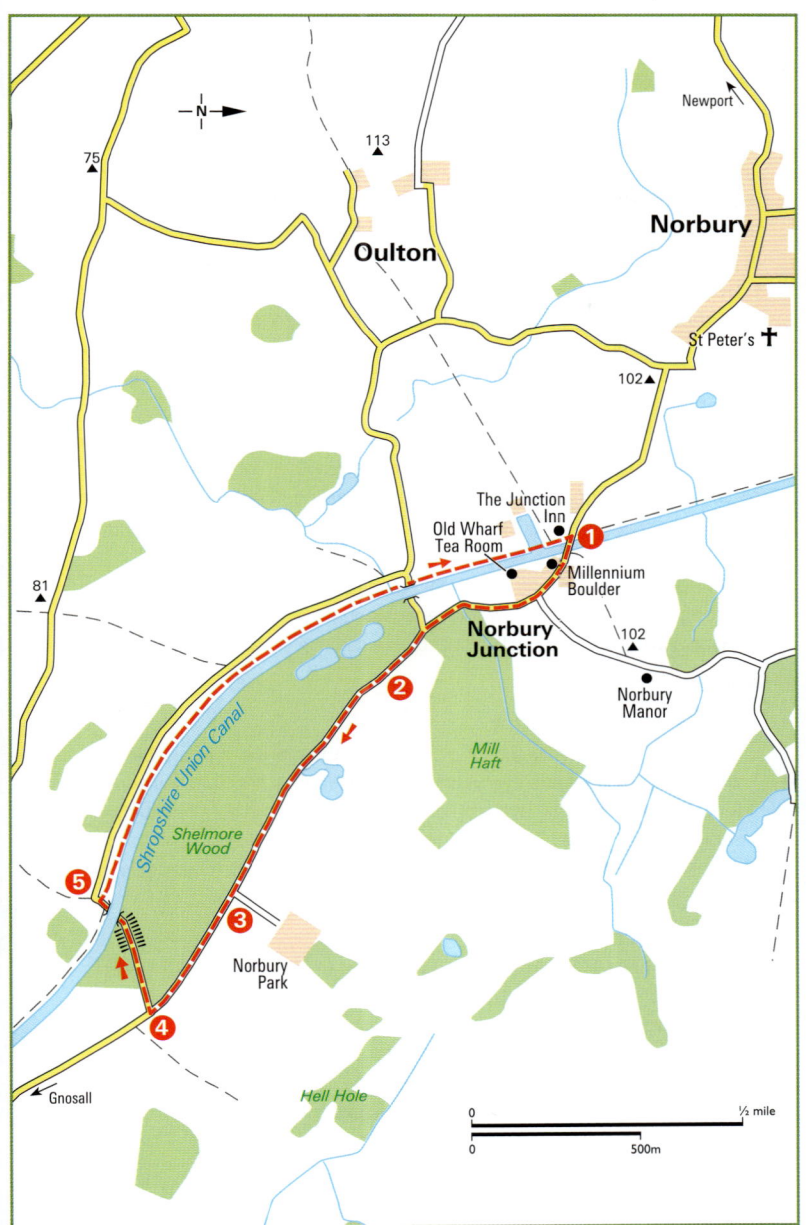

1. From The Junction Inn, follow the road towards Gnosall over the canal and bear right, past the canal boat chandlers (and boat hire). On your right you pass one of the Norbury Boulders, originally transported by glacier from Scotland some 20,000 years ago, then the final 2 miles (3km) from nearby Gorse Farm rather more recently by low-loader. It's part of a linked walk past five boulders, the Norbury Millennium Boulder Trail. This one is the biggest, and shows dark 'xenoliths', fragments of the magma chamber wall incorporated into the granite as it solidified 400 million years ago. Continue to the point where the road heads sharp right under the canal, and go straight on up the wide gravel track.

2. When this track veers right into Shelmore Wood, keep going straight on along the edge of the wood, shortly coming to a gap in a high, tree-dotted hedge. Go through this gap onto an earth path with a line of conifers on the left masking a plantation of young oak trees, and the much older Shelmore Wood on your right. In spring and early summer, listen out for woodpeckers.

3. The path joins the concrete driveway from Norbury Park Farm on your left. Keep ahead, carrying on along the edge of Shelmore Wood as far as the Gnosall road. The cottage at the corner here shows a patchwork of stone and two ages of brickwork, the more regular patterning of the extension being less ancient than the main house.

4. Turn hard right on the road down a short hill. The cutting here shows the erosive power of people: the roadway has carved itself into the bedrock during the couple of millennia that people have been using it. At the bottom beware of cars as you walk through the tunnel (stop here and shout or sing: the acoustics are extraordinary).

5. Go through a gate on the left and up some steps to the canal. At the top turn left along the tow path. Follow the canal along its high embankment, finally crossing a brick arch over the disused side canal and back to The Junction Inn.

Where to eat and drink

The Junction Inn is a welcoming pub beside the marina. It offers bar snacks and main meals every lunchtime on Monday and Tuesday and lunchtime and evening every other day of the week. An outside hatch serves ice creams, and the beer garden overlooks the canal. On the opposite side of the canal is the Old Wharf Tea Room, open daily all year round for snacks and hot meals.

What to see

Along the edge of Shelmore Wood you might spot what look like street lamp covers lining the path. These are pheasant feeders, designed to let the birds reach the grain inside while keeping out the wind and rain. The pheasants are hand-reared. In winter the grain is placed deep inside woods, where there's shelter from the elements, while in spring and summer you'll find feed hoppers at the edges of the woods, where the cocks establish their territories to attract the hens.

While you're there

At Norbury Wharf, opposite the pub, you can hire a narrowboat for a day's outing on the canal. There's also a gift shop where you can buy all manner of canal memorabilia. The Izaak Walton Cottage, 6 miles (9.7km) northeast, is also worth a visit. Walton was the author of *The Compleat Angler* (1653), the popular and enduring, fishing book. The 17th-century cottage is now a museum to his life and work; it includes a first edition of his book. Open on Sundays from May to September.

ABBOTS BROMLEY

DISTANCE/TIME	5.25 miles (8.4km) / 2hrs
ASCENT/GRADIENT	525ft (160m) / ▲▲
PATHS	Roads, grass trails and gravel tracks, many stiles
LANDSCAPE	Farmland and village
SUGGESTED MAP	OS Explorer 244 Cannock Chase & Chasewater
START/FINISH	Grid reference: SK081245
DOG FRIENDLINESS	Keep on lead at all times
PARKING	On street parking in Abbots Bromley
PUBLIC TOILETS	None on route

The existence of Abbots Bromley can be traced back to long before the Norman Conquest of England in 1066, through a number of references in charters and wills dating from that time. The first market charter was granted in 1221 for a weekly market and an annual two-day fair to be held in the village, and this fair survives today in the form of a rare and slightly unusual ritual. One theory on the obscure origins of the famous Horn Dance is that it derived from an ancient fertility rite, another is that the dance celebrates the establishment of ancient hunting rites.

The Horn Dance was first performed at the Barthelmy Fair as long ago as 1226. This was originally held on the feast day of St Bartholomew, one of the Apostles and the patron saint of tanners, but an alteration to the Gregorian calendar in 1752 changed this date to 4 September. Today, it's held on the first weekend after the 4th, with the dance proper taking place on the Monday.

According to custom, six pairs of ancient reindeer horns (or more accurately antlers) are collected from St Nicholas's Church just before 8am by a small entourage of dancers comprising – among others – a fool, a hobby horse, a bowman and Maid Marion. The first dance of the day is performed on the village green with music provided by a melodion (a small reed organ similar to an accordion). Then a tour of the nearby villages, farms and pubs ensues with the final dance taking place back at the village green. In addition to the Horn Dance proper, this colourful procession also features displays of morris and clog dancing. Other attractions include exhibitions and craft stalls. Each year the dance attracts hundreds of visitors from all over the world.

Abbots Bromley is also linked to a number of notable legends. The Goats Head pub was once patronised by infamous highwayman Dick Turpin, who is believed to have stayed the night there after stealing a horse from Rugeley Fair. And then there is the story of the Bagot goats: these black-necked beasts used to roam Bagot Woods to the north of the village and were first given to Sir John Bagot by Richard II, in return for the hunting he enjoyed here. Legend has it that as long as the herd is maintained the Bagot family shall survive.

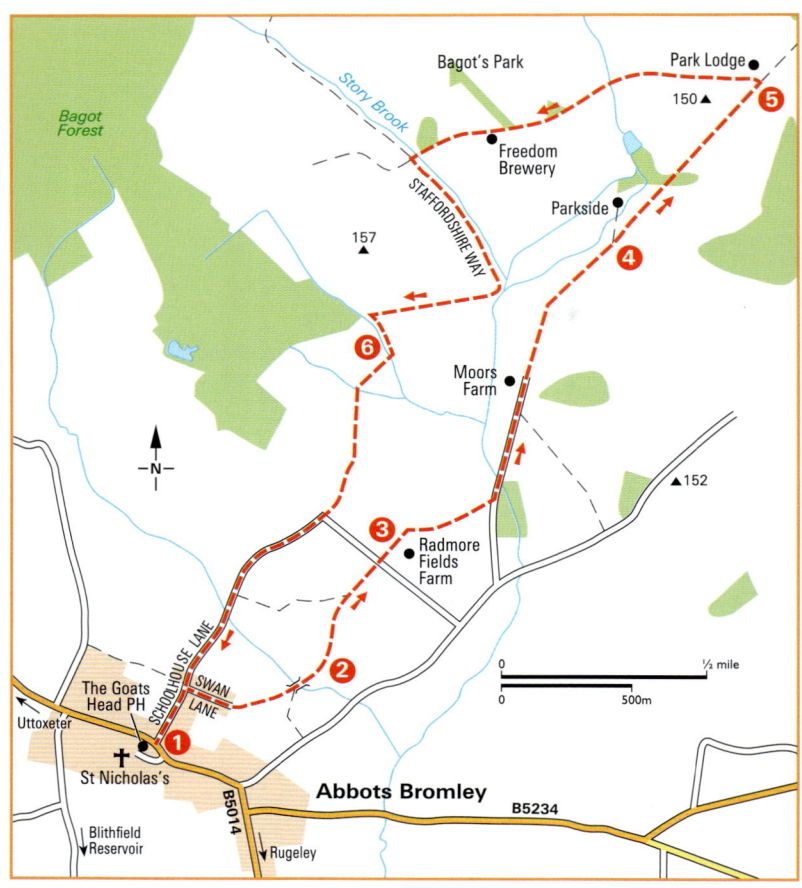

1. From the wooden Buttercross, by The Goats Head, cross the road and go up Schoolhouse Lane. At the top of the hill turn right along Swan Lane, and when you get to the end head right along a path to a gate. Head diagonally left across the field to a gap in the hedge. Go through this gap and continue across the next field to a footbridge. After the footbridge keep following the faint grassy trail to a stile near the top right-hand corner of the field.

2. Bear slightly left across the middle of the field to another stile. Carry on straight up the next field, keeping a hedge just to your left, across a series of stiles and fields, until you get to a road. Head straight across the road, following a footpath sign and, just as the track heads hard right, go straight on over a concrete stile and across the next field.

3. After another stile, follow the curve of a field to the right as far as a metalled road. Go left here, following the road and track as far as Parkside farm gate. Just before this gate, go through a gate on the right, and then left through another series of gates.

4. Continue across the field, with a hedge to your left, before crossing a funnel-shaped section of meadow to the small wood on the far side. Follow the path diagonally right through this band of trees to a pair of footbridges and another stile. Leaving the wood behind, head for the far right-hand corner of the field.

5. At the road opposite Park Lodge turn left. Just after crossing Story Brook head left. At the far left-hand corner of the field, follow the hedge round to the right and cross a small copse. Continue to follow the fence towards the corner of Bagot Forest and then go left, through the hedge. With the hedge now on your right, walk around the edge of the field, swinging left, to go through another clear gap in the hedge.

6. With Bagot Forest to your right, follow the Staffordshire Way footpath signs across the wide field ahead, aiming for the bottom end of a sloping hedge. When you reach it turn left and follow its right side up to a gate at the top of the field. Carry on straight along the track as far as a metalled road. Go straight on to get back to the start.

Where to eat and drink
There are several pubs to choose from in Abbots Bromley. The Goats Head is arguably as friendly and welcoming as any, with timber beams throughout and excellent food served lunchtimes and evenings on weekdays and all day at weekends. There is also The Crown, The Coach and Horses and Bagot Arms, also along the main road.

What to see
The wooden Buttercross (opposite The Goats Head pub and named after the produce once sold under it) would have been at the heart of the once thriving market and is thought to have been built in 1339. However, architectural historian Nikolaus Pevsner, in *The Buildings of England, Staffordshire*, gives a more likely date of the 17th century.

While you're there
Blithfield Reservoir, just to the west of Abbots Bromley, has been designated a Site of Special Scientific Interest (SSSI) thanks to the significant part it plays as a refuge for wildfowl and waders such as yellow wagtails, Canada geese, great crested grebes and herons. The shoreline at the north end of the causeway makes a very pleasant spot for a picnic, and in the summer there is often a takeaway food outlet selling snacks, hot and cold drinks and ice creams.

RUGELEY AND COLTON

DISTANCE/TIME	3.5 miles (5.7km) / 1hr 30min
ASCENT/GRADIENT	180ft (55m) / ▲
PATHS	Roads, grass trails, tow path and gravel tracks, several stiles
LANDSCAPE	Farmland, hilltop and canal
SUGGESTED MAP	OS Explorer 244 Cannock Chase & Chasewater
START/FINISH	Grid reference: SK045185
DOG FRIENDLINESS	Keep on lead near livestock
PARKING	Side-street parking near St Augustine's Church, Rugeley
PUBLIC TOILETS	None on route

Although Rugeley's existence can be traced back as far as Saxon times, today there's precious little evidence of the town's medieval past apart from the ruins of St Augustine's Church, built in the 12th and 13th centuries. Oddly, when it needed rebuilding in the 19th century, the decision was taken to choose a new site and leave the original to the elements, with the result that the parish had two churches for the price of one.

Apparently, though, no amount of building to the glory of God could deliver one local character from a life of infamy. Doctor William Palmer, the son of a timber merchant, married Ann Brooks in 1847. She subsequently bore him five children, but four died mysteriously in infancy. Ann's father also died under suspicious circumstances and, when her grieving mother came to stay, she too was dead within the space of a week. Later, when William owed money to a bookmaker, the bookie suddenly became very ill and died before he had a chance to collect his cash. In the meantime, William took out insurance policies for his wife and brother, but they both died soon after the first payments had been made. The insurance company refused to pay out, so – heavily in debt – William went to the races with a friend by the name of John Parsons Cook. As luck would have it, Cook won, but unfortunately died before picking up his winnings. So who do you suppose showed up to collect them? Why, Dr William Palmer of course!

By this stage, it wasn't just the insurance company who were crying foul, and Palmer was arrested for Cook's murder. The newspapers of the time called it the 'Trial of the Century' and for weeks it was headline news. After over a month in court Palmer was eventually found guilty and was publicly executed in Stafford at 8am on Saturday 14 June 1856, in front of a crowd of 10,000. But that wasn't the end of William Palmer. So notorious were his crimes, and so voracious was the press in reporting them, that he endured for more than 100 years as a waxwork model in Madame Tussaud's Chamber of Horrors. Remarkably, it stayed there until 1979.

One apocryphal story tells how the people of Rugeley were so horrified by the scandal surrounding the trial that they petitioned Parliament to have the name of the town changed. The Prime Minister considered the petition and agreed the town name could be changed, but only if they named it after him; the problem was, his name was Palmerston.

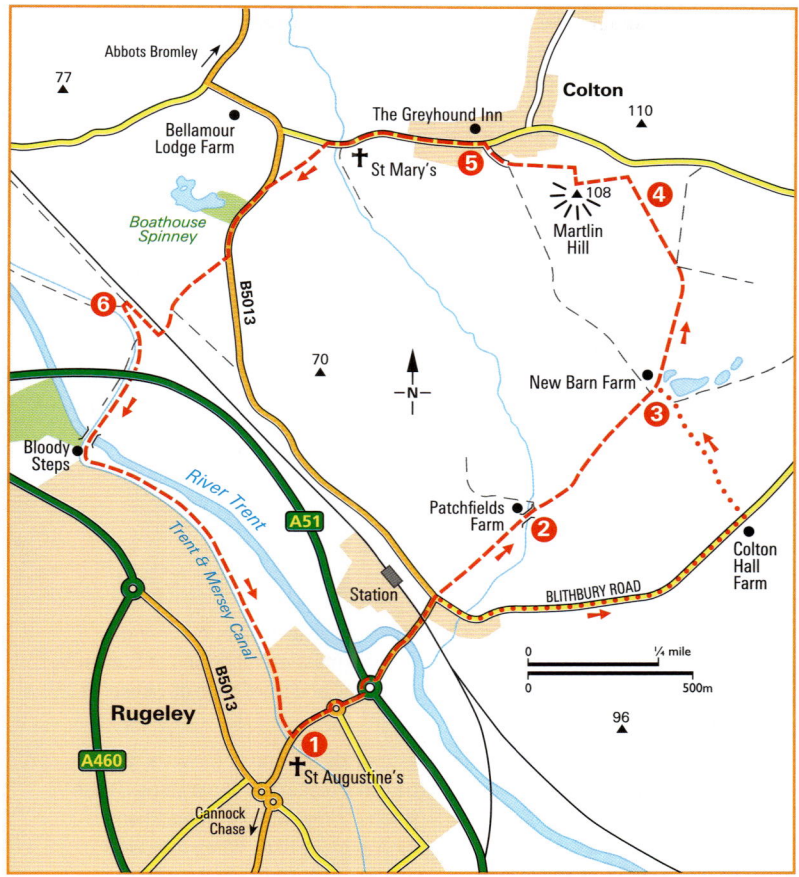

1. From St Augustine's Church head right along the B5013 towards the river. After going over two roundabouts, the river and under the railway, continue straight on along the track. When you get to Parchfields Farm, go over a stile on the right and across a field to a pair of stiles and a footbridge. (Note: if you want to avoid the bull and cows that are occasionally in this field, take the road route via Blithbury Road and after 0.5 miles (800m), opposite the entrance to Colton Hall Farm, turn left along a stony track to New Barn Farm and re-join the route at point 3).

2. Cross the footbridge and head diagonally left across the field to its far corner. Head over a stile here and straight along the right-hand edge of the field, keeping the hedge just to your right. At the end of the field, follow the yellow footpath arrows right and then left and continue in the same direction on a field track to meet the access track of New Barn Farm.

3. Turn left, passing to the right of the house onto a green track. Pass a pool, bearing slightly right, along the edge of the field, keeping the hedge to your right-hand side. The hedge curves round to the left and, after a further 220yds (201m), go through the gate in the top right-hand corner of the field. Continue in the same direction, again keeping the hedge to the right, until you get to the top of this field.

4. Go through a gate and turn left behind a big shed for about 100yds (91m) to cross a stile on your right. Turn left alongside this fence, up to the top of Martlin Hill. At the summit turn 90 degrees to the right and follow the fence down to a stile on the left. Go over and head downhill to a stile in the bottom right corner. Join the short track ahead, which becomes Martlin Lane, into Colton.

5. Turn left and walk all the way through the village. Just after a small bridge, as the road bends right, bear left onto a footpath. Head straight out across the field on a faint path. Follow this footpath until it brings you out onto the B5013 and then go left for 150yds (137m). Just after the road bends left, turn right, down a wide gravel track which crosses over the railway line before turning hard right for another 150yds (137m), to reach the canal.

6. Without crossing the bridge, head left along the canal tow path and follow this all the way to the B5013. Just before you reach the bridge go up a ramp and then right, along the canal, back to the start.

Where to eat and drink
The Greyhound Inn in Colton is a friendly and charming pub, serving a range of snacks and traditional main meals most evenings and at Sunday lunchtimes. It's open 4–11pm every weekday and from noon at weekends.

What to see
Just after the canal crosses the river towards the end of the walk, you see the tow path on the far side of the canal leading to some steps. These steps were the scene of another infamous crime, when a woman named Christina Collins was murdered by three men in 1839. When they were caught, one was hanged, one was deported to Australia and the third was sent to prison. Christina's body was buried at the new St Augustine's Church.

While you're there
Nearby Cannock Chase offers some of the best mountain biking in the Midlands. With miles of wide gravel track and lots of free parking, it's ideal for both a short potter and an all-day epic. There's a bike centre and hire shop at Cannock Chase Cycle Centre next to Birches Valley Visitors' Centre, just west of Rugeley.

CANNOCK CHASE AND SPRING SLADE LODGE

DISTANCE/TIME	4 miles (6.4km) / 1hr 30min
ASCENT/GRADIENT	361ft (110m) / ▲▲
PATHS	Gravel tracks, dirt paths and roads
LANDSCAPE	Heather and woodland
SUGGESTED MAP	OS Explorer 244 Cannock Chase & Chasewater
START/FINISH	Grid reference: SJ980181
DOG FRIENDLINESS	Beware of cyclists at all times
PARKING	Ample parking at start point; Glacial Boulder car park on Chase Road
PUBLIC TOILETS	None on route

At the beginning of the 20th century Cannock Chase was very different from the way it is now, due to centuries of deforestation. A long history of iron smelting and the consequent demand for charcoal and then coal had left the landscape almost treeless.

But the bleak landscape reflected bleaker times. With the outbreak of World War I, the Chase seemed the perfect place for an army training camp and, between 1914 and 1918, 250,000 British and Commonwealth troops passed through here on their way to the trenches. Many would not return.

The camp occupied much of the area of this walk. There were training areas and firing ranges and also a railway, sewage works, prisoner of war camp, powerhouse and pumping station, and quarters for troops and officers. Equally important were the veterinary hospital at Chase Road Corner (horses were still a large part of military life) and the Great War Hospital at Brindley Heath, for wounded soldiers brought back from the front. Many German, British and Commonwealth soldiers who died in the War Hospital were buried in the Commonwealth War Graves Cemetery, which today is a quiet, contemplative, immaculately preserved place. Equally moving is the German War Cemetery, very close by. It was established by the German War Graves Commission, an organisation charged with caring for the graves of victims of war and tyranny. The commission was asked by the German government to take care of over 1.4 million graves, in 343 cemeteries throughout 24 different countries.

After the German-British War Graves Treaty of 1959, most of the German soldiers in cemeteries around Britain were exhumed and transferred to the cemetery at Cannock Chase, and today it is the only German war cemetery in the UK. It is the final resting place for 2,143 servicemen who died in World War I and 2,797 who died in World War II. In all, 1,307 Germans remain in other British cemeteries (including the Commonwealth Cemetery here) and are looked after by the Commonwealth War Graves Commission. Read the poem on the wall of the visitor centre; it says it all.

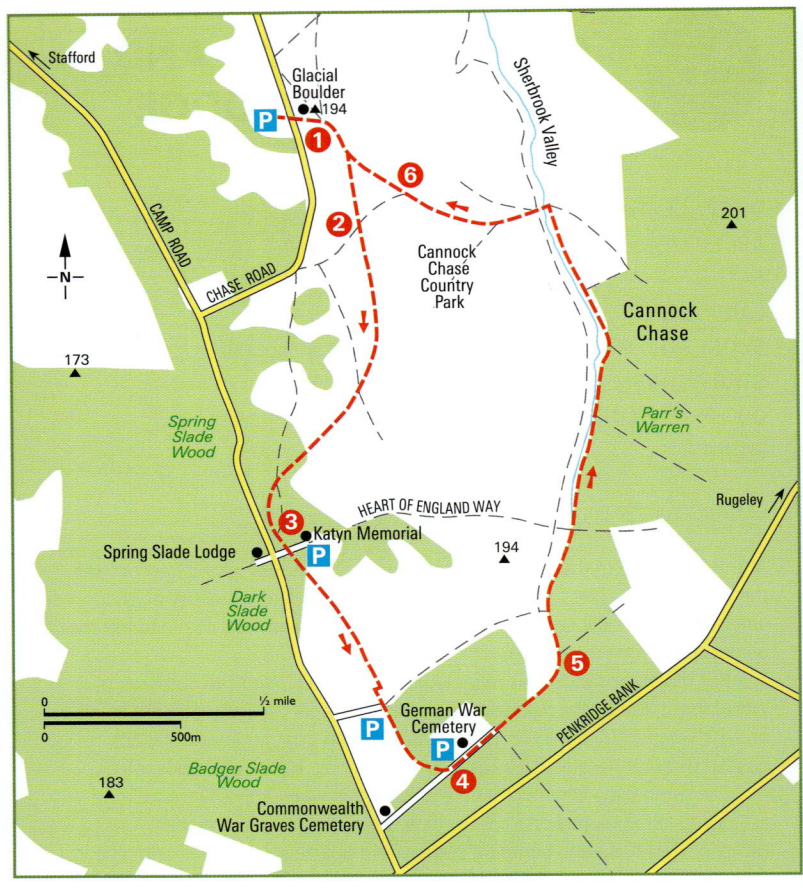

1. From the Glacial Boulder, walk away from the road along a narrow path past the trig point and then turn right along the wide gravel track. When you get to a fork, go right, following the Heart of England Way footpath sign.

2. At a crossroads of paths, keep ahead (ignoring a footpath to the right). At the next path junction, again carry straight on as the path curves gradually around the right. Continue along this track across several more path crossroads until your path enters trees and curves round to the left alongside the road. Where another wide track comes in from the left, go straight on rather than taking the shortcut down to the road on the right. Soon you meet the narrow surfaced road opposite Spring Slade Lodge. (The Katyn Memorial is just up to the left here; see While You're There.)

3. Cross the side road, and walk up a dirt track and across a path crossroads. After about 500yds (457m) you come to a T-junction which requires a dog-leg right then left to keep going in the same direction and across the end of a car park. Continue in this direction to a second car park and, as the track curves around to the left, another metalled road.

4. Turn left past the German War Cemetery. In 100yds (91m) the road becomes a wide gravel track. Continue for another 0.25 miles (400m) down into the woods, and when you get to the fork go left down into the head of Sherbrook Valley.

5. Continue along the bottom of the valley for a mile (1.6km), staying to the right of the stream and ignoring all paths off, until you get to a track junction with a ford down on the left. Cross the stream using the stepping stones. At the junction on the other side, head away from the stream following a stony track slightly left around the bottom of a hill ahead, rather than a path slightly right, straight over the top of it. Follow this track as it curves round to the right, up onto the plateau.

6. Continue across the plateau until the path starts to descend the other side, at which point you rejoin your original path, heading right, back to the Glacial Boulder and the car park.

Where to eat and drink
Spring Slade Lodge is a great place to stop for refreshments in the summer, with plenty of outside seating, but its indoor tea room is also popular in the winter (currently open daily, 10am–4pm). It offers hot snacks and tasty main meals.

What to see
To the right of the German Cemetery building are the massive grave stones for four Zeppelin crews shot down over England in World War I. They were originally buried in Potters Bar, Burstead and Theberton. Much harder to find are the graves of the 90 unknown soldiers; one near the centre is marked simply: *'Zwei unbekannte Deutsche Soldaten'* (two unknown German Soldiers).

While you're there
The Katyn Memorial, just a short walk from Spring Slade Lodge, is a tribute to the 25,000 members of the Polish armed forces and professional classes executed in 1940 in Katyn Forest, near Smolensk and at other locations in Poland, Ukraine and Russia, by the Soviet secret police on the orders of Stalin. The Poles had been prisoners of war following the Soviet Union's invasion of Poland. Polish visitors thought the birch and pine forests of Cannock Chase reminded them of those 16,000 miles away in Katyn and therefore it would be an appropriate place for a memorial.

COPPICE HILL AND THE FREDA MEMORIAL

DISTANCE/TIME	4.25 miles (6km) / 2hrs
ASCENT/GRADIENT	246ft (75m) / ▲
PATHS	Form paths and gravel tracks, no stiles
LANDSCAPE	Woods and heath
SUGGESTED MAP	OS Explorer 244 Cannock Chase & Chasewater
START/FINISH	Grid reference: SJ979192
DOG FRIENDLINESS	Very good, but be alert for bicycles and deer
PARKING	Brocton Coppice car park off Chase Road
PUBLIC TOILETS	None on route

Near the start of the walk is a monument to Freda, canine mascot of the New Zealand Rifle Brigade which was stationed on Cannock Chase during World War I. Freda was a Dalmatian adopted by the brigade at this time and it's said that she accompanied them to the Battle of the Somme in 1916. However, another story suggests that in fact she might have been found and brought back while the soldiers were in France. Certainly the warmth and companionship of their four legged friend must have been some comfort, or at the very least a distraction, from the horrors on the battlefield.

Over 70 New Zealand soldiers are buried at the Commonwealth Cemetery on Cannock Chase, which was also the last resting place for Freda who died in 1918. Her collar, bearing the inscription 'Freda of the NZ Rifle Brigade', is kept in the Army Museum at Waiouru, New Zealand. Freda's grave continues to attract visitors, some out of curiosity and others on organised military history tours. In 2010, Freda featured in an Armistice Day ceremony when dogs and their owners were invited to gather at her grave to honour Freda and other working and service dogs like her.

From the start of the walk at Coppice Hill as far as point 2, above Mere Pool, you are walking along the trackbed of a one-time military railway, constructed during 1915 by the West Cannock Colliery Company to serve the huge Brocton and Rugeley military camps that were established on the Chase. It continued north to Milford and south all the way to Hednesford and was primarily used to move supplies and munitions, since the two camps were the size of small towns. The railway was sometimes called the 'Tackeroo' Express, and although no-one is quite sure of the origin of this unusual name it may have emanated from the New Zealand troops and have a Maori derivation. One suggestion is that it possibly comes from the Maori term 'tutakarerewa' meaning to be alert, unsettled and apprehensive. Although the line was dismantled soon after the war its embankments and cuttings can still be made out today. One of the embankments crosses high above Mere Pool (sometimes called Mere Pit), which once used to be the sewage works and sludge beds for the military camp. Today it's a lovely, tree-lined pond that's a valuable wildlife refuge, a far cry from a century ago when thousands of troops must have made Cannock Chase seem a far from peaceful place.

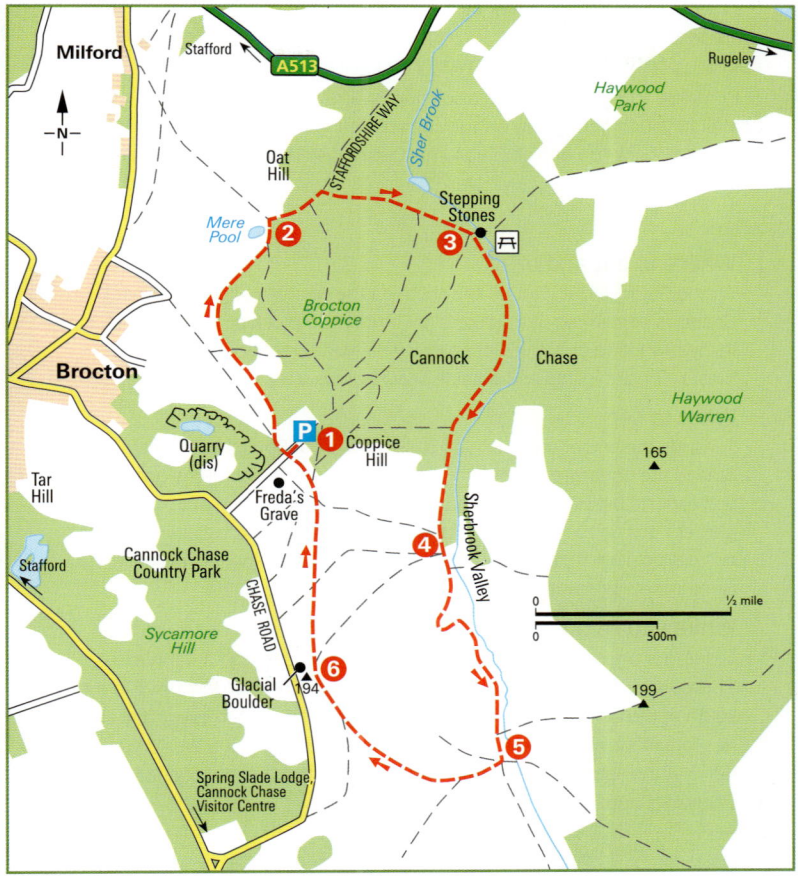

1. From the far car park by the metal barrier walk back down the road for 50yds (46m) and turn right before you reach the wooden sign for Freda's Grave. Join a broad, sunken track and stay on the main road left of Brocton Coppice and ignoring all paths off. It swings right, then left above Mere Pool.

2. At the path junction on the far side go hard right for track downhill (signposted 'Punchbowl'). When you reach the bend of a much wider track go right and follow this to a path junction by stepping stones.

3. Don't cross the stepping stones but continue straight on, following the broad track along the foot of the Sherbrook Valley. The birch trees recede and the heath becomes more open. Near a picnic bench two tracks come in from the right.

4. Carry on along the main route, again keeping straight on at another junction. With the brook still on your left, follow the track as it kinks right and continue until you reach a 5-way junction of tracks.

5. Take the second right, a wide bridleway that climbs gently into the middle of the heath. Keep right at a fork as it curves right and continue along this main route over two path junctions. Go right on to a wider track to reach the Glacial Boulder, partly hidden by trees near a trig point over to the left.

6. Continue along this popular track northwards, with Sherbrook Valley now across to your right. Ignore all turnings off left and right and stay on this route all the way back to Coppice Hill. A short, signposted path leads to Freda's Grave nearby.

Where to eat and drink
Spring Slade Lodge, just off the route on the western edge of Cannock Chase, is something of a walkers' institution, so much so that it even has its own walking group. It's open every day for a variety of snacks and meals. There's inside and outside seating, plus a take-away serving hatch.

What to see
Towards the end of the walk you pass the Glacial Boulder, partly hidden among the undergrowth near a trig point. The large boulder is granite and experts believe it originated in Scotland, before being scoured out by glaciers during the last ice age and deposited nearby. It was placed in its current position in the 1950s and rests on the base of what was once the camp reservoir tower.

While you're there
To learn more about both the natural and human history of Cannock Chase make sure to go to the main visitor centre on Marquis Drive in the south of the Country Park (follow the signposts). It's open every day and has lots more walks ideas, as well as a reconstruction of a World War I hut that the soldiers would have lived in while they were stationed on Cannock Chase.

CANNOCK CHASE

DISTANCE/TIME	3.5 miles (5.7km) / 1hr 15min
ASCENT/GRADIENT	270ft (82m) / ▲
PATHS	Gravel tracks
LANDSCAPE	Forest and forest pools
SUGGESTED MAP	OS Explorer 244 Cannock Chase & Chasewater
START/FINISH	Grid reference: SK018172
DOG FRIENDLINESS	Can be off lead, but beware of bikes
PARKING	Birches Valley Forest Centre car park
PUBLIC TOILETS	At Birches Valley Forest Centre at start

Cannock Chase, a vast area of open heathland and conifer forest just to the north of Birmingham, has been the site of human activity for thousands of years. Prehistoric hunter-gatherers built massive earthworks here (see While You're There), and William the Conqueror, realising that the heavily forested area would be difficult to cultivate, declared it a royal hunting forest. As a result, anyone caught killing a small animal lost an eye or one hand, while anyone caught poaching deer was executed.

The precedent set by William I protected the Chase from being exploited for timber, and it remained a hunting forest until Tudor times. Under Henry VIII, however, the Chase was given to William Paget, later the Marquis of Anglesey, who secured a licence to fell trees for iron smelting in 1560. Marquis's Drive, running more or less right across the chase, is a reminder of his legacy, but it was his deeds rather than his name that had the greatest impact on the landscape.

Iron smelting relied on vast quantities of charcoal to fire early blast furnaces. With the help of water-powered bellows, a mixture of charcoal, limestone and cinders was burned to melt the iron ore, which was then poured into troughs as cast iron, an alloy of carbon and iron. This mixture was very brittle, and even more charcoal was needed to burn off the carbon so that it could be hammered into wrought iron. The bars of iron produced in this way were then heated a final time, to be rolled flat and slit by a water-powered mill. By the end of the 16th century, the process was refined enough to produce items like nails, locks and chains. But the new technology came at a price, and by 1610 Cannock Chase had been almost completely deforested by voracious charcoal-burners.

It was still treeless 240 years later when the Cannock Chase Colliery came into being. The area was first mined for coal in 1298 but it wasn't until the height of the Industrial Revolution that it became big business. With coal came people, and the increase in population pushed back the boundaries of the remaining green areas further still.

Mining continued well into the 20th century, and it wasn't until the 1920s and 1930s that trees began to be systematically replanted in the area. By the end of World War II, coal mining was confined to larger pits, and many of the smaller pits were closed. In 1958 much of the woodland and heather was declared an Area of Outstanding Natural Beauty (AONB), and since then most of it has returned to nature.

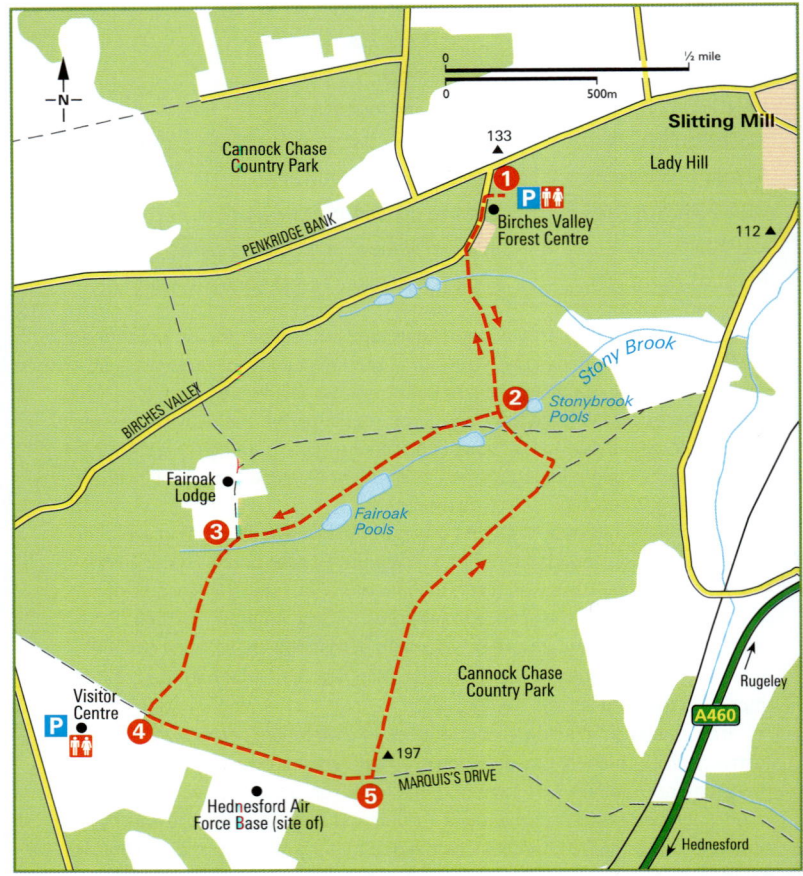

1. From the car park at the Birches Valley Forest Centre, turn left along the metalled road (Birches Valley) past a row of houses. After 200yds (183m), turn left along a wide gravel forest road. Stay left on the main track here, avoiding a less obvious grass track up the hill to the right. In 0.5 miles (800m) you reach a track junction just before Stony Brook.

2. Turn right, with a small sign for Cannock, along another smooth track. At once fork left, on a track along the valley floor. One of the small Stonybrook Pools is on your left; 300yds (274m) later you emerge into more open ground alongside two reservoirs, the Fairoak Pools. About 350yds (320m) after the second pool, you reach a major track junction.

3. Here turn left, following cycle signs for Cannock. In 100yds (91m) the main track bears right, ignoring smaller paths off to left and ahead. The path runs uphill, with clear-felled ground to the left and mature conifers to the right (these too may soon be felled). Ignore lesser paths off left and right, and walk on to a junction at the top of the slope, beside a trail bikes signboard. Go straight across for another 150yds (137m) to meet a metalled, car-free road, Marquis's Drive.

4. Turn left along Marquis's Drive (or the bike path alongside). After 0.25 miles (400m) you pass the entrance to the disused air force base of Hednesford on your right. From this point Marquis's Drive becomes unsurfaced. It heads gently uphill and bends left. About 0.25 miles (400m) from the air base entrance, and just before the very top of the slope, a smaller track turns off left, with a blue bridleway arrow.

5. Turn left on this long, straight track, which dips downhill between the rows of conifers. At the bottom of the hill, turn left along a wider track, keeping ahead to Stony Brook. Cross the stream and continue ahead (Point 2), retracing the route to the car park.

Where to eat and drink
The Grounds Café Birches Valley (at the Birches Valley Forest Centre) is open daily throughout the year and sells snacks and refreshments, including sandwiches, wraps, soup, cakes, ice cream and speciality coffees.

What to see
Cannock Chase is home to five different species of deer: fallow, muntjac, red, roe and sitka. Spot the posts with reflective strips alongside the roads that cross the chase. The strips are set at an angle, so that when they're hit by the glare of car headlights, they bounce an arc of red light into the surrounding woods. Nearby deer are stopped in their tracks, preventing them from running into the path of the car.

While you're there
The Castle Ring, just a few miles southeast of the visitors' centre, dominates the highest point on Cannock Chase and offers impressive views. Enclosing an area of more than 14 acres (5.6ha), this vast earthwork comprises a triple rampart of steep banks and deep ditches, thought to have been built between 2,000 and 3,000 years ago as either a beacon or a fortress.

HISTORIC BREWOOD

DISTANCE/TIME	5.75 miles (9.2km) / 2hrs
ASCENT/GRADIENT	75ft (23m) / ▲
PATHS	Tow paths, grass trails and roads, several stiles
LANDSCAPE	Canal, farmland and reservoir
SUGGESTED MAP	OS Explorer 242 Telford, Ironbridge & The Wrekin
START/FINISH	Grid reference: SJ881088
DOG FRIENDLINESS	Must be kept on lead near livestock
PARKING	Walkers eating at the Bridge Inn can use car park; street parking in Brewood
PUBLIC TOILETS	Brewood village centre

The first thing you need to know about Brewood is that it's pronounced 'brood', and getting this right first time round will instantly endear you to locals. The name – Breude in the Domesday Book (1086) – is from the Celtic bre, or hill, and the Old English wuda, meaning wood.

It was during the Roman occupation of Britain that the line to the north of Brewood was established as a main transport route when Watling Street was built, from London (Londinium) all the way to present-day Wroxeter, just to the west of Shrewsbury. It was one of dozens of major roads built by the Romans across Britain, the longest of which were the Fosse Way (from Exeter to Lincoln), Ermine Street (from London to York) and Watling Street itself, built in the first years of the invasion (AD 100), and later extended to Chester.

Roman roads in Britain were an extension of a systematic network connecting Rome to the four corners of its vast empire, built principally as a means of moving its great armies quickly and efficiently across occupied countries. In order to do this the roads had to be exceptionally well constructed. They were usually built on a raised embankment (to allow adequate drainage), made out of rubble obtained from drainage ditches dug on either side. Next came a layer of sand, or gravel and sand, sometimes mixed with clay; and finally the whole thing was metalled with flint, finer gravel or even the slag from the smelting of iron. The finished road was often several feet thick, cambered to allow water to run off it and with kerb stones on each side to channel any excess water.

Given the complexity of the roads, the huge distances covered and the realisation that every single inch was laboriously built by hand, the fact that many Roman roads – or at least their foundations – still exist today provides mute testimony to the mind-boggling efforts of their builders.

In addition to being well designed and well maintained, Roman roads almost invariably followed straight lines. Today's A5 follows the route of Watling Street for much of its length, and you only have to glance at an atlas to see how much straighter it is than any modern road. This was achieved by lining up marker posts, and the result meant both faster journey times and a much more efficient communications network. It's worth noting that the Shropshire Union Canal, which bisects Watling Street just to the north of Brewood, was built along similar principles, raised on great embankments and built in a series of straight lines, ultimately to improve travel times.

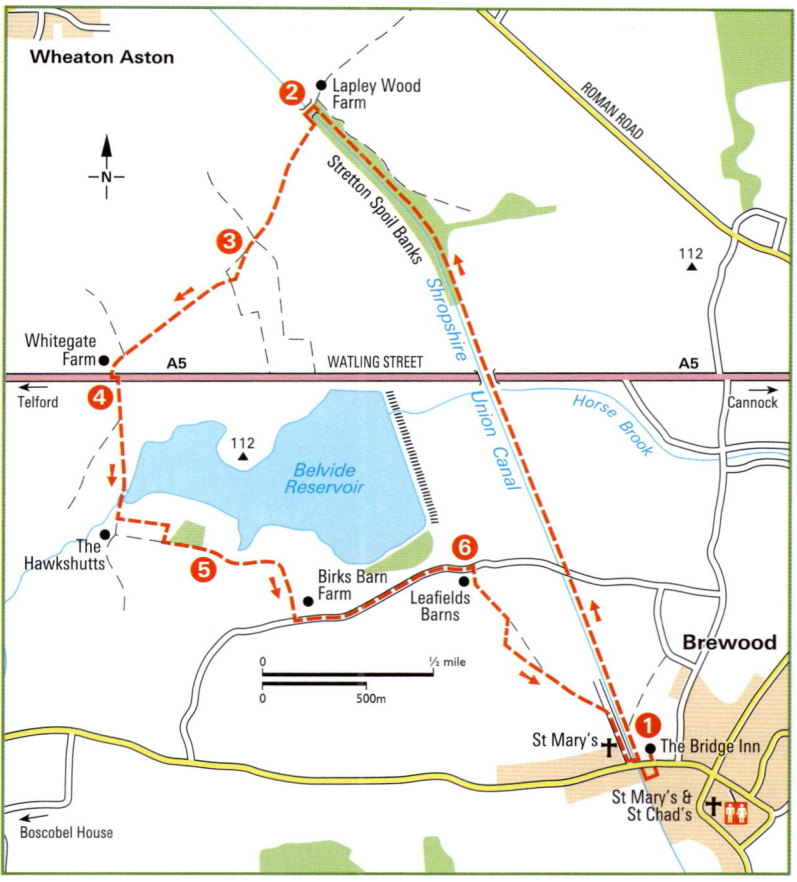

1. From The Bridge Inn car park, go straight across the main road and down some steps to the canal. Go right at the bottom of the steps and follow the canal tow path to pass over the A5 and then through Stretton Spoil Banks to Bridge No. 17 near Lapley Wood Farm.

2. Cross over the bridge and, at the concrete track, turn left for 100yds (91m). Just after this track bears right, go through the gate in the hedge to your right. Follow the hedge along the edge of the field and then along a dirt trail along a thin strip of woodland.

3. At the end of the trees, go through the gate directly ahead and then diagonally left across a field to its left-hand corner. Go through another small gate and keep ahead along the left-hand edge of the field. At the end of this very large field go through the gate and across another small field to the edge of Whitegate Farm. Skirt round the left-hand edge of the courtyard to reach a gate onto the A5.

4. Take care crossing this busy main road and then head left for 50yds (46m) before turning right along a metalled farm road. Follow this as far as The Hawkshutts. Opposite the corner of the garden wall, go left through a gate. Keep ahead to the right of the hedge, and then across a field, to pass along the right-hand edge of the wood ahead (the wood has a pond in it). Continue across the next field to a gate ahead.

5. After going through the gate, bear right along a path through bushes and trees and through the gate into another field. Bear slightly left here, aiming for a cottage with tall chimneys, until you get to a gate and a gravel-surfaced farm track. Turn right, along this track past Birks Barn Farm to a road. Turn left and walk for 0.5 miles (800m), as far as Leafields Barns.

6. Go over a stile on the right, then after a second beyond a driveway go diagonally left across a field in the direction of the church steeples until you get to a stile. Cross the stile and head right, around the edge of the field, to a line of trees down the middle. Head left here, following the line of trees as far as a field track. Go ahead up the track to the canal and then turn right, back towards St Mary's Church and the start.

Where to eat and drink
The Bridge Inn is a warm and welcoming pub, pleasantly situated beside the canal. It serves a tasty and reasonably priced range of hot and cold snacks and main meals, available at lunchtimes and evenings daily. Dogs and walkers are welcome.

What to see
Colonel Carless, a Brewood soldier who fought alongside Charles II at the Battle of Worcester in 1651 and hid with him in the oak tree, is buried in Brewood Church cemetery. The church itself, dedicated to St Mary and St Chad, owes its surprising size to the fact that successive Bishops of Lichfield owned a medieval manor near Brewood.

While you're there
Boscobel House, 3 miles (4.8km) to the west of Brewood, is famous for the part it played in the Civil War: Charles II, determined to reclaim the English throne when his father was executed on the orders of Parliament in 1649, fought the Parliamentary forces at Worcester two years later, but his army was routed. Charles fled and was forced to seek sanctuary at the hunting lodge of the royalist Giffard family, hiding himself in an oak tree. Today, another oak grows on the same site, and the house, managed by English Heritage, is open to the public.

AROUND LICHFIELD

DISTANCE/TIME	2.5 miles (4km) / 1hr
ASCENT/GRADIENT	Negligible
PATHS	Roads, surfaced paths and dirt trails
LANDSCAPE	Town centre and parkland
SUGGESTED MAP	OS Explorers 232 Nuneaton & Tamworth; 244 Cannock Chase & Chasewater
START/FINISH	Grid reference: SK118095
DOG FRIENDLINESS	Must be kept on lead near roads
PARKING	Multi storey near bus station
PUBLIC TOILETS	Town centre locations and Beacon Park

The story of Lichfield begins soon after the death of Christ. In about AD 300, during the reign of Roman Emperor Diocletian, 1,000 Christians were martyred in this area. The name Lichfield, which means 'field of the dead', commemorates the event. As a martyr shrine, it soon became a centre of Christianity, and in AD 669 the first Bishop of Mercia, Chad, established his seat here. Although Chad only lived as a bishop for three years, such was his zeal and holiness that he converted many to Christianity.

When Chad died in AD 672, he was buried close to the existing Church of St Mary. It wasn't long before his shrine became known as a place for miracles, and in AD 700 a new church dedicated to St Peter was built to receive his body. Later, a Norman cathedral was built on the same site, but a new Gothic cathedral was begun in 1085, this time dedicated to St Chad. Finally, after 150 years, the greatest cathedral in all the land was finished.

Imagine you're a peasant living near Lichfield when the cathedral is first completed. You have a small wattle and daub (wood and mud) house, some leather jerkins and sackcloth shoes. You might have seen a small Saxon or Norman church before, but if you live out in the country, you've probably never seen a stone building in your life, let alone one higher than two storeys.

You hear people talking about a new church being constructed in nearby Lichfield. They say it's built of stone and reaches up to the heavens, but nothing you've heard can prepare you for the sheer scale of what you find when you make your pilgrimage, on foot, to this new house of God. No fewer than three gigantic spires soar into the sky and when you get close, approaching the vast west façade, it's so big that it feels as if it's falling on top of you (try this as you're walking up to it yourself).

The cathedral as we see it today has hardly changed from the one exalted by Christian pilgrims and peasants 800 years ago. If anything, it was probably even more impressive in those times. Much of the stonework was painted silver and gold and the interior would have been more foreboding, lit only by the stained-glass windows of medieval times. Most of the stained glass in the cathedral today dates from the 19th century and is much lighter.

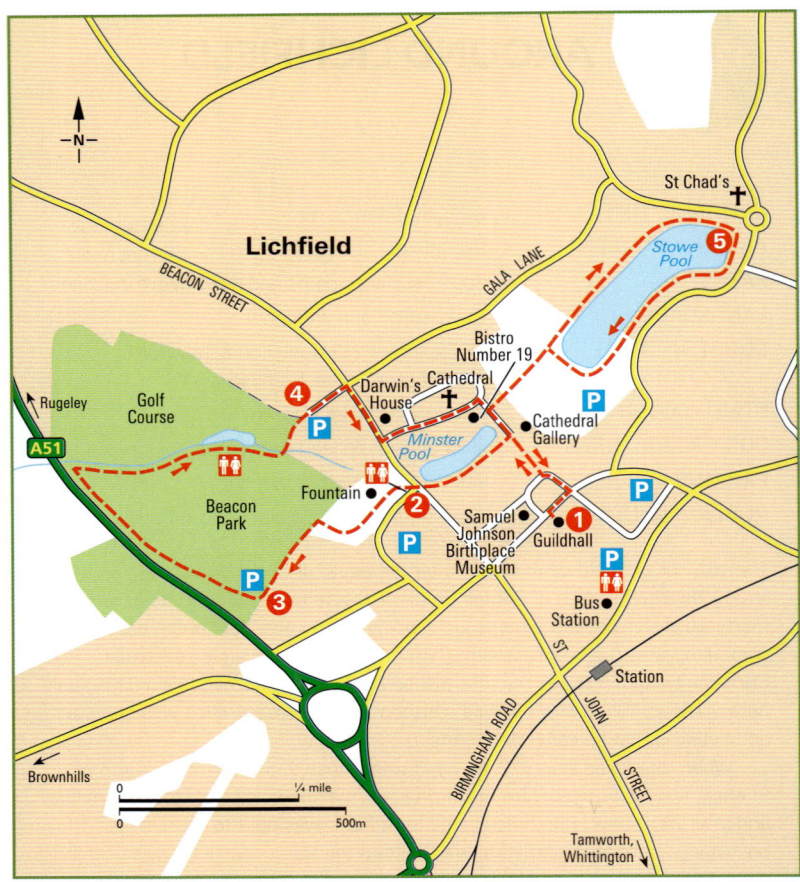

1. With your back to the Guildhall walk right and take first left down Conduit Street and go ahead to Market Square. Walk straight along Dam Street, past a series of tea shops and cafés, until you get to Pool Walk. Go left here, keeping Minster Pool on your right-hand side, until you get to Beacon Street.

2. Go diagonally right over Beacon Street to the public toilets and the entrance to Beacon Park. Pass a fountain, and keep to the left of the bowling green and then the playing fields, on a path along the left edge of the park.

3. Pass through a car park and then bear right, following a tarmac cycle path to the far end of the playing fields. After the path has entered the narrow band of trees, and just before the A51, turn right along a gravel path and carry on to the golf course at the far end. Just before the footbridge onto the golf course, turn right and follow the small brook back along the edge of the playing fields until you reach a small lake. In the summer it's possible to hire boats here for a potter on the water. Continue past the lake before crossing a footbridge to the left to pass through a small car park into Shaw Lane.

4. Follow Shaw Lane to Beacon Street, turn right for 150yds (137m) and then left along The Close to reach the cathedral. If you're not in any rush, it's worth doing a quick circuit of the cathedral inside and out, before continuing. There's an excellent shop with leaflets and guides and a free leaflet is also available, which describes the cathedral's highlights. Bear to the right of the cathedral and, at the end of The Close, just after Bistro Number 19, go right down Dam Street and then immediately left down Reeve Lane. Keep right on a hedged path ('no bikes') to Stowe Pool. From the far end of Stowe Pool you can look back at the cathedral's spires and see right through the windows from one side to the other, giving the impression that they're lighter and more delicate than stone.

5. Continue on the popular surfaced path all the way round the edge of Stowe Pool and return to Dam Street. Turn left past the end of Minster Pool to retrace your steps to the Guildhall at the start.

Where to eat and drink
There are many cafés, pubs and other places to eat and drink in the city. Bistro Number 19 is located opposite the cathedral and serves all day breakfasts, brunch, roasts, desserts and drinks both hot and cold.

What to see
The Cathedral's chapter house boasts the Lichfield Gospels, an illuminated Latin manuscript from the eighth century. It's hard to imagine that the elaborately decorated pages of this ancient book were written, painted and bound more than 1,200 years ago. The Chapel of St Michael is where the campaigns of the Staffordshire Regiment are commemorated. It also contains a book of remembrance with names of the men who fell in the two World Wars.

While you're there
Lichfield is a pretty market town with great shopping and plenty to see. Among the highlights are the Samuel Johnson Birthplace Museum, commemorating the life and work of the celebrated writer who, along with a number of famous sayings, was responsible for the first comprehensive English dictionary. Also worth visiting is the house of Erasmus Darwin (1731–1802), the grandfather of Charles Darwin, who was a brilliant doctor, scientist, inventor and poet.

AROUND WHITTINGTON

DISTANCE/TIME	9.3 miles (15km) / 4hrs
ASCENT/GRADIENT	465ft (142m) / ▲
PATHS	Roads, gravel and sand tracks, dirt trails, may be muddy after rain, several stiles
LANDSCAPE	Farmland and forest
SUGGESTED MAP	OS Explorer 232 Nuneaton & Tamworth
START/FINISH	Grid reference: SK158083
DOG FRIENDLINESS	On lead near livestock and roads
PARKING	Ample roadside parking in Whittington
PUBLIC TOILETS	None on route

Whittington Barracks, just south of the village of the same name, has been the home of the Staffordshire Regiment since 1881. The regiment dates back to 1705, when the 38th Foot was raised at the King's Head Hotel in Lichfield by Colonel Luke Lillingston, and it first saw active service fighting the French and Spanish in the West Indies. The raising of other regiments over the next 120 years led, through a complex process of change and reorganisation, to the formation of the Staffordshire Regiment after World War II, and its recent amalgamation into the Mercian Regiment. It was conferred the title of the Prince of Wales's in 1876, following the presentation of colours by the Prince of Wales (later crowned King Edward VII). All of this history, and much more besides, is related by the fascinating Staffordshire Regiment Museum at Whittington Barracks, with memorabilia from the many campaigns the regiment has been embroiled in. Perhaps the most interesting of the displays is the one dedicated to the story of those in the regiment who have been awarded the highest wartime honour.

The Victoria Cross was first established by royal warrant in 1856, to recognise acts of uncommon valour during the Crimean War, 1854–56. It was ordained that it should 'only be awarded for most conspicuous bravery, or some daring or pre-eminent act of valour or self-sacrifice or extreme devotion to duty in the presence of the enemy'. All VCs are forged from the remains of bronze cannon, captured either during the Crimean War or during the First China War. The metal is guarded by 15 Regiment in Donnington, secured in vaults and rarely removed; the most recent issue of metal, sufficient to make 12 medals, was made in 1959. It's thought the remaining metal is enough to make a further 85 medals; given that only 15 have been won since the end of World War II, it can be expected that this will suffice for many years to come. In all, 1,358 Victoria Crosses have been won, and of these, 1,156 were awarded before the end of World War I. At least three witnesses are needed for recommendation. All medals require royal assent and are presented by the reigning monarch. The inscription on front of the VC states simply: 'For Valour'. It has been estimated that the chances of surviving a VC action is 1 in 10.

Of the 11 members of the Staffordshire Regiment who have been awarded the VC, probably the most famous is Lance Corporal William Coltman, a stretcher bearer during operations at Mannequin Hill in France on 3 and 4 October 1918. Hearing that wounded men had been left behind during a retreat, Corporal Coltman went forward alone in the face of relentless enemy fire, found the casualties, dressed their wounds and carried some of them to safety on his back on three occasions. For the next two days and nights he looked after the wounded constantly. He later became the most decorated NCO of World War I.

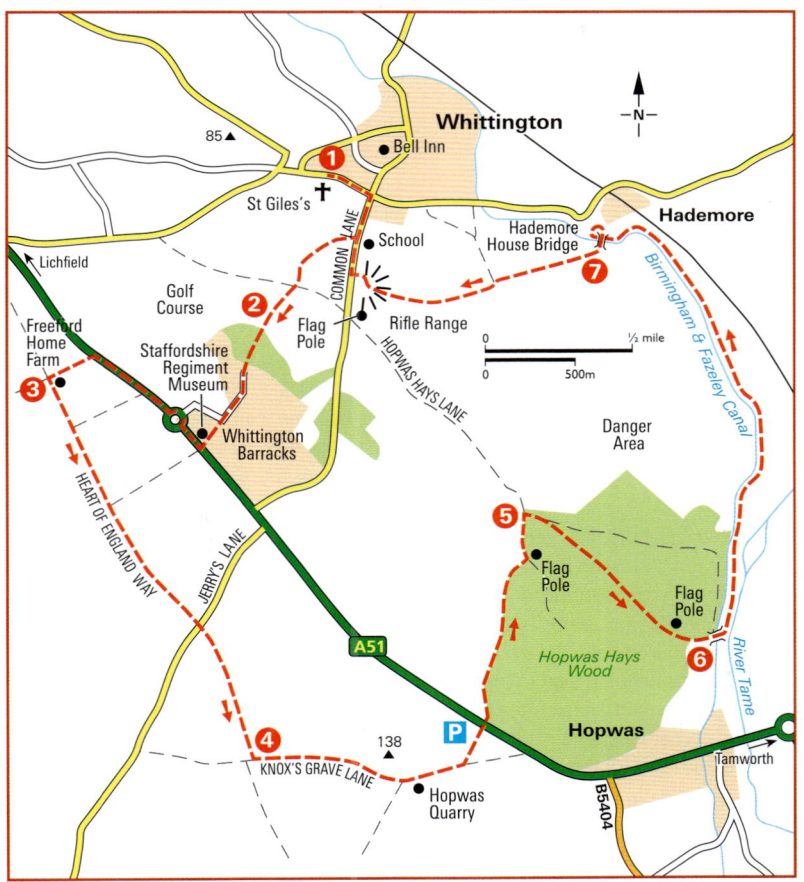

1. From St Giles's Church head into the village to a crossroads and then turn right for 250yds (229m) along Common Lane until you get to Sandy Lane. Turn right on this wide earth track until it bends hard right, and here go ahead through a gate and continue in the same direction to the corner of a wood.

2. Go through a swing gate and head slightly left through the wood, on a small brambly path, ignoring bigger paths setting off to left and right. At the residential tarmac road bear left to a wider road, and then right, to pass the Staffordshire Regiment Museum and go onto the A51. Turn right and walk along the pavement for 700yds (640m), passing a roundabout on the way. At South Lodge turn along a wide track to Freeford Home Farm.

3. Turn left onto the earth track of the Heart of England Way. Where a track joins from the left, move slightly right through a gate onto an enclosed grass track. Keep ahead for 0.75 miles (1.2km), through several gates and across a horse gallop, to a metalled road. Cross onto a hedged path, which passes a small square of trees on its right then crosses a farm track. Another 500yds (457m) brings you to the junction with Knox's Grave Lane, a wide sandy track.

4. Turn left along here and then fork right at the top of a field to reach the corner of the sand and gravel pits. An abandoned tarmac road ahead threads between the pits on either side, down the dip and then up the other side. At the top of the rise, cross the stile on the left onto a field-edge alongside the gravel pit. At the far side of the field, cross a stile and the A51, and then go straight up the track to a T-junction. Turn left and follow the edge of Hopwas Hays Wood for 0.5 miles (800m). At a range flagpole, bear left to a major track junction at the corner of the wood.

5. Turn hard right at the major 4-way junction, almost back on yourself, for a slightly sunken track up through the woodland. At the top bear right and stay straight along this wide dirt and gravel track, ignoring any smaller paths off to the left or right. The path drops through the woods to pass a range flagpole. Keep following it round to the left to the canal bridge.

6. Cross the canal and turn left along the tow path. Walk for 1.75 miles (2.8km) to pass under Hademore House Bridge. In another 50yds (46m) turn right, up off the tow path. Return to the bridge and cross over the canal. Continue straight ahead along a wide, sandy track for 100yds (91m) and then turn right along another sand track between poly tunnels, as far as a gap between two hedges.

7. Go through the gap and continue in the same direction, with a hedge on your right, following a track and then a path until it goes between two hedges along a narrow dirt trail. At a T-junction with a wide track, turn left and then immediately right, along another narrow dirt trail to the right of a hedge. Beyond an iron gate and a military firing range sign (see warning below). Follow the footpath sign to the right along the faint grass trail around the edge of the field, keeping the hedge on your right. Carry on to the far right-hand corner of this field where the hedge meets a small cottage and the metalled road (Common Lane) leading back into Whittington.

Warning If the red flags are flying, keep out! The area around Hopwas Hays Wood, marked by red triangles on Ordnance Survey maps, is a military firing range open to the public when it's not in use. Towards the end of the walk, just before you get to Common Lane, if you look back over your left shoulder you'll see the rifle range itself stretching 800yds (732m) to the target area at the far end.

Where to eat and drink
The Bell Inn in Whittington serves a selection of bar snacks and main meals, lunchtimes and evenings.

What to see
The Coltman Trench, named after Lance Corporal William Coltman, is one of the highlights of the museum, and it goes some way to recreating conditions in the trenches. The figures mentioned, however, are incomprehensible. On 1 July 1916, the first day of the Battle of the Somme, 60,000 soldiers died in a single day. When the war ended on 11 November 1918, more than 9 million people had been killed.

While you're there
The regimental chapel situated off the south transept of Lichfield Cathedral features dozens of banners and colours from the regiment's long tradition of foreign campaigns. At the entrance is a stand surmounted by a figure of St George, which bears memorial books containing the names of men who fell in the World Wars.

ALREWAS & NATIONAL MEMORIAL ARBORETUM

DISTANCE/TIME	6 miles (9.7km) / 2hrs 15min
ASCENT/GRADIENT	Negligible / ▲
PATHS	Firm tracks, canal towpath, pavement, no stiles
LANDSCAPE	Flat river valley
SUGGESTED MAP	OS Explorer 245 The National Forest
START/FINISH	Grid reference: SK182146
DOG FRIENDLINESS	Off lead on towpath and tracks, but on lead on streets and in the National Memorial Arboretum, where you must stick to the described route
PARKING	National Memorial Arboretum pay-and-display car park (open summer 10am–5pm, winter 10am–4pm)
PUBLIC TOILETS	National Memorial Arboretum

The National Memorial Arboretum describes itself as the UK's living Centre of Remembrance, a 150-acre (60ha) site of maturing woodland next to the River Tame south of Burton upon Trent that is now home to over 400 dedicated memorials. The centrepiece is the Armed Forces Memorial, a simple but stunning piece of architecture whose walls contain the names of every member of the Armed Forces killed since World War II. There are memorials remembering not just specific squadrons and battleships but also the likes of the Merchant Navy Convoys and Army Dog Unit, as well as marking the particular contribution of Commonwealth forces. Each memorial is subtly different, whether in the artistic design of a statue or tree planting, while some incorporate living willow and even picnic areas.

However, there are plenty of memorials scattered around the large site that have no military connection but are every bit as poignant. They include memorials to civil services such as Police and Ambulance personnel, the Royal National Lifeboat Institution, as well as the Quakers, YMCA and those killed in the Twin Towers tragedy. There's also the Children's Woodland, where individual trees have been sponsored by families and schools and dedicated to babies and children who have passed away. Near the visitor centre is the Millennium Chapel of Peace and Forgiveness, the only place in the UK where the Act of Remembrance is observed every day of the year.

Since the site was first developed in 1997, over 50,000 trees have been planted and the Arboretum is beginning to take shape as a 'living tribute'. In many cases the type of tree has been deliberately chosen. For instance, The Beat is an avenue of Horse chestnuts, funded by every Police force in the UK, since the first truncheons were made from chestnut and several of the trees along the avenue were grown from conkers taken from the home of Sir Robert Peel, founder of the Police Force. In another area, the Golden Grove celebrates the lives of couples who married at the end of World War II and who commemorated their 50th anniversary by dedicating trees. All the trees in the Grove have either golden leaves, stems or fruits such as the golden stemmed ash.

The National Memorial Arboretum is open daily and entrance is free. There are paths and trails aplenty and you can wander about discovering the woodland memorials at random, or else buy an official guide from the visitor centre to help you find your way about.

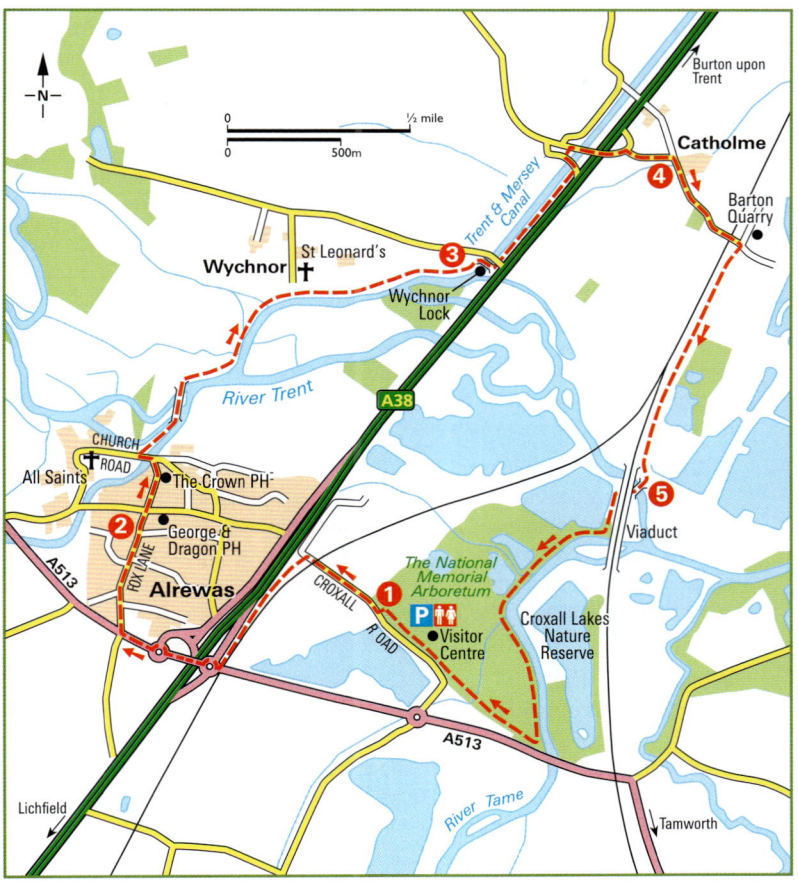

1. Leave the main gate of the Arboretum and turn right along the pavement of Croxall Road. At the end, after crossing the railway line, turn left and follow the A38 pavement up to the roundabout junction. Turn right, cross the bridge, and take the second turning on the right (Fox Lane) through the centre of Alrewas.

2. At the junction at the end go straight over and continue down Post Office Road, past The Crown pub. At the end turn left on to Church Road, cross the bridge and turn immediately right on to the canal towpath. Now follow this route for 1.25 miles (2km), across several footbridges and under two bridges until you reach Wychnor Lock.

3. Cross Bridge 43 to switch to the opposite bank and continue beneath an old road bridge. Immediately after the next bridge (number 41) go right, up a grassy bank and over a low metal barrier. Turn right and cross the canal via the road bridge. On the other side turn right for a footpath through trees that cuts the corner. Now turn right and cross another road bridge back over the canal and A38 and follow the road until the bend, where you turn right for the lane to Catholme.

4. At the T-junction turn right and follow the wide track over the railway. On the far side go right by the public footpath sign, opposite Barton Quarry entrance. Follow this broad, straight track with the railway on your right until you reach a blue painted footbridge across the River Tame.

5. Cross the bridge and on the far side turn right to go beneath the railway viaduct. Immediately turn left and walk along a narrow grassy strip. At the end turn right on to a gravel track that follows the river bank around the edge of the Arboretum, past plantings and memorials. Continue along this route until, approaching a road bridge, the track swings right and returns to the start.

Where to eat and drink
The café and restaurant at the National Memorial Arboretum is open daily and ideal for post-walk tea and cake, or even a hot meal. At Alrewas the George & Dragon and The Crown are both welcoming local pubs with outdoor seating and serve food every lunchtime and evening.

What to see
On the walk you pass a couple of active quarries. The Trent Valley has long been important for sand and gravel, which has been extracted for over 200 years, and although it clearly continues former flooded sites have been returned to nature and are now important wildlife reserves, such as Croxall Lakes on the far side of the River Tame from the Arboretum.

While you're there
If you head south on the Trent & Mersey Canal from Alrewas you come to Fradley Junction, where it meets the Coventry Canal. This attractive and bustling location is a mecca for canal-goers and sightseers alike, with a café, pub and information centre. There are audio trails and guided walks, and even Fradley Pool Nature Reserve nearby.

CHASEWATER

DISTANCE/TIME	3 miles (4.8km) / 1hr 15min
ASCENT/GRADIENT	75ft (23m) / ▲
PATHS	Gravel tracks
LANDSCAPE	Lakeside and heathland
SUGGESTED MAP	OS Explorer 244 Cannock Chase & Chasewater
START/FINISH	Grid reference: SK040071
DOG FRIENDLINESS	Can be taken off lead
PARKING	Parking at Chasewater; follow signs 'Chasewater' off A5
PUBLIC TOILETS	At Chasewater Innovation Centre

Originally Chasewater was a natural reservoir called Norton Pool, but little is known about its history prior to the late 18th century; with its poor acidic soil, heathland and forest, it was unsuitable for cultivation. But during the Napoleonic Wars (1803–15) there was a drive throughout the country to increase food production for the army, so areas of heathland and forest went under the plough.

In 1797 a dam was constructed to turn the pool into a feeder reservoir for the Anglesey Branch Canal, newly built to carry coal from local pits to Birmingham and beyond. As the canal had little natural catchment, any extra water in winter was lifted back from the canal into the reservoir by a steam-driven pump. The valve house of this remains today, on top of the dam wall.

With the arrival of the railways in the second half of the 19th century, canals were – quite literally – overtaken by the new technology. A network of tracks in the area included the causeway across the water, which carried coal from Cannock Chase. Mining around Chasewater continued well into the 20th century, but by 1950 it was an industry in decline, leaving a desolate landscape of disused railways, sidings and pit waste.

Even back then, the local authority had the foresight to transform Chasewater into an aquatic pleasure park, complete with funfair, big wheel and miniature railway. The funfair is no more, but the park now features a waterskiing centre, as well as sailing and windsurfing. For those who prefer their leisure pursuits a little more leisurely, there are displays at Chasewater Innovation Centre (free admission, open daily all year).

But the most significant achievement of the reclamation programme is its thriving wildlife. Today, much of the area has been designated as a Site of Special Scientific Interest (SSSI). In summer, when the water is low, the sediment along the shore makes an ideal feeding ground for birds such as herons, pied wagtails and ringed plovers. The stringy mat of weed over the exposed beaches is the rare but aptly named shoreweed. During winter, coots, mute swans and a vast roost of gulls are best watched from the south shore in late afternoon. Cormorants and Canada geese are also common, and great crested grebes can often be spotted displaying in spring. Some 230 different bird species have been noted here.

Heathland favours acid-loving plants; areas reclaimed from mining support only coarse grass and little in the way of wildlife. Natural grassland, though, boasts a rich variety of plants, such as lichens, mosses and cowslips. Finally, there are the bogs – disliked by walkers, but, as a habitat, appreciated by naturalists.

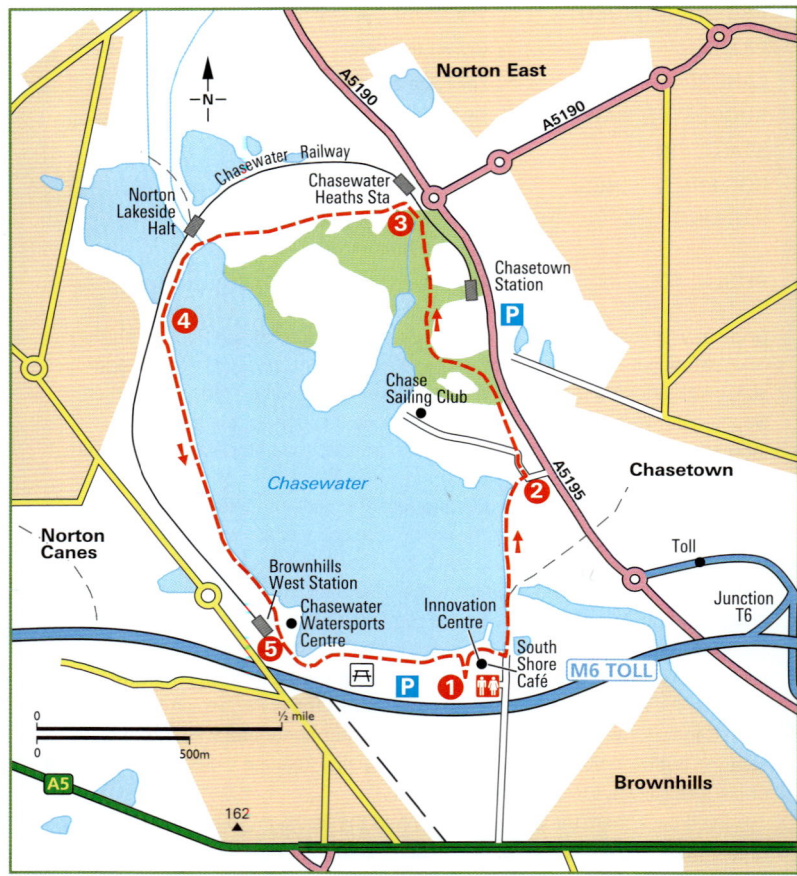

1. From the car park, go past the Innovation Centre and adjoining café down to the shore of the reservoir, and turn right. Bend left around the corner of the reservoir, and follow the tarmac path along the top of the concrete dam. At its end, drop to the right, off the path, to join the road running round to the left, towards Chase Sailing Club.

2. After 220yds (201m), as the road turns hard left, carry straight on along a wide gravel track, following cycle route signs. Keep following this track around, ignoring a path to the left, then forking left alongside the busy A5195 road. The wide path is sometimes gravel, sometimes tarmac. It passes to the left of some sports pitches, then bends right to pass alongside what looks like a pond but is in fact a corner of the reservoir. Finally it turns away from the reservoir, with a small stream on its left, to reach Chasewater Heaths Station.

3. Don't cross to the station, but stay on the wide tarmac path as it veers left, back towards the reservoir. It crosses open heath, to rejoin the railway at the start of its causeway across the north end of the reservoir. Turn left, alongside the railway, to cross the causeway.

4. Turn left on a wide dirt path along the shoreline. There are some carved picnic benches along this shoreline if you want to stop for a rest or a bite to eat, or just to watch the world go by. The sound of the steam train is carried across the water. The shoreline itself is reinforced by the roots of the tough willow trees that grow there.

5. The path becomes tarmac as you pass to the left of Brownhills West Station, then pass around to the right of the Chasewater Watersports Centre at the reservoir corner. Bear left off the main tarmac path to join a well-made gravel one along the shoreline. This path even ventures out on decking across the water of a tiny bay, before arriving at a swan pond just in front of the Innovation Centre. Pass around (or through) the Innovation Centre to the car park.

Where to eat and drink
The South Shore Café, adjoining the Chasewater Innovation Centre, is open daily, all year round. It serves a range of snacks and light refreshments, including freshly made sandwiches and a salad bar. In the summer, you can take an ice cream out onto the waterfront.

What to see
Boggy areas can be divided into two types: true bog, which supports sphagnum moss and acid-loving plants like cotton grass; and fen, which is alkaline and harbours reed mace and, in early to mid-summer, slender pink or white marsh orchids.

While you're there
Chasewater Railway operates along the only remaining section of the old Cannock Chase coalfield network. The steam-powered trips can be taken around the water from Brownhills West to Chasetown Station via Norton Lakeside Halt and Chasewater Heaths Station. Brownhills West has been built in traditional Victorian style and has a gift shop and a station buffet serving hot and cold snacks. The return trip takes an hour, with both diesel and steam-hauled trains running most weekends throughout the year. For more details go to www.chasewaterrailway.co.uk.

TRYSULL'S VINEYARD

DISTANCE/TIME	6.25 miles (10.1km) / 2hrs 15min
ASCENT/GRADIENT	270ft (82m) / ▲▲
PATHS	Roads, grass and dirt trails, gravel tracks, several stiles
LANDSCAPE	Village, farmland and escarpment top
SUGGESTED MAP	OS Explorer 219 Wolverhampton & Dudley
START/FINISH	Grid reference: SO852943
DOG FRIENDLINESS	Keep on lead near livestock
PARKING	Roadside parking in Trysull; also Hunters Green near village hall
PUBLIC TOILETS	None on route

The Halfpenny Green Vineyards is situated on the southern-facing slopes of Upper Whittimere, to make the most of the sun all year. The area was first planted in 1983 with the idea of producing wine for personal consumption, but the fine quality of the results led to it becoming a thriving business; and an astonishing 50–60,000 bottles are produced here every year.

The vineyard is one of hundreds in the UK, most of them in the south of England or south Wales. Winemaking is enjoying something of a revival in this country, thanks largely to improved methods and a rigorous application of science in overcoming the problems of drought, disease and lack of sunshine. Since the Romans cultivated vines here almost 2,000 years ago numerous attempts have been made to make English vineyards a viable alternative to their continental counterparts, but almost without exception these efforts ended in failure.

It wasn't until after World War II that research chemist Ray Barrington Brock set himself the mission of discovering which varieties of grape could cope best with the vagaries of the British weather. His work inspired others to follow suit, and in 1955 the first English wine to be made commercially since World War I went on sale.

Since then, there has been a steady increase in the number of vineyards and labels. However, in recent years this trend has levelled off, partly because many vineyards were established with little knowledge of the science involved. It has been said that the best way to earn a small fortune is to start with a large fortune and buy an English vineyard. Today though, there are numerous thriving vineyards throughout the south, despite the fact that in England only two years in every ten are 'good' years, with four average and four poor, again largely due to problems associated with weather. The most successful vineyards are well-sited with respect to sunlight and soil, grow appropriate varieties for the conditions, and are managed as scientific and commercial enterprises.

Wines labelled as 'British' are made in the UK from imported wine concentrate and are usually of poor quality. To be labelled 'English', wines must be made from grapes grown in England, with the wine itself also made in England. Time was when turning one's nose up at English 'plonk' was justified, but if the wine at Halfpenny Green is anything to go by, domestic wine is now flowing more strongly than ever.

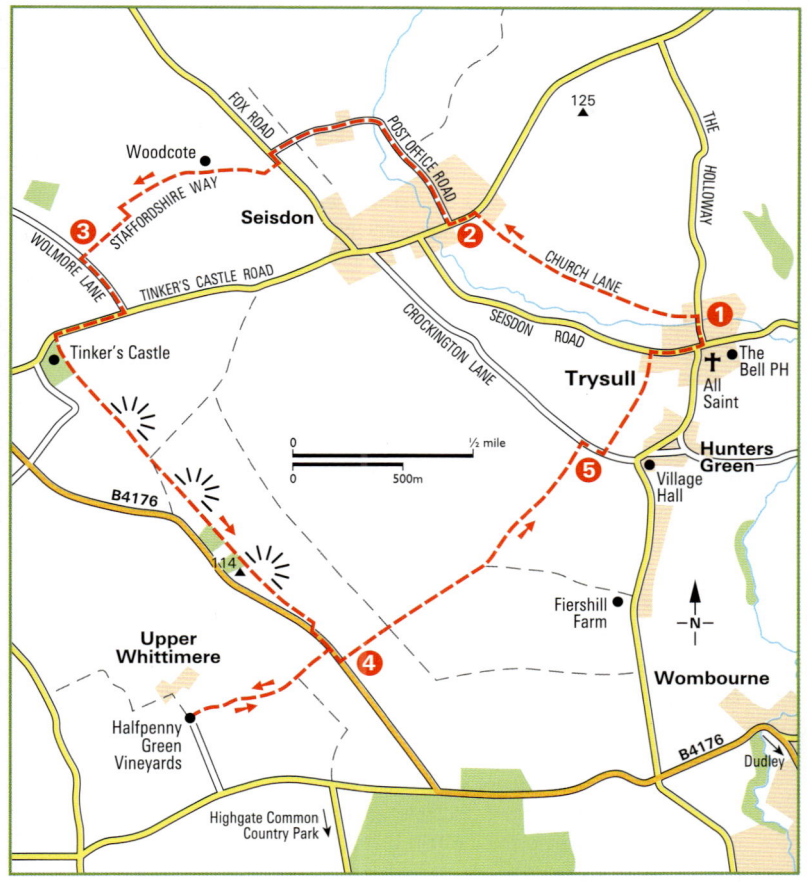

1. From All Saints Church, head north along The Holloway for 100yds (91m) and, just after crossing a small brook, turn left along Church Lane. This soon becomes a farm track, then a hedged path that may be muddy after heavy rain. Emerging at Seisdon, turn left along the road (there is no pavement here, so exercise caution), and then take the first road on the right, Post Office Road.

2. Follow this road all the way round to a T-junction with Fox Road. Turn left, then immediately right at a bridleway signpost. Follow this track past the crumbling sheds of Woodcote. At the top of the lane (Staffordshire Way marker), go through a swing gate to continue along a narrower dirt trail with a hedge to the left. At the corner of the hedge follow the path left around the edge of the field and then immediately right up to a metalled farm driveway, Wolmore Lane.

3. Turn left along this to a T-junction, then right along Tinker's Castle Road. At the top of the hill, just before Tinker's Castle house with its mock battlements, head left up a path between a wall and a fence. The path runs ahead along the wooded ridge top for 1.25 miles (2km) to join the B4176. The road ahead continues the walk, but first, opposite the junction, head right along a wide field track (signed as a public footpath) to visit Halfpenny Green Vineyards (where there's a tea room and restaurant, gift shop and craft centre). Return to the B4176 and (arriving from the vineyard) recross the road, then turn right along it for 50yds (46m), then turn off left at a footpath sign.

4. Go straight across the middle of the field to a stile, cross a track, then follow the hedge just to your right in the same direction. At the far right-hand corner of this field keep going straight on, aiming for a very large holly bush in the hedge ahead. Go through a wide gap in the hedge and bear slightly left on a faint field path, crossing the bank of a former hedge and down to a stile onto Crockington Lane. (If this field is impassable because of crops, you can bear right along the hedge to Fiershill Farm, but this means a longer walk along the road into Trysull.)

5. Turn right along Crockington Lane for 100yds (91m), before turning left through a kissing gate. Go straight on across this field to the far side and then down a track between houses to Seisdon Road. Turn right here, back to the start.

Where to eat and drink

The Bell in Trysull is an excellent village pub offering food at lunchtime and in the evening, every day. Bar snacks such as jacket potatoes, pies and baguettes are served at very reasonable prices, and there's also a full restaurant menu. The interior is friendly and relaxed, while the picnic tables have a fine view of All Saints Church.

What to see

As you walk along Wolmore Lane (Point 3), check out the huge holly bushes that have got away from the hedge trimmer and formed themselves into trees. English holly can grow up to 50ft (15m) or higher. The male and female flowers are produced on different plants. In order for bees and other insects to pollinate female flowers and so form berries, male trees need to be planted within 100ft (30m) or so.

While you're there

Highgate Common Country Park, south of Trysull, offers a wide expanse of open heathland and forest, with numerous trails criss-crossing the area and plenty of perfect picnic spots.

THE WOMBOURNE RAILWAY WALK

47

DISTANCE/TIME	4.25 miles (6.8km) / 1hr 30min
ASCENT/GRADIENT	360ft (110m) / ▲▲
PATHS	Roads, gravel and dirt tracks, several stiles
LANDSCAPE	Disused railway, meadow and hilltop
SUGGESTED MAP	OS Explorer 219 Wolverhampton & Dudley
START/FINISH	Grid reference: SO870939
DOG FRIENDLINESS	Must be on lead in fields and on roads
PARKING	South Staffordshire Railway Walk car park, Bratch Lane, Wombourne
PUBLIC TOILETS	None on route

Referred to in the Domesday Book as Womburne, Wombourne's name is thought to mean 'winding stream' (the Anglo-Saxon 'burn' is still used in Scotland and Northumberland to mean a brook). At that time (1086) it was reported as having a population of just 26 people, and by 1641 that number had barely risen above 100. Clearly, this was not a booming town, and despite a number of small industries making their mark on the village in subsequent centuries – agriculture from the 1750s, horticulture around 1800, and sand-mining and nail production from about 1850 – it served as little more than a stop-off on the Staffordshire and Worcestershire Canal throughout this time.

The canal was one of the first to be built in Staffordshire, designed by engineering genius James Brindley. It was well placed for the Potteries, carrying goods to and from Bristol, Gloucester and the West Country via the River Severn. Later, in the 1830s, it faced stiff competition from the Worcestershire and Birmingham Canal and the Birmingham and Liverpool Junction Canal, but still continued to make a profit until the 1860s. By then, however, the impact of the railways was beginning to bite, and the canal ceased to be a significant transport route by the turn of the century.

As it turned out, the local railway fared little better, again thanks to competition from bigger, inter-city lines. The South Staffordshire Railway, serving the rural areas to the west of Dudley and Wolverhampton, was owned by Great Western Railways. Building started in 1912, but – due in part to the interruption of World War I – it was not completed until 1925. Right from the start the line wasn't very successful, and passenger services were withdrawn by 1932. During World War II, following the D-Day landings in June of 1944, it was used to transport wounded Allied soldiers to hospitals in the area, and after the war it was used for transporting goods.

Following the nationalisation of the railways in 1948, it became a part of the Western Region of what was then British Railways, but the continued decline in traffic during the 1950s and 1960s resulted in its inevitable closure. The last train ran in 1965. The rail company's loss, however, was the public's gain. Today, the old line has been converted into a popular walking and cycle path, called the South Staffordshire Railway Walk, through quiet, rolling farmland, the flat, all-weather surface making it ideal for wheelchairs, pushchairs and family cycling. The route along the railway line can be extended in either direction by continuing along the Pensnett section in Dudley or the Valley Park section in Wolverhampton.

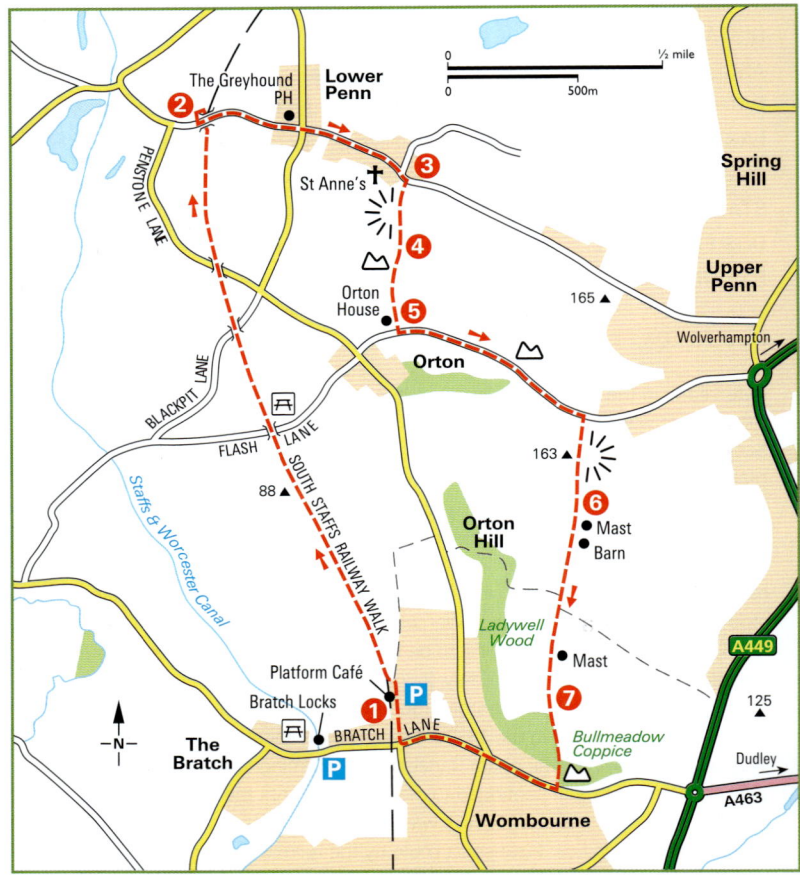

1. From the far end of the car park, walk the few paces on to the disused South Staffordshire Railway line, beyond the former station and platform. Head right and continue along the gravel track for 1.5 miles (2.4km), passing over Flash Lane, Blackpit Lane and Penstone Lane (there are picnic benches near both Flash Lane and Blackpit Lane if you're in need of rest and refreshment).

2. Immediately after the first bridge you go under, turn left up a short track to the road, and then head left over that same bridge and along the road for 0.5 miles (800m). It's usually quiet but there are one or two blind corners, so care needs to be taken. Pass The Greyhound pub in Lower Penn on your left, and continue over the crossroads towards Upper Penn.

3. Pass St Anne's Church and black-and-white timbered Rose Cottage, both on your right. Opposite a barn, take a gate on your right. A footpath sign indicates the path across the field to another kissing gate. Follow a grass path ahead across the next field to yet another kissing gate.

4. Through this gate go down some steep wooden steps and through a kissing gate. Continue down the steep, well-worn trail (this gets very slippery when wet) to reach the bottom of the field before crossing a stile. Stay on the narrow dirt track ahead; it might be thick with greenery in the summer, but there should be an obvious passage through.

5. At Orton House, turn left along the narrow, single-track road for 0.5 miles (800m); again, it's very quiet, but take care on blind bends. The road steepens up to the top. Just after the brow of the hill, turn right along a wide track (a public bridleway) past a wide house. This hedge-lined route offers great views of the rolling green hills of the Black Country to the east, the Shropshire Hills to the west and the Malvern Hills to the south.

6. Follow the track as it passes to the right of the communications mast and a large concrete and steel barn. When the track goes hard left, cross a stile ahead and continue in the same direction across the middle of the field to the near end of Bullmeadow Coppice.

7. Turn down left for a few steps, then right on a path through a corner of the coppice to an open meadow. Ignore a path to the left; keep straight on along the wood edge to the field's corner. Here go right for a narrow path down the steep and sometimes slippery hillside. At the edge of Wombourne turn right along Bratch Lane and go straight over a crossroads to return to the car park at the start.

Where to eat and drink

If the weather's fine then there's no better place to have your lunch than at Bratch Locks picnic site, right by the canal. The Platform Café, at the start of the walk, offers hot drinks and snacks as well as breakfast and lunch. Open Wednesday to Saturday 10am–3pm.

What to see

Towards the end of the walk, see if you can spot the tower of Wombourne village church. Although the 14th-century building is of little interest architecturally, it's thought to be unique in its dedication to Saint Biscop, a Benedictine monk born in 628 AD and famed for his travels and the pictures and manuscripts he collected en route.

While you're there

Bratch Locks, on the Staffordshire and Worcestershire Canal just west of the start point, are well worth visiting. This three-tiered stair, negotiating a 30ft (9m) rise, is arguably the highlight of Brindley's canal. Two large side ponds were built to accept excess water diverted from the two upper locks.

KINVER'S ROCK HOUSES

DISTANCE/TIME	5.4 miles (8.7km) / 2hrs 35mins
ASCENT/GRADIENT	787ft (240m) / ▲▲
PATHS	Wide gravel tracks and dirt paths
LANDSCAPE	Woodland and escarpment top
SUGGESTED MAP	OS Explorer 219 Wolverhampton & Dudley
START/FINISH	Grid reference: SO835836
DOG FRIENDLINESS	Can be taken off lead
PARKING	Verge car park on Compton Road, Kinver
PUBLIC TOILETS	None on route

The impressive sandstone ridge to the southwest of Kinver has been occupied in one way or another since 2500 BC, and impressive earthworks, believed to have been built around this time, still exist near the summit.

The views from the summit are indeed tremendous, and it must have seemed an impressive vantage point on which to build defences. The Malvern Hills and the Long Mynd are visible on a clear day and, at times, it may be possible to see the Black Mountains. But for all its breathtaking views, the real interest on Kinver Edge lies below the summit, in small houses carved into the rock.

Of these, by far the most impressive are the dwellings at Holy Austin Rock, a short walk to the east of the car park. Legend has it that it was named after a hermit who lived near the site. The first written reference to people actually living in these rock houses is believed to be in a book written in 1777. The author, seeking shelter from a storm, encounters 'this exceedingly curious rock inhabited by a clean and decent family', before going on to describe the rooms as 'really curious, warm and commodious'.

By the beginning of the 19th century there were several rock houses and by 1861 there were 11 families in residence, the increase almost certainly due to the demand created by the local iron works. When these went into decline at the end of the 19th century, the houses were gradually abandoned, although two families continued to live there until the end of World War II, and the last occupants didn't move out until 1963.

It was in the 1980s that plans were drawn up to renovate the houses to their original state, a task achieved with the help of postcards from 100 years earlier. The rebuilding was completed in 1993 and the site was again occupied, this time by a National Trust custodian. While this house is private, the rest of the site is open to the public during daylight hours all year round. Visitors may be surprised at just how cosy the houses feel – its due to the combination of thick sandstone and fireplaces keeping them warm in winter and cool in summer. Today, Holy Austin Rock has also been designated as a Site of Special Scientific Interest (SSSI) for its sandstone, which was formed from solidified sand dunes 250 million years ago.

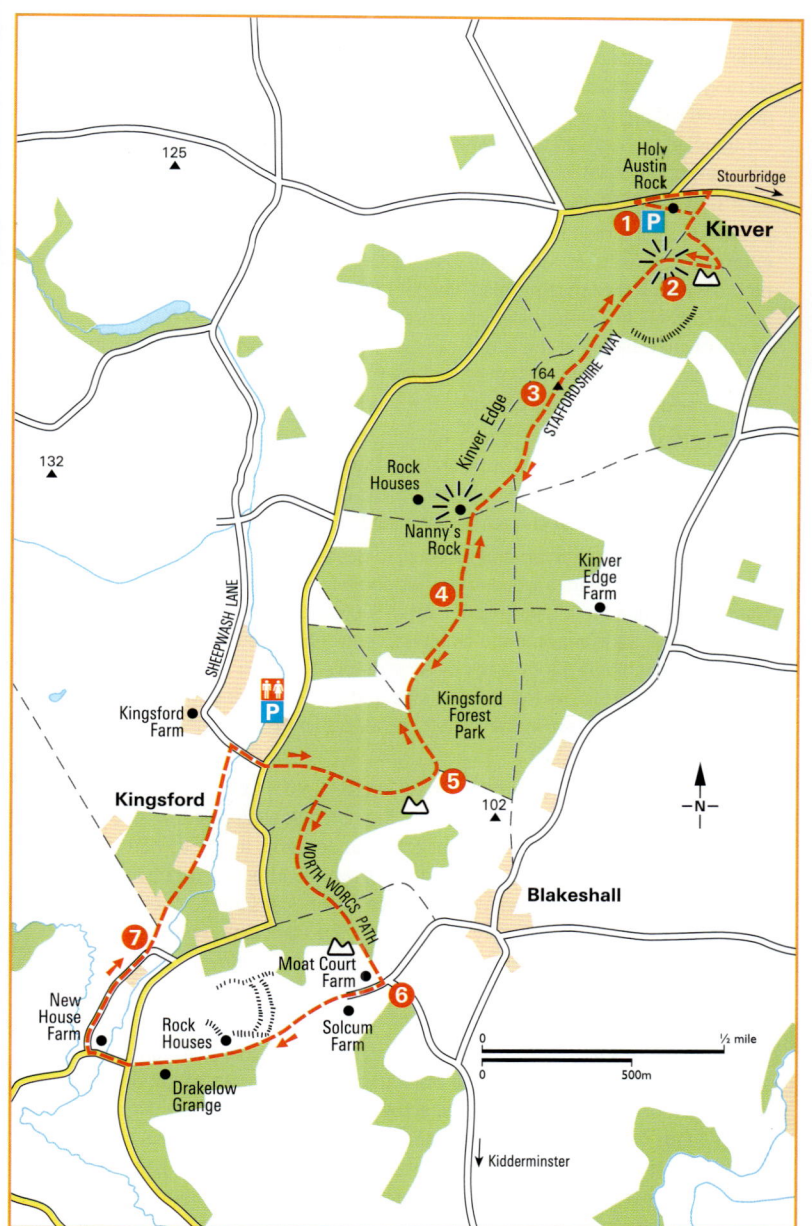

1. From the wide roadside car parking, head back along the road towards Kinver village. Just after going right at a fork in the road, follow public footpath signs to the right, up a short track into the woods. Once you're in the woods proper, take the obvious path up left to a small clearing and then turn 90 degrees to the right to follow the short, steep path to the v ewpoint above Kinver.

2. From the viewpoint, continue along the top of the escarpment, following a wide, gravel track running more or less along the uphill edge of the ancient rectangular earthworks to the left, with views across the Severn Valley glimpsed through trees to the right. From the corner of the earthworks, continue on the wide and well-walked track through intermittent woodland, with new and distant views opening up on either side. Carry on along the escarpment top, to pass the trig point.

3. Staying on the highest path, continue for 0.25 miles (400m), when the path enters woodland. In 60yds (55m), just after a path joins from the left, a steep path down to the right is marked 'danger cliff edge'. Following this down for about 40yds (37m) would take you to Nanny's Rock. The main route descends gradually to the gate at the National Trust boundary before a small clearing. Here a signpost for the Staffordshire Way (back towards you) and the North Worcestershire Path (ahead) marks the county boundary.

4. Continue along the escarpment. Keep to the main (higher) track and follow waymarkers for the North Worcestershire Path. The path turns down left around a small covered reservoir, then turns back up to the ridge crest. Turn left, down to the corner of an open field.

5. Turn right, past a barrier and a bench, to descend a fairly steep path. Where this path meets a wooden barrier and a more obvious sand track at right angles, head left, gently uphill. After 300yds (274m) you come to another path junction. Bear left onto the smallest, central path, following the yellow arrow. On reaching a sandy track go straight over, coming shortly to a steep hill. When you get to the top, cross a stile and continue along the field edge, with a fence to your left. In the far left corner of the field, go through a gate onto the road.

6. Turn right (marked No Through Road), passing Moat Court Farm on the right and, shortly after, Solcum Farm on the left, following a yellow arrow down a dark and heavily wooded track. As you descend, the steep bank to the right forms the remains of Iron Age earthworks. After a brick shed on the right, look up right to spot another group of cave houses, these ones far less developed than the ones at Holy Austin Rock. The earth path emerges onto a concrete track past the recently built, half-timbered Drakelow Grange. At the road junction beyond, continue straight on and take the first right at New House Farm. Carry on to where the surfaced road turns to the right.

7. Follow the tarmac track bearing left, in a few steps taking the right fork. At the end of the houses, when the track turns up, continue straight on to the right of a fence, following the yellow arrows with a stream on your right. A gate leads onto the tarmac lane below Kingsford Farm. Turn down right until it meets a bigger road. Go straight across and up a footpath just to the left, by a Forest Park sign. When this path meets a wide sandy bridleway, continue across, retracing your steps back to point 5 and then back to the start.

Where to eat and drink
The Tea Rooms at the Holy Austin Rock houses continue the tradition of 1777, in the top level of houses, with rock-carved back rooms. They are open from Thursday to Sunday, 11am–4pm.

What to see
Nanny's Rock, just below the path, provides an exciting viewpoint and a great place for a picnic. Continue down past it on the steep and somewhat rocky path (take care here) then turn right on a wider path to reach a set of simple carved-out cave dwellings. Like the Nanny Rocks above, they are heavily graffitised by incompetent rock carvers – what will the geologists of future eras make of these 'trace fossils'?

MODDERSHALL

DISTANCE/TIME	10 miles (16.1km) / 5hrs
ASCENT/GRADIENT	836ft (250m) / ▲▲
PATHS	Field paths, lanes, woodland tracks, 26 stiles
LANDSCAPE	Rolling farmland and woods
SUGGESTED MAP	OS Explorer 258 Stoke-on-Trent & Newcastle-under-Lyme
START/FINISH	Grid reference: SJ926368
DOG FRIENDLINESS	Good in woodland and on enclosed tracks, but on lead around farms
PARKING	Roadside lay-bys in Moddershall
PUBLIC TOILETS	None on route

Although Moddershall comes across today as serene and largely unspoilt, the presence of the huge mill pond below the Boar Inn at the start of the walk is an indication that this small valley was not quite as peaceful as it now seems.

During the Middle Ages there were almost certainly a number of corn mills and possibly fulling mills (where cloth is cleaned in water) along the valley, but local activity really took off after 1720 when flint grinding for the local pottery industry began. Imported flint was ground into a powder and added to the local red-coloured clay to produce a highly sought-after white or light cream ware. Moddershall soon became an important part of the wider activity centred on the Potteries, which included Josiah Wedgwood's famous pottery at Burslem. Later the mills also began grinding bone, which was another recognised additive of fine china.

In total there were nine mills around Moddershall, all located in the valley of the tiny Scotch Brook and described as one of the most intensively exploited watercourses in Staffordshire. The brook flows into the River Trent at nearby Stone and the narrow valley was ideally suited for damming and mills. One of the most striking mills stood next to the present-day Boar Inn and was called Boar Mill. It was built in 1798 and was the highest of the nine.

The mills were powered by water wheels, Boar Mill having a wheel that was 18ft in diameter wheel and 4ft wide. One of the few wheels that still survive is called Top or Splashy Mill. It earned its name from having two water wheels side by side, one overshot and the other undershot. Records show that most of the mills were still supplying the pottery industry in the 1930s, but with the privations of wartime they gradually began to close. Boar Mill continued until the 1950s and a few others until as late as the 1970s.

Part of this route forms a section of the Stone Circles Challenge Walk, devised by local group Stone Ramblers to encourage more people to walk and enjoy local paths. The 36-mile countryside route joins up a string of attractive villages and hamlets, including some on this walk like Moddershall, Hilderstone and Fulford.

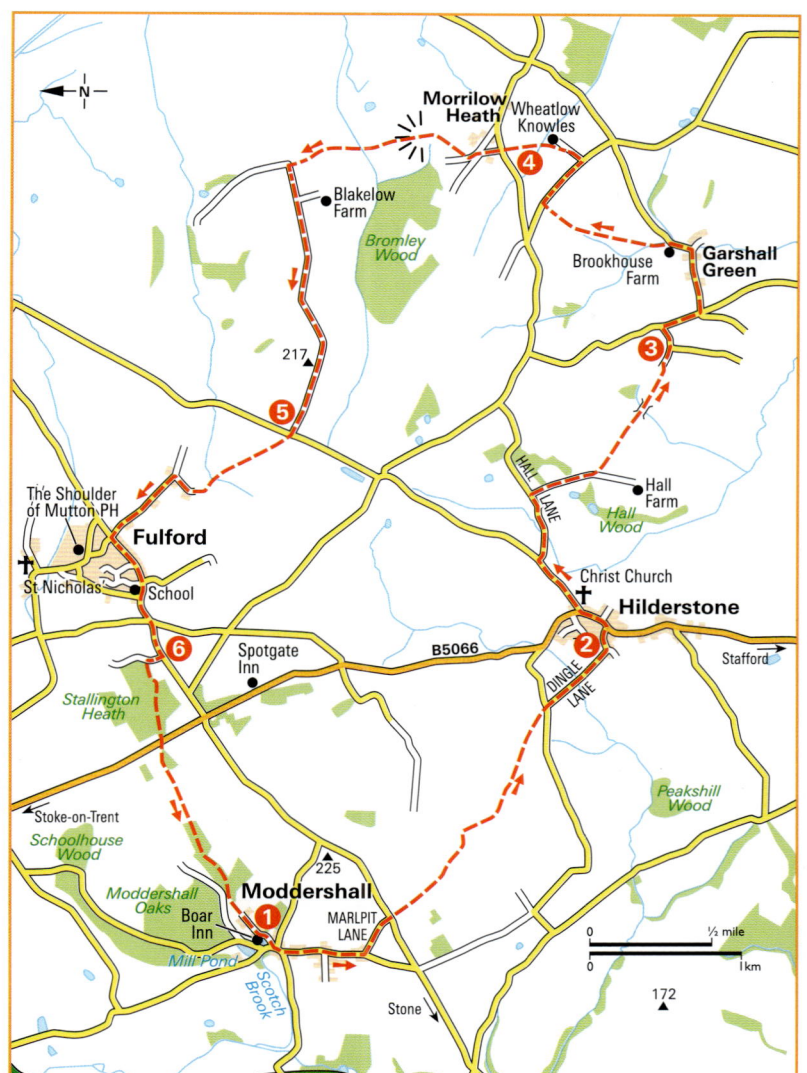

1. From the Boar Inn walk up the road past the small duck pond and through the village. Turn left on to Marlpit Lane and at the end cross the road for field paths ahead through successive fields. Cross a bridleway, go around a young plantation, then by a pylon go right, around a field edge to a stile. Beyond this head half left across a field for a road and down the lane opposite into Hilderstone.

2. Turn left on to the main street and continue up past the church. Go right into Hall Lane, then right again on to a track for Hall Farm. When you are about 275yds (251m) from the farm go left, by a yellow waymark on a telegraph pole. Go straight across a series of open fields, between three mature trees, and continue as far as a footbridge. Go up a field edge, through a farmyard and along its drive to reach a lane.

3. Go ahead and turn right, through Garshall Green. Turn left at crossroads by a post box, then at the ford by Brookhouse Farm turn left alongside the brook. Veer right beyond the stile for a rising path through a number of fields. Turn right on to a lane, then left down the drive of Wheatlow Knowles. Keep left of the building and beyond a spinney go up through a field to the road.

4. Go straight over for a dirt track, ahead at a crossroads, then in 50yds (46m) go right over a stile for a broad hedged strip. At the end head across a wide open valley, aiming just to the right of distant Blakelow Farm. Half way down stay left of a hedge and beyond the brook go half right (not the tempting farm track) up to reach a lane. Go left and follow the lane to the very far end.

5. Go across the main road for a tree-lined track. At the far end continue to the right of a farm and swing left on its drive, past houses. At Fulford turn left and walk along the road past the school and out of the village.

6. Turn right on a track signposted 'Wood Farm'. Go left on a footpath through woodland, keeping close to the boundary on the left. Cross the main road and continue opposite, going right beyond the second kissing gate down a field for a popular valley bottom path through woodland. This eventually emerges on a lane which leads back to the start.

Where to eat and drink
The Boar Inn at Moddershall is the obvious place for a drink. The Shoulder of Mutton in Fulford, just to the east, and passed on the walk, is open every day of the week and serves food at lunchtimes on Friday to Sunday and every evening except Sunday. Alternatively, The Spotgate Inn, where you can dine in a Pullman carriage.

What to see
St Nicholas Church at Fulford and in the early 1800s earned a reputation as the Gretna Green of North Staffordshire due to the number of runaway couples married there. In 1828 as many as 84 couples tied the knot, although curiously most of them appeared to come from one small part of Stoke-on-Trent.

While you're there
On the far side of the Trent Valley, north of Stone, is the Trentham Estate. The centrepiece of this popular visitor attraction is the award-winning Italianate garden, but on top of this there are miles of parkland and woodland walks around an ornamental lake, plus great views from a hilltop monument. There's also a maze, aerial walkway even a monkey sanctuary.

KINVER TO WHITTINGTON

DISTANCE/TIME	3.25 miles (5.3km) / 1hr 15min
ASCENT/GRADIENT	360ft (110m) / ▲▲
PATHS	Grass tracks, field paths, roads and dirt trails, many stiles
LANDSCAPE	Field, meadow, woodland and canalside
SUGGESTED MAP	OS Explorer 219 Wolverhampton & Dudley
START/FINISH	Grid reference: SO848835
DOG FRIENDLINESS	Keep on lead in all fields
PARKING	Small car park at Kinver Lock; otherwise off Kinver High Street
PUBLIC TOILETS	None on route

Given the part canals have played in the Staffordshire landscape over the past 250 years, it seems appropriate that the final walk in the book should include at least a short section of artificial waterway, even if it isn't the walk's highlight. It seems fitting too, that the Staffordshire and Worcestershire Canal was designed and built under the apparently omnipotent eye of James Brindley, whose name is associated with so many of the walks in this volume, and who perhaps did more than any other single person to shape the landscape and fortune of the county.

The Staffordshire and Worcester Canal was one of Brindley's earliest projects; it was officially opened in 1772. Essentially, it was part of his so-called 'Grand Cross', a visionary scheme to connect all of the major ports (Bristol, Hull and Liverpool) by linking the Severn, the Trent and the Mersey. The canal begins at the River Severn before rising slowly to Aldersley Junction, near Wolverhampton, where it connects with the Shropshire Union Canal. It then continues as far as the Trent and Mersey Canal at Great Haywood near Shugborough. Its highlight has to be the three-tier lock at The Bratch, near Wombourne.

Despite James Brindley's best efforts, the highlight of this walk has to be the Manor House of Whittington, a timber-beamed house built in 1310 that now serves a very reasonable pint – and also has a handy selection of spirits. It was originally owned by Sir William de Whittington, then lord of Kinver, and grandfather of Dick Whittington, who became Lord Mayor of London.

The house was later inherited by ancestors of Lady Jane Grey, who spent some of her childhood here, before her life was plunged into turmoil. She was fourth in line to the throne in Henry VIII's will, but thanks to the scheming of her Protestant father-in-law, a royal advisor, she was crowned Queen ahead of Henry's daughter Mary, who was Catholic. She ruled for just nine days, before Mary, with strong popular support, seized the throne and had her imprisoned in the Tower of London. Less than a year later, aged just 16, she was beheaded. During the reign of Mary's successor, Queen Elizabeth I, Jane was celebrated as a Protestant martyr. Today, her ghost is said to still haunt the inn staircase. Meanwhile, the apparition of Dick Whittington has been spotted, in a black coach galloping soundlessly south towards Kidderminster.

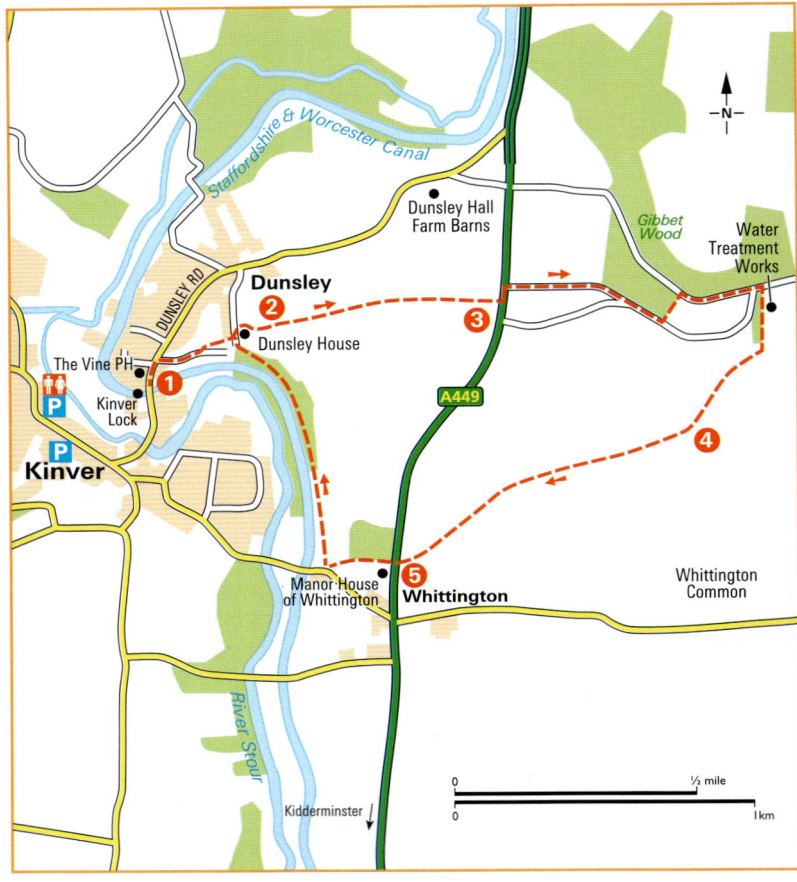

1. From The Vine pub beside Kinver Lock, go up Dunsley Road for 100yds (91m) and turn right along a gravel track ('Gibraltar') between houses. In 200yds (183m) bear left up a fairly steep path through woods to the corner of a driveway. Turn up left, and then right just after Dunsley House, along a short dirt and grass track.

2. At the track's end keep ahead over a stile, with a tall hedge on your right. Continue straight ahead from stile to stile across one small field, then down over another small one and two very large ones to a final stile on to the A449.